W9-CIG-914

Dark Union

The Secret Web of Profiteers, Politicians, and Booth Conspirators That Led to Lincoln's Death

Leonard F. Guttridge
Ray A. Neff

John Wiley & Sons, Inc.

To Augusta Mae Neff

This book is printed on acid-free paper. ∞

Published by John Wiley & Sons, Inc., Hoboken, New Jersey
Published simultaneously in Canada

All photos Neff-Guttridge Collection unless otherwise specified. Pages 212 top, 218 top: Library of Congress; pages 213, 215 bottom: Notman Photographic Archives, McCord Museum of Canada, Montreal; page 216 top: NARA, LAS Files, Microscopy 599, Roll 3, Panel 1208; page 221 top: NARA, LAS Files, Microscopy 599, Roll 3, Panel 114; page 221 bottom: Museum of the Confederacy, Richmond, VA; page 222 bottom: Illinois State Historical Society Library; pages 227 top, 229: Photo by Neff-Guttridge, original at Ford's Theatre, Washington, D.C.; page 231: National Archives, Cotton and Captured Property Records, No. 17468; pages 233 bottom, 234 bottom: *History of the United States Secret Service* by Lafayette Baker (1867); page 234 top: Naval Historical Center, Washington, D.C.; page 235 top: Records of the Columbia Historical Society, vols. 29-30, Part 7, 1928; page 235 bottom: National Museum of Health and Medicine, Armed Forces Institute of Pathology; page 240 bottom: Clay County Historical Society, Brazil, Indiana; page 242 top: Archives of Indiana State University, Terre Haute, Indiana.

Library of Congress Cataloging-in-Publication Data:

Guttridge, Leonard F.
Dark union : the secret web of the profiteers, politicians, and Booth conspirators that led to Lincoln's death / Leonard F. Guttridge, Ray A. Neff.
p. cm.
ISBN 0-471-26481-4 (cloth)
1. Lincoln, Abraham, 1809–1865—Assassination. 2. Conspiracies—United States—History—19th century. 3. United States—Politics and government—1861–1865. I. Neff, Ray A. II. Title.

E457.5.G87 2003
973.7'092—dc21

2003005319

Printed in the United States of America

10 9 8 7 6 5 4 3 2 1

Contents

Acknowledgments

Following our acquisition of Lafayette Baker's *Colburn's* volume and related discoveries at Philadelphia City Hall four decades ago, and then the prize of the Potter Papers, the prospect of following through with additional research was intimidating, yet irresistible. It indeed proved an often formidable labor and one that never could have approached completion without the generous assistance of people and organizations to whom we are much indebted.

Our thanks go to the administration of Indiana State University, Terre Haute, Indiana; to Doctor David E. Vancil, librarian and head of Rare Books and Special Collections of the university's Cunningham Memorial Library; and to his associate Dennis J. Vetrovec. Both were most helpful in arranging for the addition of our research material to the library's holdings.

We also appreciate the ever-competent services provided by the researchers at the National Archives and Records Administration, with a special nod to Michael Musick, his colleagues, and the staff of the Old Military branch. The Library of Congress, despite budgetary constraints and other problems, remained over the decades a superlative setting for historical research.

Here we spent countless hours in the Manuscript Room, where assistance is invariably courteous and prompt. Special thanks go to the Brown Library, Washington, North Carolina, for its information on the Demills of Civil War–era New York, and to the Archives of New Brunswick, Canada, for data on the Chaffey shipping company. Other libraries unstinting in their aid include the Fairfax County Library Reference Division and the Alexandria Library, Special Collections, both of Virginia; the Illinois State Historical Library, Springfield, Illinois; the Martin Luther King Library, Washington, D.C.;

the Lilly Library, University of Indiana, Bloomington; and the Rome Floyd County Library, Rome, Georgia. We also thank the New York Public Library and the New-York Historical Society.

Our personal gratitude is due to the following people, who know the measure of their help and inspiration without our stating it here: Jan K. Herman, historian of the Navy Medical Department, Washington, D.C.; Douglas Greer, M.D.; and Jack Towers, Morris Questal, Jean Guttridge, and Marty Deblinger. Finally, we acknowledge with love and gratitude the patience and the encouragement of our families.

Introduction

The irony of it all is that Abraham Lincoln loved a good mystery. As an itinerant lawyer, the future president seldom rode far without a volume of Shakespeare or Robert Burns in his saddlebag. No less a favorite of his was America's prime specialist in stories of deduction and the macabre: Edgar Allan Poe. Lincoln's political campaign biographer reported as much. Such was the candidate's mathematical mind, he took particular delight in the absolute and logical method of Poe's tales and sketches, in which "the problem of the mystery is given and wrought out in everyday facts by a process of cunning and analysis."

As deviously wrought as anything conjured by Edgar Allan Poe were the perils lurking ahead for the would-be chief executive. Seeking his country's highest office predestined for this ambitious prairie lawyer the role of victim in a meshing of events whose sinister scope, had it all been fiction, few might have relished more than he. Homespun member of the bar, reluctant war leader, Great Emancipator, and peace-loving martyr—these are the familiar images of the sixteenth American president, as portrayed by some historians. But with a clarity provided by fresh research, we see him now in a new and troubling shape, that of a crime fiction fan caught in a real-life trap of such complexity as to rival any innovation of the detective story's progenitor and master.

Books confined to the first of our history's four presidential murders have scarcely exceeded three dozen in number—in most cases, so duplicating each other that significant facts have been left unexplored and myths perpetuated.

A noteworthy example is found in a fairly modern reproduction of the trial proceedings of the accused conspirators to Lincoln's assassination. A respected popular historian wrote an introduction to it, in which he set forth the entries that John Wilkes Booth, while a hunted fugitive, had scribbled in a pocket diary. As quoted in this introduction, they contain the line "And for this brave boy, Herold, here with me . . ."

Early in 1977 we were permitted by the U.S. National Park Service to examine Booth's diary, page by page, subjecting each to concentrated photoanalysis. The techniques used involved a variety of filters and emulsion, and innumerable exposures were made. Our purpose was to ascertain whether any of the pages contained invisible writing. None did. But neither did the assassin write "Herold" anywhere in the little book. David Herold was one of the four eventually convicted and hanged as conspirators. The omission of his name, and indeed of any identifiable reference to him, allows for at least the possibility that the brave boy with Booth was someone else.

The writer of that introduction, Philip Van Doren Stern, was by no means the first to wrongly insert Herold's name among Booth's words. It had been done at the outset when the diary, after two years of concealment and with almost half of its pages clearly knifed or scissored away, was released by the War Department to an impatient press and public.

Still earlier, within hours of official reports that Booth had been cornered and shot, the myth began concerning his alleged last words. The various versions differed substantially, which was itself sufficient to stir doubt. Yet they have been repeatedly cited, despite the denial of the officer commanding Booth's captors that there were any such last words. And it was the stated conclusion of the highest military medical authority that the dying man was incapable of intelligible speech.

In the same class of spurious history is the presumption that the fugitive's body, brought to the Washington Navy Yard thirteen days after Lincoln's murder, was positively identified as that of John Wilkes Booth by the actor's close friends, stage acquaintances, and relatives. Reference to the War Department's detailed record of those strange proceedings on the iron-hulled USS *Montauk* is all that is required to show that just fourteen people were permitted to view the body, that all but four of these were connected with the War Department, that none had anything to do with the theater, and that not one was an intimate friend of Booth's, much less a relative.

Rather than repeat doubtful material, writers might have pondered more the questions surrounding Abraham Lincoln's murder or at least asked themselves why, for generations, these have remained unexplained. On this point, there are several answers: For one thing, dangerous tongues were stilled in short order; close-mouthed contemporaries took their secrets to the grave; and backyard bonfires destroyed an inestimable wealth of evidence. Documents that survived, brimming with new intelligence, waited a century or more to see the light of day. Some rich collections are still blocked from view, moldering in basement trunks or the blackness of attics.

Valuable papers in federal archives have been ignored, wrongly interpreted, or discounted because of lack of context or have simply escaped notice. And for decades, researchers were denied access to them. Before the last restrictions were lifted from government files concerning events of the second half of the nineteenth century, the middle of the twentieth had come and gone. Nothing can be served now by mincing words. What standard history books have to say about the assassination of Abraham Lincoln is substantially rooted in pure myth and faked or incomplete testimony.

Things scarcely could have turned out otherwise. Before the last of the ceremonial funerals with which twelve cities from Washington to Springfield, Illinois, bade the slain leader farewell, imaginations were astir and pains taken to falsify the record of what had occurred and why. The enduring sham first took form under the dictates of Edwin McMasters Stanton, secretary of war. This is not to charge Stanton's motives as other than patriotic. The fact remains that the recourses he apparently deemed necessary to the Union's best interests called for tactics of deception, in the employment of which evidence was doctored or destroyed, photographs were cropped or blacked out, news organs manipulated, corpses misidentified, and witnesses silenced.

The countless studies of Lincoln's life generally agree when dealing with his death. Only now and then can an undercurrent of doubt be detected when the biographer reaches that final chapter. In all of Lincoln literature, few titles shake loose, for close inspection, the inconsistencies in standard accounts of Lincoln's death. Writers have overlooked what amounts to a substantially new cast of characters, varying from smugglers, spies, and government sleuths to financiers, political intriguers, and seductive mystery women with a lethally provocative pen.

The source material for our story, strengthened by collections easily accessible in public archives, is broad and diverse. It ranges from a rogues' gallery of unpublished photos, deciphered intelligence locked within a nineteenth-century military tome, the private memoranda of a respected Midwest university professor, and the correspondence of a prestigious judge from the same region, to the tape-recorded memories of a centenarian whose enterprising father, unmentioned by any history book, played a pivotal role.

Conventional accounts of the Abraham Lincoln murder case run more or less as follows: The president was shot in the back of the head by the actor John Wilkes Booth on Good Friday night, April 14, 1865, while seated in the state box at Ford's Theatre, enjoying a performance of the comedy *Our American Cousin.* He died hours later in a house across the street. His assassin leaped from box to stage and broke a small bone in his left leg but managed to escape through the rear of the theater into an alley, where his horse was waiting. Twelve days later a military posse, led by government detectives, cornered Booth in a tobacco barn in Virginia, but he refused to surrender and was shot to death by a cavalry sergeant after the barn had been set on fire. Booth's body was brought back to Washington and, under War Department auspice, routinely identified. According to the military tribunal appointed by Secretary of War Stanton to try Booth's alleged accomplices, the assassination and a simultaneous physical assault on the secretary of state elsewhere in the city were elements of a general plot against the Northern government, instigated by political leaders of the Rebellion.

The military court convicted eight people of aiding Booth, four of whom were sent to prison, and the others, including a widow, Mary Surratt, were hanged.

The true story of our first presidential assassination is far more complex, one reason perhaps why historians have not ventured deeper into its examination. At any rate, successive generations have known too little about it. And a tragedy deserving sound affirmation and a genuine script has instead come across more as half travesty, half shadow play.

PART I

The Profiteers

CHAPTER 1

The Riddle of the *Colburn's* Volume

One of the most popular haunts of Philadelphian bibliophiles in the 1950s was Leary's Book Store. Standing on Ninth Street opposite the post office, its shelves and counters crammed with as many as 300,000 volumes, Leary's advertised itself as America's largest retail outlet for rare books. It had a soft-sell policy and would no more have employed a high-pressure salesman than hired a known shoplifter. Customers were invited to browse all they wanted to, and any who were reluctant to leave empty-handed could at least have carried off a complimentary lithograph entitled *The Bookworm,* ready for framing.

This is where our quest began, on the second floor of Leary's Book Store one afternoon in April of 1957. Not that either of us, at the time, had Lincoln's murder in mind. The occasion was a routine forage among the Civil War collections, and the item we bought was selected because it contained an account, by an officer of the British Royal Engineers, of a visit to General George Meade's Union Army of the Rappahannock. For fifty cents the book was ours.

Colburn's United Service Magazine and Military Journal was required reading at Sandhurst, West Point, and other academies where young men were schooled for command. Bound sets filled the shelves of retired generals and army chiefs of staff. A forum equally for theorists and sentimentalists, *Colburn's* mingled reviews of the latest advances in military science with anecdotes of service life in peace and war, travel articles, and memoirs reliving the dash and glory of old campaigns. The bound set bought in Leary's Book Store was Part Two of 1864, embracing the months May through August. Its pages, except for the article on Meade, were no more than cursorily glanced at until the following summer, when a number of them were seen to contain figures and letters penciled along the inner margins, close to the binding. Ray Neff was then conducting research at the office of the medical examiner for the City of Philadelphia. He showed the book's pages to a chief investigator, Patrick Kmat. To Kmat, who had served in army intelligence during World War II, the writing appeared to be a cipher. Kmat knew an expert in cryptography, who was then shown the *Colburn's* volume and who confirmed Kmat's suspicions. He gave instructions for translating it.

The system used was of a "sliding" variety, in which the key pattern is shifted at intervals to make solution all the tougher. Translation taxed patience and perseverance but was duly accomplished. And the first part of this cipher, found on page 181 and dated "2-5-68," struck a distinct note of alarm. "I am constantly being followed. They are professionals. *I cannot fool them.*"

There was yet more: tiny dots under certain letters in essays on an invasion of Denmark and a voyage to Tenerife. The letters formed these words: "It was on the tenth of April sixty-five when I first knew that the plan was in action." What followed was a detailed charge that Abraham Lincoln's secretary of war had fostered a plot hatched among influential persons in the North to have the president kidnapped and, if necessary, killed. On page 107 the decoded words included "Ecert had made all the contacts, the deed to be done on the fourteenth." Correctly spelled, the name was that of Thomas T. Eckert, Secretary Stanton's close aide and chief of the military telegraph. Pages 119, 120, 127, and 245 yielded this startling allegation: "I know the truth and it frightens me. I fear that somehow I may become the sacrificial goat. There were at least eleven members of Congress involved in the plot, no less than twelve army officers, three naval officers and at least 24 civilians, of which one was a governor of a loyal state. Five were bankers of great repute, three were nationally known newspapermen and eleven were industrialists of great wealth. The names of these known conspirators is [sic] presented without comment . . . in Vol. one of this series. Eighty-five thousand dollars was contributed by the named persons to pay for the deed. Only eight persons knew the details of the plot and the identity of the others."

The final words, secreted within an account of artillery experiments along the east coast of England, formed another distress signal: "*I fear for my life,* LCB."

At this point, every page in the book had come under close scrutiny. Several marginal portions seemed oddly discolored. Subjected to ultraviolet radiation, one of the spots glowed purple. At first, exposure under the lamp produced nothing. Several days of additional experimenting were required before an application of tannic acid brought forth a name: L. C. Baker. The writing had been done with an "invisible ink" not unknown to secret agents in the Civil War. Its ferricyanide base would ordinarily have become visible after an hour's exposure to bright sunlight. But it had lost this property with the passage of many years, which explained why it had not responded to the ultraviolet lamp.

The imperiled encipherer? Lafayette Charles Baker was an intimidating figure, docketed by historians, when noticed at all, as a federal lackey doing Stanton's undercover work, with the official designation War Department special agent or provost marshal, chief of its detective bureau. Baker had launched countless campaigns against alleged enemies of the Union, arresting military bounty brokers, uncovering sexual immorality in the Treasury Department, and raiding liquor and gambling saloons. He had also directed the pursuit of John Wilkes Booth. After the war, he had infuriated Andrew Johnson by posting gumshoes on White House grounds to spy upon the president's female visitors. This impertinence hastened his departure from government service, and Baker retired to Philadelphia, where he died in July 1868.

The question remained. Did the handwriting that had given the *Colburn's* volume a dimension of mystery belong to Secretary Stanton's chief detective? We found Lafayette Baker's will at Philadelphia City Hall and a codicil to it in the same file. Upon the advice of a member of the Pennsylvania Historical Society, Chief Investigator Kmat contacted Robert F. Fowler, editor of a national magazine specializing in Civil War subjects. Fowler obtained the services of Stanley S. Smith, former officer of the Pennsylvania State Police and an examiner of questioned documents, who finally reported that the signature "Lafayette C. Baker" in the left margin of page 574 of the *Colburn's* volume and those on Baker's will and codicil were of the same hand. Not found, although eagerly sought, was the early 1864 *Colburn's* containing, according to Baker, the names of conspirators in the plot against Lincoln.

That codicil indicated likelihood of a court hearing. We talked with Charles Hughes, Philadelphia archivist (the city's first), already noted for his rescue of important historical documents lost for years and in danger of destruction. Hughes had, for instance, found the original deeds that secured for the City of Philadelphia clear ownership rights to Independence Square and the site of Independence Hall. Promptly interested, Charles Hughes referred us to Ernest DeAngelo, register of wills, for authority to go into the City Hall basement, accompanied by appropriate staffers.

After a week of exhaustive rummaging amid piles of faded documents and moldering ledgers, we found the shorthand record of a hearing "In the matter of a paper propounded as a codicil to the Last Will and Testament of Lafayette C. Baker, deceased." The hearing was conducted before W. Marshall Taylor, register of wills, on October 14, 1872. Further search revealed the handwritten transcripts of the hearing's shorthand text, and this in turn led to the discovery of additional transcripts typed in 1936 under the federal Work Projects Administration. Charles Hughes saw to it that the entire material was brought above ground and microfilmed.

It was this record of a court hearing, dealing with an unprobated codicil to Baker's will, that most quickened pulses. Viewed alongside what had been found in the *Colburn's* book, the document portrays in arresting detail a former public official who knew too much, who had determined to mask his dangerous knowledge in cipher and secret ink, and while so engaged had raced an agonizing death at the hands of someone beneath his own roof.

Further tests on the *Colburn's* volume were conducted at the U.S. National Archives and Records Administration (NARA) by questioned documents specialists from the United States Post Office, the Department of Defense, and the FBI. All reached the same conclusion: The signatures, dots under letters, and numbers in margins were the work of Lafayette Charles Baker.

The release of a portion of these discoveries in the fall of 1961 touched off a mild furor. Edwin Stanton and Lafayette Baker became, briefly, front-page news. The *New York Times* published a letter from one of Stanton's descendants, angrily defending the secretary's good name. A professor of history was apparently so eager to veto the findings that he confused them with the enduring controversy over the death of Napoleon Bonaparte, for he sailed into print attacking "veterans of the 'Lincoln was murdered' hypothesis." Hypothesis? But such hapless irrelevancies aside, the general response among Lincoln scholars and professional historians reflected keen, if guarded, interest in what was unearthed to date and an almost unanimous recommendation that the digging continue.

It did, with caution. A British writer on Lincoln's assassination called the new revelations "the most extraordinary discovery in this field." David Kahn, in a definitive work on cryptography, contemplated as a possible result of it "a reappraisal of one of the cruelest moments in the whole of American history." Wrote Victor Searcher, author of *Lincoln's Journey to Greatness,* "The new data on the Lincoln murder . . . underscores the fact that all has NOT been told." And the reaction of Ralph T. G. Newman, Lincoln authority, manuscript dealer, and founder of the Civil War Round Table, was an admission of belief that Stanton took advantage of Lincoln's murder to "further his own ends . . . that he did, to some extent, 'cover up' details of the crime. One thing is definite now—the case is not closed."

This was all very well. Enough was known of Baker's duplicity for us not to place much credence in his cipher-shrouded accusations. Baker was capable of playing an elaborate and malevolent joke on his boss or anybody else against whom he had a grievance. Some suggested that Baker's charges were the product of a senile brain. He was only in his forty-second year when he framed them, but his physical health *was* certainly questionable. He was taking belladonna and bromides to guard against the epileptic fits that had plagued him in youth, and the discoveries in Philadelphia's City Hall make clear that Lafayette Baker had been so dosed with arsenic that the medicinal leeches his doctor pressed behind his ears fell away lifeless.

The man Lafayette Baker accused of engineering Lincoln's removal as part of a plot to seize power was himself something of an enigma. Like the future president's, Edwin M. Stanton's career had begun in legal practice. He had an early courtroom encounter with Lincoln and at that time spoke of him with contempt. When he joined Lincoln's cabinet in the second year of the Civil War, some who knew both men expected that it would be only a matter of time before Stanton gained the upper hand. Yet their wartime relationship would be recalled by others as, at least outwardly, marked by cooperation and mutual esteem. It was well known, however, that Stanton cultivated a close liaison with Lincoln's most active political foes and, according to one of Stanton's own aides, was in "continual argument" with the president over his disposition to let the South off lightly once the war had ended. On at least two occasions, Stanton overruled the chief executive. Indeed, the two men had a working agreement that the secretary could ignore White House directives whenever he saw fit, and he is said to have torn up such notes in front of visitors.

Unlike the torrid anti-rebel outbursts of his radical cronies in the Republican Party, self-revealing rhetoric seldom escaped Edwin Stanton's lips. But his public attitude toward the insurrectionist South was as retribution incarnate. Some lauded him as an indefatigable war bureaucrat, devoted to the Union. He was feared by others as a would-be despot. Friends ascribed his sour personality to asthma. The deaths of his daughter and his first wife, and a brother's suicide, may have warped his character. A former law partner is said to have argued that if it should prove necessary to replace the Constitution with a military dictatorship, Stanton would be just the man. According to General Ulysses S. Grant, the secretary held little regard for the Constitution during those years of extreme national crisis.

A deciphered entry in Lafayette Baker's *Colburn's* volume reads: "Address Earl Potter, Ladoga, Indiana." A decade-long hunt revealed that Earl Potter managed Baker's National Detective Police. The

Virginia-born Potter had been a tracer of missing goods for a Norfolk shipping firm until the outbreak of war. His antisecessionist views compelled him to leave the state for his safety's sake, and he joined Baker's then modest little detective corps after its transfer from the Department of State to the War Department.

The ostensible function of the NDP was to track down spies, contrabandists, traitors, and defrauders of the government. Its command post at 217 Pennsylvania Avenue conveniently faced Willard's Hotel, a setting for much wartime intrigue, and among its other Washington installations was a four-floor building on Tenth Street in the southeast quarter of the capital. Here, Earl Potter's younger half-brother Andrew ran the Secret Services division, which assembled photographs and dossiers on hundreds of Americans, well known and obscure alike. That Tenth Street address was the nerve center of a clandestine corps that compensated in industry for what it lacked in manpower. At peak strength the NDP's undercover section numbered no more than 400 agents, couriers, paid informers, and a small but effective band of female spies, all operating in territory both north and south of Civil War battle lines. What Americans knew of the NDP was learned mainly from its roving agents, who showed little regard for constitutional rights and due process when following a "case." This attitude had started at the top with Baker, who, in his capacity as NDP chief, was answerable only to Secretary Stanton. Too often for his own good, he flouted even this limited allegiance, acting as if he were a law unto himself.

Specialized branches of this early federal bureau of investigation included a cipher room and a telegraph service, a photography division, and a gun shop. In 1863 a mounted police unit was added, armed, and equipped for local raids on nests of crime, vice, and subversion. It was organized as the First District of Columbia Cavalry; was commanded by Lafayette Baker, who had a colonel's rank; and was snubbed by the regular army. When the Civil War ended, the NDP's controversial activities diminished, but many of its agents remained in federal employ until Edwin Stanton's death in 1869. Afterward, as Richard Wilmer Rowan says in *The Story of Secret Service,* "Most of Baker's operatives scattered over the land as a new and insinuating plague of private detectives."

Documentation that would have secured for these original G-men a safe niche in the appropriate annals had also become scattered, buried, or destroyed, leaving few clues to the role they played in the drama of Lincoln's murder. But two men made sure that all was not lost. Shortly after the war, Earl and Andrew Potter—the service was rife with Potters—spirited a large quantity of sensitive NDP files, reports, and correspondence out of Washington and into rural Indiana. By the early 1870s, in the course of an extensive probe into a number of "strange deaths" in the wake of Lincoln's murder, the two agents added fresh quantities of documents to what already constituted a rich hoard of research material. There it all remained, stored near the small town of Ladoga, in gently rolling farm country some thirty miles west of Indianapolis, infrequently disturbed and engaging the attention of one person alone, Andrew Potter.

The remnants of what had been Secretary of War Stanton's secret police force held periodic reunions after the turn of the nineteenth century. Potter, one of the last survivors, continued his detective role, it seems, until his death at age ninety-two. Although he knew close state secrets of the Civil War era, lingering questions haunted him for the often unhappy balance of his long life. Combining what he continued to ferret out of equally aging contemporaries with the solid mass of NDP records in his grasp, he strove to form and fit together a tale of Lincoln's murder that he knew to be utterly at variance with conventional accounts.

Forty years after his death, we purchased the remains of the Potter collection. More than a decade following disclosure of the material that Lafayette Baker had secreted in the *Colburn's* volume, we had acquired other relevant material from Baker sources and elsewhere, photographic as well as documental, the written harvest supplemented by almost 1,500 tintypes, ambrotypes, daguerreotypes, cartes de visite, and glass plates. And on the face of it, here indeed was abundant indication of a series of events disturbing enough in their nature, doubly so inasmuch as the evidence had never been permitted to see the light of day.

The story now shaped up this way: To head off national bankruptcy and to finance the Union war effort by restoring American cotton to the international market, Lincoln had sanctioned, at great political risk, semiclandestine trade deals between Northern investors and owners of Southern cotton. When the Richmond government held out for direly needed meat instead of greenbacks as payment, representatives of both sides met secretly in neutral Canada to negotiate a mammoth exchange of pork for cotton. At the time, the negotiations had Lincoln's quiet endorsement. But in early 1865 Lincoln began to vacillate in regard to trading with the enemy, which, along with the imminent end of the hostilities, threatened the huge profits at stake. Simultaneously, the radical Republicans, the extremists of Lincoln's own political party, became enraged by his forgiving attitude toward the South. Determined to save the Union from the postwar course this attitude foreshadowed, they plotted to remove him from office.

Hourly more desperate as the Civil War neared its end, these elements merged into an unholy alliance. Simultaneously, holdouts from the crumbling Confederacy hoped to seize victory from the jaws of defeat by kidnapping the North's commander in chief. Once Lincoln was carried off by these rebel hotheads, a congressional junta in Washington would take control of the government, and the cotton deals would go through. The Northern interests bent on Lincoln's departure promised his abductors discreet aid, which ranged from a selective parole of rebel secret service agents in Union captivity to moored brigs on standby in quiet backwater coves. As a conspiracy, it was slipshod and improvised. But with powerfully motivated men involved and political survival and windfall profits at stake, it was altogether expedient and even foreseeable.

Unfortunately for these interests, a go-between or factotum with connections on every side was the unstable actor John Wilkes Booth. He was at Ford's Theatre, as was Lincoln, on the night set for seizing the president and spiriting him from Washington. But the actor's mind was obsessed by more than just abduction. And the derringer bullet he exploded into the president's brain incriminated politicians, bankers, Wall Street speculators, and even some of Lincoln's personal friends, not to mention his successor in the White House.

Booth was pursued across southern Maryland and into Virginia. But he was not cornered and shot to death in a burning barn, as promulgated by Secretary Stanton's War Department and fobbed off on posterity. The interests with so much to hide had permitted Booth to escape. A luckless substitute was slain and buried in his name, a stunning transposition of identities only whispered of at the time and destined for generations of concealment.

Although it utterly contradicted standard history, Andrew Potter's scenario was too persuasive, too logically detailed, for instinctive dismissal. So here had loomed a formidable challenge. There was no escaping it, no easy path of compromise. If the story as presented by the War Department secret police papers and our follow-up research was not true on every salient point, the usual accounts of Lincoln's murder must and should prevail. If it *was* true, then a trick without parallel has been played on history. Getting at the truth would surely be a task of unpredictable length and labor. No short cuts were permissible. The detective documents and other newfound material that appeared to support them would have to be checked against independent evidence—and particularly that which anybody could readily look up in international and regional archives. The effort must be exhaustive, the search conducted just as diligently to refute as to corroborate. Double-checking became the order of the day.

CHAPTER 2

Montreal: A Prelude

Throughout much of the nineteenth century, one of Canada's largest and most fashionable hotels was Montreal's St. Lawrence Hall. It occupied an entire block of St. James Street with two hundred well-ventilated suites popular with foreign dignitaries, international businessmen, and British royalty. During the latter two years of America's Civil War, it also catered to a more secretive clientele, serving as a safe and luxuriant habitat for agents from both sides of the fratricidal bloodbath.

In the main lobby barbershop, Americans regularly gathered, "submitting their cheeks," an observant guest noted, "to the barber's razor and their ears to the latest news." Although Montreal's newspapers editorialized, "We must keep the war away from the shores of Canada as we do from those of Great Britain," Confederate spies and sympathizers met beneath the crystal pendants of the dining room's gas-lit chandeliers, around the grand piano in the plushly furnished second-floor lounge, or around the tables in the basement billiard parlor. And as often as not, they were under the steady watch of the U.S. North's federal detectives. No history book can depict what precisely occurred during a closed-door business conference held in the St. Lawrence Hall on Wednesday, October 19, 1864. But we now know of the circumstances surrounding it. At the time it was the culmination of months of clandestine activity. Couriers had risked life and limb to deliver messages. Agents of both sides in the war courted danger by dealing personally with each other behind battle lines. Speculators with an eye on huge fortunes knew they would face ruin should plans go awry. Dollars by the million were at stake.

* * *

Rain had drenched Montreal for days. The sidewalk fronting St. Lawrence Hall's noble entrance bustled with arrivals and departures and baggage-laden porters, as horse-drawn carriages drew up, one after another, along the sodden curb. Inside, guests thronged the lobby, which included a post office, a telegraph bureau, and newspaper stalls. Others drank at the hundred-foot-long bar or sat reading the *Montreal Herald* in the slope-backed armchairs that lined the walls, spittoons within easy reach between every two chairs.

The newspaper reported that business houses in Liverpool faced disaster, due to reduced cotton shipments from America. Telegraphed dispatches from New York relayed news of fighting near Chattanooga, of Philip Sheridan's devastating ride through the Shenandoah Valley, the body count climbing to rival that of the summer's carnage at Cold Harbor.

On October 14, thirty-nine-year-old Robert Daniel Watson checked in, writing "Liverpool" as his destination. If his narrow, bearded face expressed both eagerness and apprehension, it was because the deal, whose planned closure Watson was in Montreal to attend, bore uncertain hazards, as well as a promise of profits greater than any he had so far enjoyed as one of the American Midwest's most prominent farmers, livestock owners, and merchant capitalists. Watson was assigned to Room 196.

Doctor Luke Blackburn, a Confederate physician who had fought cholera and yellow fever on two continents, reached the St. Lawrence Hall the next day. At forty-eight and with whitening hair, he was the oldest of the group assembling in Montreal to finalize negotiations. Blackburn's concerns were humane. Earlier that year, he had served on a committee to study the health of Union captives. He knew the horrors of Andersonville. His efforts to promote a mass exchange of prisoners had been thwarted by the reluctance of Jefferson Davis, the South's leader, to free enemy soldiers whom he feared could become once more fit for combat. Another obstacle was Abraham Lincoln's inability to counter the opposition of his secretary of war and of General Ulysses S. Grant to any plan for a huge military swap. Blackburn had reminded his government in Richmond that food, shelter, and clothing were scarce enough for the South's civilians and armies. How, then, to keep alive more than one hundred thousand Union prisoners? "If we hold them throughout the winter," he wrote on August 29, "at least 20,000 will die before June the first, 1865. We cannot justify this in the eyes of God or man."

More than six feet tall and with a ruddy complexion, Nathaniel Beverley Tucker signed in with some difficulty. He wore a black glove on his right hand to conceal the stump left by an amputated thumb. Tucker's affable manner betrayed no hint of a lifetime of vicissitudes. Briefly a prewar newspaper editor in Washington, where he still had influential friends, and in Europe a failed businessman, Beverley Tucker espoused the Southern cause. It was while serving in the Home Guard, defending Richmond, that he accidentally cut his thumb by drawing a rusty sword from its scabbard. When the wound became inflamed, there was no time for proper treatment.

Jefferson Davis had at last approved, reluctantly, a policy permitting the exchange of Southern cotton for Northern supplies across the battle lines. Large-scale deals were most safely negotiated from a neutral base. Tucker had mercantile experience and knew how to make contact with businessmen on both sides of the war. Even though it meant leaving his wife and eight children, he was eager to perform some valuable service for the Confederacy. So he was a natural choice to sign an agreement with the Bureau of Subsistence in Richmond, committing him to secure vast amounts of Northern meat in return for cotton.

In early April, thumb bandaged, Tucker had boarded a blockade-runner that, by detouring via Bermuda and the Bahamas, took him safely into Halifax, Nova Scotia. Here a doctor cut off the thumb but warned against further travel. Even so, Tucker sped inland through snowstorms by open sleigh. Finally settled in Canada, he busily engaged himself making contacts. They were extensive. He refused to let pain impede him. Nor was he defeated by news that Richmond authorities had denied his wife's appeal to join him in Canada. In June he wrote to his brother, "I have abiding confidence in our noble Lee . . . and our brave and devoted army. . . . but how many anxious hours I pass, and how much I deplore the separation from all I love."

That same month Tucker expressed surprise and displeasure on learning that two other Confederate agents, styled "commissioners," had arrived in Canada under vague orders to make mischief for the North.

In August the Confederate president Jefferson Davis sent Jacob Thompson, a wealthy Mississippi lawyer, and Clement C. Clay, a former United States senator from Alabama, to Canada for an expected six months' stay, during which they were to foment mischief against the North from neutral soil. Both in their fifties, asthmatic, and homesick, they were an unlikely pair for the job. On a limited budget they planned hit-and-run raids on New England towns, expeditions to free Confederate prisoners of war, and active alliances with pro-South "secret societies" based in the American Midwest. Few of their projects amounted to anything serious. An exception was the St. Albans raid, coincidentally staged the same date as the St. Lawrence Hall business meeting. A band of Confederate guerrillas slipped into the Vermont town and robbed three banks, escaping to Canada with eight or ten thousand dollars. But by then, Clay's and Thompson's mood was at its lowest. "We came here on a fool's errand," Clay had only just complained to Richmond. "I feel as cheap as humiliation can make. We will leave here sadder and wiser men."

Tucker was not pleased by the presence of those commissioners. "I am on a peaceful mission," he wrote to his wife, Jane, "best achieved if I participate in nothing else." And now, in October, he could savor the prospect of an early and triumphant return home. The success of his six months' labor appeared imminent. "The negotiation here has been already completed," he reported, "and the parties are strongly backed to carry it out."

William Arthur Browning, confidential aide to Governor Andrew Johnson of Tennessee, checked in on the evening of the 15th at about eleven o'clock. Browning's role in shaping the great meat-for-cotton deal about to be closed was that of emissary; he was quick-witted and equipped with military passports ensuring him unmolested travel in the North and the South. With Nashville his base, Browning had kept interested parties in Canada, New York, Washington, and Richmond abreast of progress, frequently doing so through a privileged channel of communication—Union army telegraph lines. As Will Browning well knew, the telegraph was a valuable handmaiden of big business. Wall Street ran its own private network, providing speculators with advance data on the progress of the war. New York financiers were often better informed about battles than Washington, Richmond, and even field commanders were.

Browning was an effective spark plug in the commercial undertaking, a self-proclaimed envoy without portfolio, ostensibly exploring avenues for peace—above all, a get-rich-quick artist who had worked closely with the livestock owner R. D. Watson from the inception of the super-deal. A photo of the twenty-nine-year-old Browning with his family shows him clean-shaven; in another, his face appears adorned with a jet-black beard so heavy as to compel suspicion of a disguise. Certainly, he signed the St. Lawrence Hall register with a false name, D. A. MacDonald, the same alias he had used on his many stays in Montreal since the beginning of the year.

Will Browning's room was No. 132. Just ninety minutes before him, a guest was booked into Room No. 150. This guest used his real name, penned in a bold hand—John Wilkes Booth. An American actor almost as well known in every Canadian metropolis as in those of his own country, north and south, he had no occasion for subterfuge. His presence at the St. Lawrence Hall was to help Will Browning push ahead with the meat-for-cotton plans. He also had something else in mind but, having so far done little about it, felt safe from suspicion. This was just as well, because the principal objective of his mission to Montreal was hoped-for cooperation in a scheme of his own, one spelling danger for Abraham Lincoln.

In addition to his personal quarters at the St. Lawrence Hall, R. D. Watson had rented a large room on the second floor to serve as the group's conference chamber. What they were about to discuss would not have enjoyed unanimous approval, in either Richmond or Washington. But Beverley Tucker, for one, knew how to challenge opposition from his constituency. His words would be to the point. "Where are we to look," he would ask, "for indispensable supplies if not through the cupidity and avarice of our enemies?"

Gratifying them was abhorrent to him, but it made sense to capitalize on Northern greed when the alternative was starvation for General Robert E. Lee's fighting men.

When they convened, introductions were brief. Business got under way, with James Virgul Barnes, chairman by general consent. Barnes was a shrewd-eyed thirty-year-old agent for international merchant bankers. Amid cigar smoke and brandy fumes, the meeting lasted well beyond midnight. At the outset Browning, tacitly acknowledged as representing Lincoln's government, was handed a message brought up from the telegraph bureau. It told of changed minds in Washington. Instead of payment entirely in meat on a pound-for-pound basis, half the cotton must be paid for in Union greenbacks.

Tucker protested. Half a pound of bacon for every pound of cotton, the balance made up of Yankee currency, was not what he had worked so far from home to bargain for. Arguments arose. Compromise quieted them. "I will agree to the new terms," Tucker finally said, "if the amounts on both sides are doubled." This would enable him to fulfill the promise he had made in Richmond to secure 5 million pounds of bacon. He would have wished for more. But at least, based on existing army rations, that amount could be calculated to feed Lee's famished soldiers for another hundred days.

This seemed fair enough. After satisfying Tucker that the parties he represented were "powerful and influential with the U.S. government," Will Browning continued that with their involvement, he could guarantee to supply "at least half supplies of meat, the other half greenbacks, for all the cotton your government may feel disposed to part with. If the deal falls through it will be because of your side." Everything had to be done with the utmost secrecy. "These precautions are essential for the sake of protecting the Executive, to whom we are alone indebted."

The Executive. Like everyone else around the conference table, Luke Blackburn knew who that was. He also believed that the ordeal of Union prisoners of war burdened that man's mind as it did his own. This was why he was in Montreal, to make sure of the linkage. Captives would be released on both sides, concurrently with the commercial exchange. This was part of the deal. The doctor's only stipulation was that it be delayed until the first frost to ensure that no plague from the prisons spread north through infected soldiers.

Blackburn was soon disillusioned. His attempts to discuss the subject of prisoners of war were unheeded. As bargaining chips, they had ceased to count. Neither was much notice paid to an offer from John Wilkes Booth to furnish a vessel or two from the rag-tag Chesapeake Bay flotilla he used to smuggle medical supplies into the South. The actor was told that a token cargo of three hundred barrels of Northern pork was already bound for Mobile, where cotton awaited. Assuming the success of this first step, more meat would enter the Confederacy downstream on R. D. Watson's dozen Mississippi River steamboats.

At least from Will Browning's point of view, everything was cut and dried. The United States Treasury had already imposed a 25 percent tax on whatever transactions Northern speculators arranged. The deal thrashed out in Montreal would result in still greater benefit to the North from a fall in the price of gold that economists figured would follow the reappearance of American cotton on the overseas market. This monetary gain would enable the Union to accelerate its war effort, with hopes for an early victory. On the other side, for the Confederacy, extra food would strengthen its soldiers enough to keep them in the field.

Profits beckoned from every angle. Ten million pounds of cotton would fall into Northern hands, half of it paid for in pork shipped into the South from Watson's storages and smokehouses along the Ohio and Mississippi rivers. The other half would be paid for in greenbacks at 60 percent of the going price for cotton in New York. A heavy share of the proceeds would go to Watson and his partners. Watson welcomed the prospect, after two years of selling meat to federal troops at bankruptcy prices or hiding it to avoid seizure. Modest commissions would be allotted to sundry bagmen and second-stringers. Will Browning expected a small fortune for his energetic investment. Richer rewards would go to James V. Barnes, who had induced the moneymen he worked for to deposit a $1 million surety bond against any default. Barnes had every reason to feel proud of having structured the superdeal. He estimated that its success was worth, to British interests, a staggering 250 million pounds sterling.

Beverley Tucker was elated. His only cause for annoyance was an obligation imposed on him by Richmond to consider the two "commissioners" in Canada his seniors. Neither had attended the St. Lawrence Hall conference and were not even in the building but waited miserably in another Montreal hotel for the war to end.

Tucker was under orders to get the commissioners' endorsement of his every move. Accompanied by Luke Blackburn, he hurried across town to the Donegana Hotel, where the pair lodged. To his report of success at the St. Lawrence Hall, they voiced approval, with little absorption of the details. They showed still less interest when Blackburn brought up the matter of a large-scale prisoner exchange.

Tucker drafted a jubilant report for Richmond. Had his work in Canada failed, he would be forever haunted by regrets that he had not remained a humble soldier. Instead, "I felt as thankful to God as if I had achieved a successful military campaign." The whole scheme, he wrote, was "endorsed by the highest official in the United States government." In case these words were not strong enough to impress his Richmond bosses, Tucker closed with a euphoric postscript. "I have seen with my own eyes Old Abe's written permission to pass the Blockading Squadron at Mobile, with vessels to take in meat and bring out cotton."

CHAPTER 3

Wheelers and Dealers

Over time, every Civil War engagement from Bull Run to the fall of Richmond has been meticulously chronicled, many of them even bloodlessly reenacted as entertainment, while far less attention has been given to the economic pressures that affected the combatants.

The men at the St. Lawrence Hall knew of cotton's importance to the republic's existence. Commercial covenants binding the nation as one were founded on the production and sale of cotton. Mutual profit had wedded the South's planter class to the North's shippers, bankers, and insurers and both of them to the European textile industries. These were the elements of a great trading triangle, on which for more than three-quarters of a century had rested the wealth and stability of two continents. The Civil War had shattered them.

To win foreign credit with which to buy arms and supplies, the Confederacy had at first tried to ship its cotton directly to foreign ports. The Union had countered with a naval blockade. Even then, Richmond's leaders had expected the collapse of the traditional trade structure to work in their favor. Once Europe felt the squeeze of declining cotton imports, diplomatic pressure and the threat of British and French warships off American coasts would compel Abraham Lincoln to seek peace. So hoped the South. The doors of Britain's mills closed; half a million employees in Lancashire alone were thrown out of work. In London, Liverpool, Manchester, and Paris, merchants and politicians talked more and more of entering America's war, on the side of the South.

Thus President Lincoln had to reckon with a possibility that the Confederacy would gain cotton-hungry allies. Even without the staple itself on the high seas, the South managed to use it to some advantage, arranging European loans in exchange for cotton bonds. The North had no such drawing card. The cotton remained in Southern hands. Union troops who might have "liberated" it were stalemated on battlefields from Virginia to Vicksburg. When Northern bankers staged bond-raising jamborees to help finance the war, they failed to meet goals. And foreign credit abroad was scarcely to be had in countries where Lincoln was blamed for wrecking trade. Only a resumption of the cotton flow to Europe would restore it. For the North, no less than the South, cotton had become the means of survival.

Thus the Montreal conclave. To secure Confederate cotton and resume transatlantic shipments, Abraham Lincoln had gambled his political future on a plan that all but guaranteed graft and corruption. But he saw nothing morally wrong or constitutionally sinful in trading with the enemy, providing business was confined to areas brought by force of arms under Union jurisdiction. As his secretary of the treasury, Salmon P. Chase, stated, "Let commerce follow the flag."

Commerce all but swallowed the flag. Cotton bought from the South fetched twelve times the purchase price in New York before its shipment abroad. This produced a new battlefield phenomenon: Wall Street–bred camp followers who ferreted out bales of cotton ahead of and behind each Union army push, via security leaks and telegraph. "The temptation is so great that everybody wishes to be in it, and when in, the question of profit controls all, regardless of whether the cotton seller is loyal or rebel." Those were Abraham Lincoln's own words in 1863. In almost the same breath, he egged on the practice by telling army officers to do nothing that would prevent Confederate cotton from coming through the lines. "It is deemed important to get as much as we can into the market."

By that time, Confederate leaders realized that after all, they might not be able to buy foreign allies with promised cotton. The British and the French were managing with imports, albeit of inferior quality, from India and Egypt. Moreover, after the Confederate defeats of 1863, European powers lost whatever zeal they had had for joining in the American struggle. War strategists in Richmond continued to pin faith in cotton as their ace card, but they then had to play it in a different game, one dictated by the specter of famine on the home front and, most seriously, among their fighting forces.

Swine fever in Southern states had wiped out herds. Rich grazing lands were lost to the North. Food ships crossing the Atlantic ran afoul of Union blockades. Bureaucrats so fumbled a plan to ship provisions from Bermuda and the Bahamas that tons of bacon procured there putrefied in the sun. Lee's soldiers who had survived the slaughter at Gettysburg trudged home on reduced rations. Morale sagged among them; mutiny loomed.

For Jefferson Davis, trading with Yankees went against the grain. But, finally, he had authorized field officers to barter for food, as well as for military ordnance. Quick to recognize the value of cotton as currency, quartermasters were soon buying bales for themselves and trading them for meat from behind enemy lines. The barter was at first piecemeal, but, to astute businessmen, it was apparent that fortunes could be reaped. Bales were piled up in the swamps and forests of the Deep South and on wharves in Mobile, Savannah, Charleston, and Wilmington. Northward, in the Mississippi and Ohio River basins, the walls of smokehouses bulged with salt pork. And in New York, commercial opportunism and speculation flourished as never before.

Abraham Lincoln had understood all this as the war entered its third year. Some of his generals were dead set against trafficking with the foe and sent angry letters to congressmen and even the White House. In a letter unpublished for years, Lincoln explained his thinking: "Our finances are greatly involved in the matter." A supreme effort was needed to replenish the national treasury. As crucial weeks advanced, so had a semiclandestine cotton policy of the president's own design. It was to serve "the public interest." This was Lincoln's rationale for fostering private deals between Northern capitalists and Southern cotton growers. His words gave no hint of the political minefield he would be treading. War profiteering? "If pecuniary greed can be made to aid us, let us be thankful that so much good can be got out of pecuniary greed."

To say that Montreal in late fall swarmed with spies from both sides in America's war would be to exaggerate, but not by much. Colonel Lafayette Baker's NDP prowlers were busy. Baker had fallen out of favor with Stanton in the summer of 1863, when the same line of thunderstorms that cleansed Gettysburg's battleground disrupted telegraph communication elsewhere in the eastern United States. Washington was briefly isolated. "Junius Pluvius Succeeds Where Lee Failed," ran an *Evening Star* headline. Repairs were quickly under way. Baker's men at the NDP's secret service post seized the moment to install a tap on the military wire between field commanders and the War Department.

When Stanton learned of this, he ordered NDP activity substantially curbed. Even so, Baker remained the Department's chief detective. In Montreal, after the St. Lawrence Hall business conference adjourned, one of Baker's agents, code-named Rob Rover, studied the guest book. His purpose in Canada was to nab Captain Thomas Hines, a Confederate operative believed en route from Chicago to secure Clay's and Thompson's approval and also funds, for a bold attempt to liberate thousands of Confederate prisoners of war.

Rob Rover had received an informer's tip that a man answering to Hines's description was at the St. Lawrence Hall in Room 150. He checked the register and furtively tore out a portion of the appropriate page for later examination, after which he telegraphed Baker that Hines was indeed there under a false name. Further sleuthing convinced Rob Rover that he had made a mistake. He sent his chief another wire. Hines was still in Chicago. The occupant of Room 150 was exactly who he said he was. "The man we thought was Hines is instead John Wilkes Booth, an actor from Baltimore."

Rob Rover told this to another agent, code-named "O. U. Rice" or "Our Rebel," and suggested that Booth be placed under surveillance in case he, too, was up to no good. What Rob Rover did not know was that O. U. Rice was a double agent whom the rebel commissioners trusted. Jacob Thompson allowed Rice to hide behind window drapes when Booth came to the Donegana Hotel. The double agent told Rob Rover what he had heard, and off went another telegram to Lafayette Baker in Washington. "Booth discussed with Jacob Thompson a plot to kidnap President Lincoln. The conversation was overheard by Our Rebel who was present. It is not yet known whether the rebel government is agreeable to it but the plot was hatched by Booth. I feel certain that with or without rebel government aid this man will attempt it. He should be watched."

* * *

Born on May 10, 1838, the son of Junius Brutus Booth, a powerful but increasingly alcoholic actor, Booth began his professional career at the age of twenty in the Holiday Street Theatre stock company in Baltimore. For the next three years, while his brother Edwin won acting glory abroad, Wilkes had little more than walk-on parts, and he stumbled frequently, often forgot his lines, and once had to be dragged off into the wings, frozen with stage fright. He fought hard to perfect himself and to avoid the embarrassment of public comparison with his acting brothers Edwin and Junius Brutus Jr. and their late father. He adopted the stage name "John Wilkes." In 1859 he married Izola D'Arcy Mills, a seafarer's daughter and an aspiring actress. When having a wife in tow seemed hardly to square with a romantic public image, Booth's father had settled his own spouse on a comfortable but remote Maryland farm. Following suit, John Wilkes Booth found an isolated retreat for Izola and their daughter, a hilltop home and thirty-six acres overlooking the Shenandoah River near Harper's Ferry. He christened the place Mount Olympus.

His evolution into a player of unnerving energy came almost overnight. Edwin had returned from an Australian tour, and in Richmond he got his younger brother the role of Horatio to his Hamlet. Before a packed house, Edwin introduced him in a tone some might have thought condescending. The effect on John Wilkes was galvanic. He shed all traces of inferiority and redoubled his efforts to overtake, to surpass. Edwin soon felt the competition at his heels. Writing to his mother, he said that he did not expect John to "startle the world" but conceded that his brother had certainly improved as an actor and "looked beautiful on the platform."

Even offstage, John Wilkes Booth cut a compelling figure. He moved gracefully, was of lithe physique, and, when it suited him, could soften his handsome, sometimes brooding face into the most lady-killing of smiles. It seems he was unable to discuss a subject, however trivial, without striking a pose. Men as well as women, meeting Booth for the first time, were apt to walk away dazed. The Montreal meeting was probably an exception: Among the determined men at the St. Lawrence Hall, the twenty-six-year-old actor could not have stolen that show if he had tried.

Booth supported the Confederate cause and, especially after brandy, loudly acclaimed it. But following brief prewar militia service, he kept a promise to his mother never again to don a uniform offstage. In 1863, onstage, he had excited audiences as if to outshine the more experienced Edwin. The voice could be shrill and he often raced his lines, but the nineteenth-century American stage knew no more vehement a performer. He tore through roles with such zest that fellow actors would pant for him to take it easy. As Count Pescara in *The Apostate,* "he seems to revel in rascality, to enjoy devilish tricks . . . glory like another Lucifer in the misery he has caused." And in this role, he had once stabbed himself in the arm. Yet the last act of *King Richard III* was Booth's personal tour de force. "He dies hard . . . face blackened with blood . . . a face of a thousand masks." Once he defied history and Shakespeare by tumbling the actor playing Richmond into the orchestra pit.

On Monday evening, November 9, 1863, he performed at Ford's Theatre, Washington, in a play by Charles Selby called *The Marble Heart.* Abraham Lincoln sat in the state box. The president could afford to take a brief respite from the pressure of wartime responsibilities. It was a period in the Civil War when campaigns were planned rather than fought, a relatively bloodless interval between the summer fighting at Gettysburg and the impending struggle for Chattanooga. For the time being, Lincoln's thoughts were not so crushingly burdened by high casualty figures.

To drama critics in the audience, the star of the play exhibited "a grasp of genius," was "an actor of rare merit." And at the final curtain, Abraham Lincoln joined the rest of the audience in applauding the man who would kill him.

All this time, few Americans suspected that their dynamic young thespian led a double life. One who did know was his sister Asia, to whom he had melodramatically declared, "My knowledge of drugs is invaluable, my beloved money . . . oh, never beloved until now, is the means, one of the means by which I serve the South." But only briefly did he disclose how he smuggled medicines into the Confederacy.

Booth's drugs were brought into American waters by brigs and schooners salvaged from a once-prosperous shipping concern, J and J Chaffey, based on Indian Island, New Brunswick, Canada, which contemporary guidebooks flattered as "the little sea nymph of Passamaquoddy Bay." In the mid-nineteenth century the English-born brothers Chaffey, with at least a dozen sailing ships, plied the Atlantic seaboard with ships that carried Canadian lumber, millwork, and salt fish, returning north with sugar, molasses, rum, and household luxuries. Since the Civil War's second year, under Booth's often remote but effective direction, these decrepit craft had skirted the Union blockade to creep up Chesapeake Bay and into secret unloading coves, where Confederate carriers waited to collect their cargoes of medicine for the journey into rebeldom. Serving the South in this manner assuaged any pangs of guilt the actor felt from avoiding that other theater, where blood was real and the sobbing unrehearsed. Also, the pay was good.

More recently, Booth had invested in oil, forming a partnership with a Cleveland theatrical entrepreneur named John Ellsler and an alcoholic sportsman. They had bought land in western Pennsylvania, a region attracting swarms of speculators. Booth footed most of the bill for drilling costs. Early reports from the property were not encouraging; also, the drunken partner had become a liability. And in the meantime, Booth had separated from his wife, Izola, following the birth of their daughter.

Five nights after performing in Washington before Lincoln, whom he detested, Booth embarked on a western tour that was all but ruined by wintry weather. He had accumulated funds in Canadian banks and a fortune in foreign mintage that was secreted at Mount Olympus. But wartime restrictions had prevented their conversion into ready cash.

At the Union Theatre in Leavenworth, Kansas, he gave Christmas week performances but was snowed in for days in St. Joseph, Missouri. When hotel and brandy bills consumed the last of his resources, he recouped to the amount of $150 only through impromptu readings at Corby's Hall. His poetry choices, according to the local press, included "Beautiful Snow" and "Once I Was Pure."

To begin the return east, Booth hired a horse and sleigh and "came 160 miles over the plains," he wrote to Ellsler, his Cleveland partner. "Four days and nights in the largest snowdrifts I ever saw. I never knew what hardship was until then."

He arrived in St. Louis by train, four days late for his engagement. His next stop was Louisville, and he later boasted of having used a pistol to make sure of getting there on time. When deep snow halted the train, he threatened to blow the conductor's head off if the engineer did not start up again. "I have had a rough time," he told Ellsler early in 1864, adding, "I am anxious for our business to go on, as you are. Let us push this thing through. I go from here to Nashville."

He opened in the Tennessee capital the first of February with Shakespeare's *King Richard III* and was an immediate success. And it was here that Booth first met Will Browning and was drawn into the meat-for-cotton scheme.

Browning came from a tailor's family in Washington that had befriended the Tennesseean Andrew Johnson, himself once a tailor, during his lonely days as a freshman senator. When Johnson returned to Nashville in 1862 as the state's governor-general, he had shown his appreciation by taking Will Browning with him as a private aide, designated "colonel."

Browning was demonstrably of pro-Southern stock. His father collected secessionist poetry. His brother Ringgold was an active Confederate guerrilla and a contraband runner. More than once Andrew Johnson, again out of gratitude to the Brownings, had pulled strings in Washington to get Ringgold out of the Old Capitol Prison. As governor, Johnson had quickly become immersed in the problems of his sundered state and, as a result, gave his young aide extraordinary leeway.

Browning was able to reach the right people, regardless of ideological differences. At the close of 1863 he had visited Richmond, under his alias "MacDonald," for private talks with Confederate leaders. As was by then a key element of his method of operation, he emphasized the grandiose trade and prisoner-of-war scheme, claiming that it had the backing, necessarily confidential, of President Lincoln. It was partly a result of Browning's Richmond visits that Jeff Davis had sent Beverley Tucker to Montreal. And in those early weeks of 1864 Browning had met Booth, then giving Nashville theatergoers more than their money's worth in galvanizing performances. The two young men became fast friends, finding that they had a lot in common—including philandering, although Browning had a wife and two daughters in Alexandria, Virginia.

While Governor Johnson was absent, in Washington briefing President Lincoln on the war situation in Tennessee, Booth and Will Browning conferred in the former's dressing room at the Nashville Theatre on Cherry Street or behind closed doors in the state capitol on Cedar Knob. Browning told Booth of the great meat-for-cotton scheme, which would certainly profit investors but would also achieve loftier aims, emptying hellish prison camps and perhaps even shortening the war.

It was a sales pitch that Browning had earlier elaborated during his hush-hush talks with top men in Richmond, where he was quick to recognize and build on Confederate presumptions of unbridled Yankee avarice. Trading contracts, for whose procurement Beverley Tucker had gone to Montreal, were expected to be broad enough, in the words of a Richmond bureaucrat, to "tempt cupidity or venality." American cotton sold in Europe now could fetch, in gold, six times the prewar price paid Southerners. What Northern capitalist could possibly resist the South's offer of cotton in liberal quantities as payment for his products?

This, more or less, was the engaging vision with which Browning regaled John Wilkes Booth in Nashville. As an actor of widespread eminence, Booth carried a military passport. Browning believed he could use Booth's help in the task that kept him so much on the move. Booth offered to cooperate. It was a partnership quickly put to the test. News reached both men in March of a Union cavalry raid against Richmond, aimed at burning the Confederate capital and hanging its leaders, Jefferson Davis included.

CHAPTER 4

The Dahlgren Raid

The raid was headed by Judson Kilpatrick, a twenty-eight-year-old brigadier-general whose command included such daring colonels as Ulric Dahlgren, who lost a leg at Gettysburg, and George Armstrong Custer. Kilpatrick called at the White House on February 13, the day on which Booth appeared in a dual role in his final Nashville performance *The Corsican Brothers*. Kilpatrick told Abraham Lincoln that his intentions were confined to sabotage, distribution of handbills promising amnesty to rebels who joined the Union cause, and freeing Union prisoners from Richmond's Libby prison.

Lincoln approved. Neither Secretary of War Stanton nor General Grant could be budged from their opposition to a peaceful exchange of prisoners. And though Lincoln liked the idea of demolishing prison gates, practical politics and common humanity also determined his endorsement of Kilpatrick's stated battle plan. That year, 1864, was an election year. Lincoln was aware that war-weary Northerners had begun to blame him for prolonging the conflict.

So, under a bright moon on Sunday, February 28, Kilpatrick's Third Cavalry Division, 3,500 strong, forded the Rapidan River. Six artillery pieces augmented the cavalcade. Bundles of amnesty pamphlets burdened mules plodding at the rear.

Colonel Dahlgren's advance column detoured westward to cross the James River upstream. His objectives at Richmond had little to do with remission of sin and a goodwill handshake. "Guides and pioneers," he had ordered, "with oakum, turpentine and torpedoes, and scouts and men in rebel uniform will move down with the force on the south bank. Everything depends on surprise." Mills were to be set ablaze and plenty of oakum and turpentine saved for burning "when we get into the city." Reaching the James at Jude's Ferry, the colonel found it swollen by melting snows off the Blue Ridge. Fording was impossible and the cavalry had no boats. Enraged by frustration, Dahlgren turned on his black guide and charged him with treason. Minutes later, the guide's body dangled from a tree.

In sudden rain that turned to sleet, Dahlgren's column was forced to move along the left bank instead of the right, making for Richmond from the west instead of by a swing from the south. He heard the echoes of Kilpatrick's cannon, a barrage of ominously short duration. His soldiers ploughed on, wrecking canal boats and locks, a coal mine, saw mills, and grist mills. With Richmond still four miles off, the troops encountered savage enemy fire, and visions of thundering in triumph through the heart of the city faded. Dahlgren now perceived the city to be a trap. He wheeled his force back north to rejoin the division.

He had some catching up to do. General Kilpatrick had no sooner reached Richmond's northern outskirts when he learned that rebel sharp-shooters had massed in the pines behind him. Moreover, his first artillery salvoes had drawn a heavy response from the city's breastworks. With unexpected resistance ahead and his northern retreat cut off, the general had decided not to wait for Dahlgren as planned. He hauled his troops off the Brook Turnpike, leaving sixty dead or wounded and bundles of amnesty bills behind. They hurried east across the Fredericksburg and Richmond Railroad tracks and "destroyed everything within reach," the *New York Times* said, making the best of a sorry situation.

Kilpatrick's men pitched camp in freezing meadows alongside the Chickahominy River. Reluctant to quit, the general was weighing chances of an assault on Richmond from a new direction when enemy guns opened up quite close and rebels swarmed in force from the woods around Hanover Court House. Too numbed or weary to make a stand, the Union soldiers scattered, half of them on foot as their horses stampeded.

Dahlgren's troops, meanwhile, had swung their mounts away from the outskirts of Richmond and ridden up and around the city. After crossing the now abandoned and body-strewn turnpike in icy darkness, the column broke in two. By Wednesday noon, Dahlgren had reached the Mattaponi River, twenty-five miles east of Richmond, pursued by rebel marksmen. Reduced in strength to less than a hundred men in the saddle, the detachment floundered through a racing current to the far side. The colonel was last to cross, holding off the enemy with a pistol. But gallant rearguard gestures were of no avail. The whole countryside was up in arms. Home guards, militiamen, and soldiers on furlough had banded into groups against the Yankee invaders. Confident yet of linking up with Kilpatrick, Dahlgren led his men down the highway to King and Queen Court House, headlong into an ambush. Before the raid, Ulric Dahlgren had told his father that he knew of no better place for a Union officer to fall in action than in Richmond. Under crossfire, he died on a muddy road twenty miles away.

All that Wednesday, the rebels snapped at General Kilpatrick's heels. Finally, he shook them off, and, joined by survivors of Dahlgren's party who gasped out their own melancholy tale, he led his men to the safety of Union lines along the York River. He had suffered more than three hundred casualties, and the prisoners supposed to have been freed were in a fix worse than ever. Cramped living space and civilian resentment over sharing meager rations with Yankee soldiers had forced Richmond authorities to explore new sites for prisoner confinement. Kilpatrick's raid speeded up plans for their transfer, to a new location in the Georgia swamplands, a place called Andersonville.

According to Richmond news dispatches, papers taken from Dahlgren's body contained orders to unlock prison barracks, then "burn the hateful city. It must be destroyed and JEFF DAVIS and his cabinet killed." The South reacted to these disclosures with fury. That the scheme had miscarried in no way mitigated its foulness. That the would-be assassins and arsonists were routed by valiant Confederates did nothing to erase the brutal true colors in which the Union's masters were at last exposed. Richmond newspapers branded them fiends bent "on a war of extermination. What more have we to dread from Yankee malice? What have we to hope from their clemency?" So much for Abraham Lincoln's readiness to pardon and embrace.

As Southerners raged on, political radicals in the North charged that faked documents had been planted on the colonel's body. In private, those fiercely anti-rebel war hawks exulted over the outcome of the raid almost as much as if the detested Richmond leaders had indeed been put to death. It purged the war of foolish chivalry and had reduced "Old Abe's" amnesty leaflets to irrelevant scraps of paper. For appearances' sake, the Union army held a formal inquiry. Kilpatrick denied any intention of political murder or unjustified arson. Dahlgren's staff officers swore to the innocence of their lost commander. These statements were made public. Kept quiet was evidence that Lafayette Baker's detectives had found, showing that Dahlgren's orders had come via General Kilpatrick from Secretary Stanton. And only among themselves did some of the North's top army officers assert their belief that the papers taken from the dead colonel were indeed genuine.

Genuine or false, they boded ill for Lincoln. The obvious consequences were grave enough. The purported disclosure of a plot to murder Confederate heads of state and set Richmond afire had roused Southerners to unprecedented anger. It guaranteed a prolonged and more bitter war and made mincemeat of Lincoln's hopes for national reunification. As events proved, it also helped seal his death warrant.

Those bleak March days were among the most distressing in Lincoln's memory. For respite, he paid a series of visits to Grover's Theatre. The featured star was Edwin Booth, and within a single week the president saw him in *Hamlet, Cardinal Richelieu, The Fool's Revenge,* and *Richard III*. Seated in his regular box, long legs stretched sideways, he could for fleeting hours forget that misfired cavalry raid and its ominous significance for the future course of the war. Mercifully, too, he was unaware of its impact on the febrile brain of Edwin's younger brother.

John Wilkes Booth had read the front-page accounts of the North's alleged perfidy on the eve of a five-week engagement in New Orleans. That the charges were true, he did not doubt for a moment. His feelings may have been acted out onstage, to the awe of New Orleans critics. His opening performances were "masterpieces of satanic dissimulation." Stalking about the bloody field of Bosworth, he was "absolutely horrifying." And then, abruptly, Booth was stricken with a strange hoarseness. It ruined, one after another, his portrayals of Gloucester, Othello, and Macbeth. So bad was his Shylock in *The Merchant of Venice* on March 25 that the manager of the St. Charles Theatre stepped before the house and announced with regret that the tragedian had a cold and must rest. Before another week, the New Orleans engagement was canceled.

Booth's throat trouble persisted. So, too, did the rankling memory of the Dahlgren raid. It threatened to rob Colonel Will Browning in Nashville of the valuable ally he had recruited into the meat-for-cotton project. When next they communicated, he tried to convince the actor that the papers causing so much recent commotion must have been thrust into Dahlgren's pockets by extremists of the South, bent on wrecking peace moves. Browning's words took some of the edge off the actor's emotions, or so it seemed. Once more, Booth consented to help him. "When you needed me," he was to recall in characteristically florid terms, "I gladly gave you succor, virtually abandoning my profession. I followed you like a modern-day Christus, seeking an end to this madness."

But he could not entirely swallow Browning's theory that the documents were a hoax rigged by Richmond's war hawks. Moreover, it suited his theatrical instinct for a vengeful role to believe otherwise. From this point on, Booth was ripe and ready for any kind of a move against Lincoln. Abduction, he had already thought of. The rebel commissioners had turned him down on that proposal, but others had thought of it as well. Three weeks after Kilpatrick's raid, the *New York Tribune* ran letters from an unnamed correspondent, alleging a conspiracy between rebel agents and Northern Copperheads—disloyal Democrats—to seize Lincoln in Washington and carry him off to Richmond. One hundred and fifty men and relays of horses were to be used. And if abduction had taken root in Booth's mind, so had the potential for murder. After the Dahlgren affair, notwithstanding Browning's attempts to mollify him, thespian Booth was self-cast in the real-life role of divine instrument to exact retribution for a tyrant's criminality.

CHAPTER 5

The Canadian Go-getter

The uproar over Kilpatrick's raid and the so-called Dahlgren papers had yet to subside when the North opened two major offensives. One marked the start of General William T. Sherman's drive into the lower South. The other was to destroy Lee's army north of Richmond. Those campaigns, both soon in trouble, gripped public attention. Early in May, one hundred thousand men under Sherman made for the Atlantic. Grant's soldiers, bound for the Wilderness, trudged through spring blossoms, the last many would ever see.

This renewed bloodshed was well under way when, at sea, the USS gunboat *Vicksburg* sighted a two-masted schooner while patrolling off the North Carolina coast. The Union captain ordered a shot fired across the stranger's bow and took her under tow. Upon boarding, he discovered that he had nabbed a mystery ship. She was no routine blockade-runner. Ship's papers identified her as the *Indian,* registered under the British flag. A coat of paint hid the name on her stern and she carried no log. There was no mate on board; the crew was made up of five blacks and a Mexican. The ship's master was J. M. Celeste. The Union naval commander described him as "suspicious."

The *Indian*'s hold contained nothing but a hogshead of palm oil, yet the captain's cabin yielded quantities of champagne and cigars and $30,000 in gold and silver. The size of the crew did not conform with the shipping list, made out at Belize, British Honduras. The *Vicksburg*'s skipper reported, "one man on board not accounted for." There was vague talk among the *Indian*'s crew of an unidentified passenger secreted on the schooner and since vanished.

Joas Miguel Celeste, of Anglo-Portuguese parentage, usually went by the name John Celestina. To his captors, he was stubbornly uncommunicative. He said little more than that he had left Matamoros, Mexico, with a cargo of cotton for Belize, and that bound next for Havana, his vessel had been swept by gales beyond Cuba into the Atlantic. Gulf Stream currents had carried her five hundred miles northward. The obliteration of the name on the ship's stern? A clumsy paint job, following repair of storm damage. Celestina refused to answer further questions, claiming immunity as a Portuguese subject.

Held as a suspected blockade-runner, he wrote appeals to the British and Portuguese envoys in Washington for their intercession. Conveniently for him, the United States Navy Department chose that moment to issue new rules protecting bona fide foreign subjects on ships seized in American waters. Celestina was at liberty within a month. And by then his mystery passenger, James Virgul Barnes, was safely ashore at Wilmington, North Carolina, and soon talking with Confederate officials in Richmond, concerning the plan Will Browning had already outlined there—the grand, clandestine program that would place them both in Montreal six months hence.

Barnes was born in 1835 in Belleville, on the Bay of Quinte, Ontario, and brought to the United States as a boy. He was about to seek his fortune in California when growing political tensions in the east offered more enticing prospects. Barnes opened an office on Wall Street, where he attracted the notice of important financiers.

Brown Brothers of New York used him. The business of that giant merchant bank was virtually at a halt because of the war's disruption of the transatlantic cotton trade. As a busy commercial traveler, Barnes had campaigned among profiteers and politicians on behalf of the big meat-for-cotton deal, following talks with British businessmen. One of his employers was Brown Shipley, a Liverpool house related to Brown Brothers and a cornerstone of the Anglo–U.S. cotton trade. His purpose that spring of 1864 was to estimate the amount of cotton under Confederate control. As bales were constantly moving across the Texas border to be exported via Mexico, his first stop after leaving England had been Matamoros, and it was there that Celestina, by prearrangement, had picked him up.

Barnes had worked for the retail "prince" Alexander Turney Stewart, a self-made millionaire who enjoyed few public pleasures, and whose mind seemed constantly to be taking inventory. He transferred hundreds of hungry families from impoverished Ireland, his birthplace, to New England, where he employed them in his textile mills at minimum wage. Stewart was the second biggest buyer of New York real estate, and no man owned more church property. His own place of worship was the office at his monumental store, and he rode to his daily devotions in a small coupe drawn economically by a single horse. Stewart's wife, who bore him no children, was seldom seen.

While on Stewart's payroll, Barnes journeyed abroad, securing contracts to supply laces, furs, brocades, carpets, chinaware, and chandeliers, all of which helped to make A. T. Stewart's block-long New York store, between Ninth and Tenth Street on Broadway, an eight-story steel-and-brick mecca for buyers of luxury merchandise.

When the Civil War began, A. T. Stewart was the country's largest dry-goods importer. His overseas chain of branches and warehouses stretched from Belfast and Berlin to the Mediterranean. His net worth in the 1860s exceeded $20 million, and he continued to profit from war contracts with Lincoln's government, while contributing regularly to Lincoln's Republican Party. Stewart exerted a singular hold over the president's wife, whose scandalous shopping sprees plunged her heavily into debt. She had indulged many of her extravagances at Stewart's emporium, and he had hinted at court action to get what she owed him. This made her fear that her insolvency would reach the newspapers and undermine her husband's re-election prospects. By early summer, 1864, Mary Lincoln was forced to a campaign of her own, a furtive dunning among recipients of presidential patronage for their help in settling her debts.

It was precisely at this time that A. T. Stewart and Barnes operated behind the scenes as top steersmen in the great plan to trade Northern meat for Southern cotton. Stewart's influence at the White House was a calculated element. Stewart and Barnes, Will Browning, R. D. Watson, Beverley Tucker—these were the principal activists in the quietly maturing commercial coup.

The secrecy so essential in the United States was not so binding in England, where financiers expressed puzzlement over peculiar dealings between Stewart and the Browns banking family—peculiar because

Stewart, a Republican, had done no business with the Browns, a mostly Democratic clan, since long before the Civil War. Outsiders figured that what Stewart was up to had to be speculation in cotton futures and that being the type to bet only on a sure thing, he was gambling on inside knowledge of a forthcoming fall in the international rates of exchange.

Such a fall, bringing relief to the United States Treasury, could occur only if American cotton reentered European markets. The Browns' stake in a resumption of that flow was self-evident. In peacetime they had been the leading merchant bankers, financing more than 70 percent of all Southern cotton exported to England.

Cotton exports or their absence directly affected the nation's gold supply. The mere prospect of cotton emerging from the South for shipment overseas would bring down gold quotations. Until the market stabilized in this manner, gold prices would fluctuate and gold gambling flourish. The gamblers included Brown Brothers of New York, who felt that they had no alternative but to indulge. Often, the price of gold rose and fell in phase with the bloody see-saw of combat. Market demands in turn regulated the war's tempo—cynics were to detect a link between the Union government's anxiety to hold down gold prices and the terrible immolation that history books would call the Battle of the Wilderness. "Of all the millions of eyes that watched the onward march of the Grand Army of the Potomac," a Wall Street plunger wrote, "none were riveted on it more closely than the gold speculators." President Lincoln, aware of this, fulminated against "those fellows in Wall Street who are gambling in gold at such a time as this," and he wished that "every one of them had his devilish head shot off."

Congressional legislation had failed to scotch the orgy. Short of big Union victories on the battlefield, the only way to strengthen the North's economy was to gain control of the South's cotton and free it on the market. This would halt the decline in the Union's gold reserves. Prescient economists, in regular contact with Lincoln (he once grumbled that their letters fatigued him), would not let him forget it. War had driven the market price for cotton so high that only if cotton was brought out of the South for sale abroad would gold quotations fall.

Hence Lincoln's encouragement of schemes to procure Confederate cotton. Near the end of June, Lincoln's private secretary wrote, "The President told me yesterday he had a plan for relieving us to a certain extent financially, for the Gov't to take into its own hands the whole cotton trade and buy up all that is offered, to take it to New York and sell it for gold."

The president's plan had become known via Ward Lamon to Wall Street speculators, who were quick to detect its unique money-making opportunities. Lamon had been a law partner of Lincoln's and was now not only among his close friends but also his self-appointed bodyguard. Most consequentially, the president's eagerness for the North to secure as much as possible of the South's cotton was soon known to James Virgul Barnes.

In Montreal he had favored Luke Blackburn's notion of a North–South prisoner exchange, but only insofar as it contributed to that different proposed barter, meat for cotton. For Barnes was an inveterate go-getter with a chilling singularity of purpose. Scarcely could this trait have been more sharply compulsive than on this occasion. The time approached when no one would have wanted to appear even remotely connected with this particular wheeling and dealing. But if any man could have justifiably claimed to be the architect of the mammoth yet furtive cotton-profiteering scheme, it was James Virgul Barnes.

CHAPTER 6

Lincoln and the Radicals

On July 4, 1864, Lincoln rode down dusty Pennsylvania Avenue to the Capitol, entered the ornately frescoed President's Room in the north wing, and sat at the mahogany table. Congress was about to adjourn. He had to consider the legislation it had passed. One of the bills before him authorized the Treasury Department to regulate cotton purchases within Union military confines. The mood of Congress was generally against unregulated trading with rebels, so "special agents" of the Treasury Department would supervise private cotton deals, the government taking 25 percent on each transaction. He signed the bill.

Lincoln also considered the Wade-Davis Bill that afternoon. This was the latest blueprint for postwar reconstruction, as drafted by the extremists in his Republican Party. Convinced of his intention to reconcile with the South when the gunfire stopped, they badgered him with their insistence that the South be treated as a conquered foe and punished.

The radicals, ultras, unconditionals, Jacobins—whatever label they wore—were bent on limiting Lincoln's power and, if necessary, robbing him of it. They swore to a fundamental conviction that in the process of national government, supremacy belonged to Congress, not the president. On these grounds, they claimed it their duty to control him. Trying hard to do so must have felt at times like running into a brick wall. They were not a tightly knit conspiratorial band. Nor were their numbers great. But they were an intimidating force within the Republican Party, quick to brand disloyal any who questioned their hard-line policies.

The war must be fought to a finish and slavery abolished. This was the stern avowal of the Joint Committee on the Conduct of the War, created by Congress early in the conflict and chaired by Ohio senator Benjamin Wade, Lincoln's most vocal critic. Wade and fellow radicals called Lincoln or his generals to account whenever they perceived a slackening of the war effort.

Yet the shooting must not end too soon. "I hope to God there will be no peace," Wade declared when the war began, "until we can say there is not a slave in the land." When the North won at Gettysburg, Senator Charles Sumner of Massachusetts eschewed celebration because "I fear our victories more than our defeats." This robust bachelor, who flattered Mary Lincoln at White House parties while mentally rehearsing speeches to ridicule her husband's policies, believed that a premature cease-fire would cause Northerners to forgive and forget. He prayed, "God save us from any such calamity."

Their bloodthirsty tirades were not mere hot air. Congressman George Julian of Indiana meant every word when he declared that the sole purpose of the conflict was total subjugation of the South. "Both our people and our army have been learning to hate rebels as Christian patriots ought to have done from the beginning." Zachariah Chandler, senator from Michigan and a member of the Joint Committee on the Conduct of the War, thought "a little bloodletting" good for the Union. Lincoln had dragged his feet on the issue of emancipation and had dared to preach lenity for the slave-masters.

Most congressional work that summer was done in a hurry but not the Wade-Davis Bill. Wade and Henry Winter Davis of Maryland had driven a hard-line piece of legislation through both the House of Representatives and the Senate, with its main theme intact. Congress, not the president, must govern the Reconstruction. "This great question," Wade had stressed in the Senate, "does not belong to the president. It belongs to us."

Minutes before Congress adjourned, emotions exploded. Lincoln had set aside the Wade-Davis Bill, unsigned. The House speaker, formally closing the session, had to shout to make himself heard above the sharp voice of Henry Winter Davis, "clear and cold, like starlight," as he fiercely denounced the chief executive.

Eight days later, Confederate cannons roared along Washington's northern outskirts. General Jubal Early's troops had crossed the Potomac and wheeled down the turnpike upon the Union capital itself. Urging Washingtonians within artillery range not to panic, Lincoln set an example with a show of personal calm on the parapets at Fort Stevens. The scare dissolved as Union reinforcements put the impudent Early to flight. Then it was politics again, with Lincoln the target in a different line of fire.

Before the month ended, the chagrined Wade and Davis drafted a sensational manifesto, accusing Lincoln of flouting the authority of Congress. Music to the ears of extremists, the manifesto's language was not all that novel. It exemplified its authors' flair for rhetoric, but it ended on a threateningly new note. Lincoln had too long presumed on his party's forbearance. He had to learn that "[the] *authority* of *Congress* is *paramount.*"

Leading radicals clustered in New England. A Boston newspaper likened them to a coven brewing mischief; it "boded no good for Father Abraham." But they would have to move fast. Two months had elapsed since the party, convening in Baltimore, had nominated Lincoln to seek reelection and selected Tennessee governor Andrew Johnson as his running mate. Then it was August, and even Republican moderates favored replacing Lincoln as standard-bearer with a more viable candidate.

The moment seemed opportune. War weariness had sapped Lincoln's popular base. The conflict had gone badly for the Union, the people losing heart (except on Wall Street, where gold prices soared). Grant's drive into Virginia had stopped short after the fighting at Cold Harbor. The government announced plans for drafting thousands to fill the gaps left by the spring butchery. Consumer prices rose. Among the crowded thoroughfares of Boston, New York, and Philadelphia; in the western metropolis of Chicago; and within the Union capital itself, soothsayers warned of catastrophe under Lincoln's continued leadership.

Richmond, on the other hand, expressed optimism. The Confederacy's vice president, Alexander Stephens, affirmed cotton as "the tremendous lever by which we can work out our destiny under Providence." Beverley Tucker in Canada was the man who grasped the lever. But hitches to the meat-for-cotton plan had to be dealt with. This called for the special talents of James V. Barnes, who, as strategist and most active drummer for the project, journeyed to and fro on both sides of the battle lines.

As the effort to replace Lincoln with a radicals' choice for the White House gathered momentum, Barnes traveled west to brief the Watson Provision Company on details of his intended commercial coup. He carried a letter of introduction from Richard Demill, a pro-Confederate lawyer and cotton broker with headquarters in a sail-loft at the rear of a four-story building, number 178½ Water Street in New York City. Demill was a native of North Carolina who, with his father and uncle, ran the New York–Savannah steamship packet line before the war ruined business. But they had remained in wartime New York, they told Southern-based relatives, without amplifying, in order to serve the Confederacy. The thirty-six-year-old Demill, who considered Abraham Lincoln a hateful tyrant, was so devoted to the rebel cause that he christened two daughters Alice Roberta Lee and Virginia. When a third followed, he named her Nina Caroline, so that the initials of her name would be those of his native state. One of Demill's brothers served as a major in the rebel army commissary.

Demill wrote of Barnes as "a man of considerable importance and in almost daily contact with men of means and substance on Wall Street." Barnes met frequently with friends of President Lincoln, "who could, if [Lincoln] was convinced, expedite the shipment of the produce north." He meant cotton.

Neither Barnes nor Demill knew much of the political peril Lincoln faced just then. Moderate as well as radical Republicans were exchanging frantic letters. Lincoln had to go. "The Baltimore Convention was stupid political suicide." Nothing but a battlefield victory could boost Lincoln's reelection chances. He himself was heard to sigh, "Without one I am a beaten man." Men of commerce were especially alarmed. Most Northern merchants, regardless of how much they blamed Lincoln's war for disrupting business, had his Republican Party to thank for banking reforms, tariff laws, homestead acts, and the subsidizing of railroads. They knew on which side their bread was buttered. Pro-business legislation would not last long under a Democratic administration. A powerful segment of the New York banking and commercial world had thus become regular Republican Party supporters. Few were outright abolitionists. Many had once defended slavery, but their thoughts now were on the hard profits at stake, not on political ideology. And whenever Lincoln seemed to falter in the war effort, the impatience they shared with radical ideologues had its own ruthless edge.

They were the backbone of the Union League. This pro-Republican sociopolitical fraternity of bankers and merchants, poets, publishers, and congressmen boasted a membership exceeding 1 million. It had also developed a marked radical slant, resulting from its infiltration by the Loyal Order of the Strong Band. Founded in Chicago by a pair of Republican extremists, the Strong Band named itself after the patriotic German *bunds* of Napoleonic times. It touted superpatriotism and boasted of "nomenclature, paraphernalia, covenants, laws and ceremonies warlike in structure." Its branches were "camps"; its officers bore military titles, the rank and file addressing each other as "comrade." The Strong Band had already served notice on the White House, letting Mr. Lincoln know that although hitherto occupied with charity work among the wounded, recruiting new blood for the Union colors, and day-to-day vigilantism, in the future "we hope to make our power more sensibly felt."

The Strong Band's militancy was too extreme even for some radicals. Republican moderates viewed the order as "a dangerous engine of imperial power," without regard for law, Constitution, or the president. Strong Band propagandists had burrowed into every big city Union League lodge. Cells flourished secretly in the armed forces and in the federal government. And however abhorrent to the mainstream of the Republican Party, the Strong Band's unblinking ardor for bold steps to save the Union attracted more and more Northern politicians, newspaper publishers, and men of finance as election day drew closer.

The abandonment of Abraham Lincoln by some of his own partisans was, in the words of a White House aide, "sort of a political Bull Run." But defeat-prone or not, the president was a difficult man to get out from under. On August 19, some two dozen radical politicians, press lords, and financiers met at the Fifth Avenue home of George Opdyke, a millionaire banker and a New York ex-mayor, and voted to call for a new Republican convention at Cincinnati. That Fifth Avenue caucus was supposed to be secret, but somehow word of it reached the White House, where it merely stiffened an already obdurate spine.

Most alarmingly for radical Republicans, the Democratic Convention, staged in Chicago, nominated George McClellan as its presidential candidate. McClellan was anathema to radicals, who, with Secretary Stanton's aid, had forced Lincoln to oust him as an incompetent commander. War-sick civilians and military veterans, still fond of "Little Mac," seemed likely to support him. Perhaps they would, but as surely as night follows day, the extremists would never allow him into the White House as commander in chief. The panic was on. A despairing radical appealed to Senator Charles Sumner: "What are you going to do in this chaos?"

Near the month's end, all signs pointed to a Democratic landslide. Visiting England earlier that summer, Edwards Pierrepont, a future United States attorney general, startled British bankers by predicting a revolution within the North and the necessary imposition of a dictatorship. Ward Lamon would recall the same approach of "a dictatorship" proclaimed by "atrocious conspirators" who sought to depose the chief executive. Lamon meant the Republican radicals.

On the 30th, drastic action was contemplated, if not openly discussed, at another "secret" New York conclave. Three dozen worried men, including industrialists, publishers, and Strong Band militants, met at 86 East Twenty-first Street, home of David Dudley Field, lawyer, political string-puller, and president of the National Bank of Commerce. No details of this gathering ever surfaced, but something of the prevailing mood of desperation was evident in a *Cincinnati Gazette* editorial that same week. Republicans, by no means all extremists, believed that "four more years of Lincoln would ruin the country." But how to prevent it? "Whatever is done should be cautiously managed." Henry Winter Davis had been one of the camarilla on East Twenty-first Street. Leaving it, he crowed privately of simpletons for whom Lincoln was a gift from heaven. "They will soon be convinced that he was on his way *lower down* and not intending to stay here much longer."

That same week Booth left New York for Washington. There he was joined by William Patrick Wood, nominally superintendent of the Old Capitol Prison and called "colonel" because Secretary Stanton had favored him with appropriate army pay and status. Wood was a stocky man of affable cunning and strident atheism. More significantly, he enjoyed a close relationship with Stanton and was, wrote one observer, "deeper in the war office than any man in Washington." Some suspected that Wood exerted a hold over Stanton. More accurately, each had something on the other.

As Stanton's most reliable tool, Wood had assisted him in more than one questionable episode—for example, the fabrication of evidence for Stanton as attorney in the prewar McCormick Reaper case. In wartime, as prison superintendent, Wood intercepted and read inmates' mail and persuaded them to eavesdrop on one another. He thus served Stanton as head of a unique "secret service" system. Within the War Department, the secretary had most often to confide in his telegraphy chief, Thomas T. Eckert. But Eckert tended to act independently, as had the Department's chief detective, Lafayette Baker. To the extent that Stanton felt he could trust anybody at the heart of the military bureaucracy, his longtime henchman Wood was the choice.

Booth and Wood slipped across the Potomac into Confederate country and sent a messenger to contact the partisan leader Colonel John Singleton Mosby and arrange a meeting. It took place at one of Mosby's northern Virginia hideouts. Booth, as "John Wilkes," was on Mosby's muster roll, although he had not served with the unit. Mosby's men had begun to specialize in capturing high-ranking Union officers. So it was natural that Booth and his companion would seek Mosby out because what they had to propose was nothing less than the abduction of the North's commander in chief.

Booth and the man from the Union War Department told Mosby that many Republicans thought that Lincoln was a losing candidate and wanted him removed. His departure would benefit both the Confederacy and the Union. As things stood, the North faced bankruptcy, while the South bled to death. "Certain elements in the Republican Party," Mosby would recall, "had decided that the best thing would be for Lincoln to be taken prisoner by the Confederates and a treaty worked out to the advantage of both sides." He signified assent hesitantly, unsure whether he was being set up in some dark Yankee plot. Wood had not mentioned his immediate boss, the secretary of war; indeed, no names were raised other than that of the intended captive.

Booth's next stop was Baltimore. He took a room at Barnum's Hotel and sent for two ex-Confederate soldiers. One was Samuel Bland Arnold, a schoolmate of his youth when both had attended St. Timothy's Hall in Maryland. They had not seen each other since 1852. Arnold was now a footloose blade, tarnished at thirty, drifting between tavern sprees and recuperative spells at his family's country home. The other, Michael O'Laughlen, would also have won no awards for solid citizenship, but he worked as a branch manager in his brother's produce and feed business. Booth told this pair that important people in the North's government had offered to pay handsomely if he would arrange the abduction of President Lincoln. He promised that capturing Lincoln would make them famous, as well as rich. The Confederacy, naturally, had no love for Lincoln, but there were also powerful Northerners who wanted him out of the way. Did not all who cherished liberty oppose him as a tyrant? Booth stressed that this was his main concern, not so much the money as a chance to strike a blow at tyranny. After more drinks and cigars, his proposal began to sound easy.

Lincoln might be seized on one of his afternoon drives or as he walked from the White House to the War Department, as was his custom. Booth told the two Baltimoreans that premises were actually prepared for the captive's confinement within a stone's throw of the White House. Here he could be held until it was safe to bear him across the Potomac into rebel lines and finally to Richmond. In Confederate hands, Lincoln could serve as a hostage for an exchange of prisoners. It was this worthy aim, Samuel Arnold later claimed, that made him hang on to Booth's words. The scheme, as outlined by the actor, was "devoid of ambition and aggrandizement, had notions of humanity and honor. After a debate of some time, and being under the effect of some little wine we consented to join him in the enterprise."

"Glorious news. Atlanta captured." Headlines the first week in September signaled Abraham Lincoln's political recovery. Reports of Admiral Farragut's ships penetrating Mobile Bay had been followed by General Sherman's telegram: "Atlanta is ours and fairly won."

A dispatch from Canada to the *Times* of London put it perfectly: "The people were depressed and discouraged. But General Sherman took Atlanta, and with the celerity of a harlequin in a Christmas pantomime who with one stroke of his wand can convert a Quaker into a grenadier, he filled the American heart with hopefulness as great as its previous despondency, opened before the delighted eyes of Mr. Lincoln a bright prospect of his re-election, and reinvigorated that love for conquest and the Union which had slumbered but not died."

The news forced radicals to abandon plans for a Cincinnati Convention, having nowhere to turn save back to the chief they had striven to dump. "Only through this course," wrote a seething Henry Winter Davis, "can any sort of hold be retained on the government. We must . . . for four years more wring from that old fool what can be gotten." And responding to a letter from Ben Wade, ending, "I can but wish the d——l had old Abe," Judge Alphonse Taft of Ohio, a future cabinet minister, wrote on September 8, "Providence must have some punishment for Lincoln. How it is to come has yet to be seen."

In the words of a White House adviser, Thurlow Weed, the revolt against Lincoln from within his own party had its roots in "a conspiracy, formidable and vicious, embracing a larger number of leading men than I had supposed possible." The revolt, thanks to the army and naval victories, had collapsed. But the radicals knew only too well that they dared not relax what grip they still retained on Lincoln. To stave off any chance of Lincoln's offering the shaken South an olive branch, Massachusetts governor John A. Andrew, war hawk and veteran abolitionist, proposed that like-minded governors of Illinois, Ohio, and Indiana join him in a descent upon the White House with appropriate arguments. "It is of the first importance," wrote Andrew, "that the President should be rescued from those who are tempting and pushing him into an unworthy and disgraceful offer to compromise with the leaders of the Rebellion." Their visit to Washington was effective, at least temporarily. Talk of possible peace overtures seemed to evaporate. Should the White House need any reminding, the Strong Band and Spartan Brotherhood, convening in the middle of October at New York's Clinton Hall, solemnly resolved, "We regard peace, at the expense of the Union and the supremacy of the laws, as the greatest possible calamity, and those who favor that measure as traitors to their country."

Abraham Lincoln had still to be saved, Governor Andrew declared, "from the infamy of ruining the country." There was no telling what he might do. His restored popularity and the Confederacy's numbed state after Atlanta might tempt him into offering the enemy peace terms. The radicals would be the saviors. To make sure that Lincoln defeated McClellan in November was the immediate duty facing them, "as practical men. I think we shall win . . . and then, how great are the duties which lie beyond." In other words, after winning the election, Lincoln would have to toe the radicals' line. Making sure McClellan never got control of the Union was only half the battle.

The Union must be safeguarded from the perils of a Lincoln victory. This was how the extremists of his party reasoned, as they gave the 1864 election campaign a coloration unprecedented, stumping across the land for a candidate they had earlier tried to displace, a galling exercise made bearable only by construing it as a rededication to the principle of congressional supremacy. The chief executive would be in their debt once the campaign smoke cleared, that debt payable on demand. And woe betide him if he defaulted.

CHAPTER 7

Lincoln and the Secret Trade Deal

With brightened prospects for success at the polls, President Lincoln swung his attention back to Southern cotton. While the nation gave thanks for military and naval victories, Salmon Chase's successor at the Treasury Department, William P. Fessenden, drafted "General Regulations for the purchase of the products of the insurrectionist states on government account," pursuant to the new trade bill passed by Congress in July of that same eventful year, 1864. Now it was September, and at a cabinet meeting on the subject, Secretary of the Navy Gideon Welles noted that "both the President and Fessenden started out with the assumption, and as a settled fact, that the cotton within rebel lines must be sought after and brought out."

Under the new procedures, the federal government would award contracts to approved applicants who claimed control or ownership of cotton in rebel territory. All that a speculator had to do was pledge delivery of the cotton he had bought (at giveaway prices) to one of seven "special agents" of the Treasury Department who were stationed at New Orleans, Nashville, and five other Union-held locations in the South. Permits signed by the president would ensure safe passage of the shipment through military lines. Payment for the cotton at three-quarters of the then-current New York price would allow 25 percent of the profit on the transaction to go into the Union treasury.

The transatlantic market price for cotton had reached up to twelve times what American merchants were paying planters for it. But to make any kind of killing, there was no time to lose. Union military gains had already shaken Northern speculators. A slippage in cotton prices had occurred, following George McClellan's bid for the presidency, an event signaling the possibility of an early cease-fire. The downward trend was sure to resume with the prospect of a peace won by Union guns. So the North's cotton profiteers had become as one with the radicals in their dread of a premature peace.

From the start, rings formed by speculators included Lincoln's close associates. One busy ringmaster was the Republican Party's top strategist, Thurlow Weed. He expected to raise campaign funds, as well as line his own pockets, in payoffs from business colleagues favored with coveted contracts and executive permits. Also prominent among the jockeying vanguard of fortune-hunters were two of the president's oldest friends. Ward H. Lamon was one of the most active in the cotton scandal. At the same time, as marshal of the District of Columbia, he devoted himself to Lincoln's physical safety. Another busy speculator, Orville H. Browning (unrelated to William Browning), was a former senator from Illinois turned lawyer-lobbyist in Washington, with full visiting privileges at the White House.

Richard Demill had men like these in mind when on September 12 he again wrote to the Watson Provision Company. True, the envisaged meat-for-cotton coup would necessitate paying out substantial amounts in commission, but it had become of a magnitude promising huge rewards. "The men we are dealing with are moneyed men, politically well placed, have [Lincoln's] ear, and can thereby assure success of this venture."

While Northerners celebrated the fall of Atlanta, commissary officials in Richmond warned General Robert E. Lee that only through a miracle could they guarantee his underfed troops enough meat to last through the coming winter. To most proud Southerners, bartering with Yankees was repugnant. But without food, their fighting men would perish. Accosted as they were by commercial agents from the North, planters and cotton-hoarding quartermasters of the Confederate army had insisted more and more on meat, instead of Yankee greenbacks, as payment for their bales.

This presented a problem to Northerners, who expected quick profit from the new federal regulations. "The matter of supplies [is] the most important of all, and I don't see how to carry it out." Thus bemoaned a speculator writing to Hanson Risley, a ward-heeler from Albany, New York, appointed Treasury Department manager of contracts and special permits. The reference was to the South's demands for meat instead of money.

It was then that President Lincoln, in the public interest, had smoothed the way for large cotton deals. Formally endorsing Secretary Fessenden's regulations, he also signed a related executive order. It stipulated that parties bringing cotton to Treasury Department agents could take back into Confederate lines, under protection of the Union flag, one-third of the cotton's value in supplies "other than contraband of war." The War Department had never specifically defined contraband of war or drafted so much as a set of guidelines. So food was not ruled out.

Few, if any, in Lincoln's administration would have dared propose that the North victual the enemy to obtain his cotton. But the cabinet had not been consulted beforehand and Congress was kept in the dark. So there it was, a White House fiat attached to the Treasury Department's general regulations like a furtive postscript—in effect, an executive mandate for broad business dealings across the battle lines.

A section of the westernmost part of the state of Kentucky is oddly severed by a sharp loop of the Mississipi River. On maps, it resembles a thumb grafted onto neighboring Missouri. It is known as Watson's Bend. The area was rich farmland owned by the Watson Provision Company, which had sold beef, pork, grain, and hay to the South. It was founded by Daniel Watson, who had farmed the area since the century's early years. In 1862 Union forces had shelled and captured New Madrid, Missouri, pushing across the river to occupy Watson's Bend.

No longer able to ship produce downstream into the Confederacy, and determined not to let the occupying forces seize it or buy it for next to nothing, the company welcomed any plan to maintain or, preferably, increase its profit. The patriarch's health failing, control had passed to his oldest son, Robert Daniel, a key figure in the meat-for-cotton deal. He would run his part of the operation from an office in New Madrid, above the Mississippi loop that girded so much of his livestock grazing land.

A. T. Stewart, the scheme's most shadowy progenitor, enlisted an old former partner, Thomas E. Henry, to set up a front, the Henry Stewart Company, which would function as general overseer as the barter gathered momentum. Its New York address, 178½ Water Street, the Demill headquarters, soon became a clearinghouse for intrigue. When in New York, R. D. Watson used it as his address, in addition to that of the Astor House. Masters of vessels in use for Booth's smuggling apparatus, John Celestina among them, called there for shipping orders. At this same location, payoffs as necessary were made to silence inquisitive Port of New York customs collectors. Throughout the Civil War, the Customs House was never immune to corruption.

James V. Barnes was a frequent visitor to Water Street. As a result of the Montreal meeting in October, he had more reason than ever to wear a buoyant smile and dispense cigars, as a clerk at the Confederate Treasury Department remembered seeing him. He and the rest of the meat-for-cotton ring, fringe investors, beside such pivotal characters as Barnes, R. D. Watson, Beverley Tucker, and the secretive promoter A. T. Stewart, might well have felt relieved at what they considered a climax to a tense summer and fall. And the political pieces in the complex but grand enterprise were in place. President Lincoln had weathered the summer storms. What Beverley Tucker had alluded to as "the Executive to whom we are alone indebted" would crown all the effort with success. Such was the situation at the start of November 1864, the month of a presidential election Lincoln was now expected to win. Among the money men, the wheeling and dealing in Montreal had bred a spirit of confidence. It would quickly evaporate, diluted by betrayal.

R. D. Watson once had an older brother, James. While the younger devoted himself to managing the Watson company at New Madrid, James had actively aided the South as message courier and smuggler of medicines. In late summer 1863 James Watson and two companions were captured near Jackson, Tennessee, by troops of the 2nd Iowa Cavalry. James and one of the others were tried as spies and sentenced to death. The third, James W. Boyd, was a Confederate army captain, for whom fate was preparing a lamentable role.

This was at a moment when R. D. Watson was seeking a reliable messenger with contacts in Richmond, Washington, New York, and Canada, someone who could be of service in the maturing meat-for-cotton project. On the eve of his execution James wrote his brother good-bye. He addressed him using the nickname by which Robert D. was known within the Watson clan: "Dear Ardy." He would be hanged the next morning. He would prefer not to die but "can take it like a man." Then James wrote:

> I have a message for you. . . . Just now I want to arrange for the disposition of my property. . . . Only have a short time left. . . . Have my saddle. . . . Never did I think I would be writing a letter such as this. . . . Have my farm sold. . . . As for the horses . . . Richard can have my buggy. . . . Reserve enough cash to pay for my funeral. . . . I do not care what you do with my hounds. . . . Sell them if you wish. . . . Only don't let anyone have them who will not care for them. Notify grandma when I am gone. . . . Sam is already free. . . . Unless I am to be hanged tomorrow . . . Randy will probably hear from Cincinnati. . . . Randy can have his pick. . . . Amos can have my gold watch. Tell Mother and Dad not to grieve. . . . Tell Judy that I have written to her. . . . When the war is over maybe she can go to school. . . . Allow her to decide for herself. . . . She is a sensible girl. . . . Help her in any way you can. . . . It will be hard for her. . . . Nelly can have her freedom. . . . Give her that packet of papers. . . . There are a number of letters from Susan. One was written the week before she died. Now I must close and say goodbye. Your loving brother—James.

What tipped off Watson to the letter's hidden intelligence was its reference to Judy. She was a family member who had died in youth, as both brothers knew. To Watson, this meant something special, the "message" James wished him to have. He noted the initial of each consecutive sentence. It was a simple acrostic that had escaped the notice of his brother's guards. James had worded the last letter he would ever write to convey the name and whereabouts of the courier so urgently needed: John Harrison Surratt, Washington.

By the time of the Montreal meeting, John Surratt had cultivated the acquaintance of certain Wall Street speculators. Ambitious to the core, he had embarked on a risky lifestyle when scarcely in his twenties. He had a brother in the Confederate army, but his own allegiance was to money, combined with adventure. Following education at St. Charles College, near Baltimore, he had inherited his father's postmastership at Surrattsville, a Maryland hamlet twelve miles south of Washington. The post office was also a crossroads tavern, which Surratt helped turn into a secessionist rendezvous. Chief Detective Baker heard of this and had him brought to Washington for questioning. The usual fate of Baker's suspects was an indefinite spell in the Old Capitol Prison or enforced espionage for the North. Surratt was freed.

He was soon carrying mail for the South. But in October 1863, aged twenty, he wrote a letter to the North's secretary of war, applying with innocent formality for a federal position. Baker's sleuths knew of his apparent service to the Confederacy but made no move to arrest him. Reticent in later years concerning his wartime activity, Surratt invoked a "holy oath" of silence, demanded of him in exchange for his life. But on at least one consequential occasion, he worked undercover for Stanton's War Department. Sharp-featured, blue-eyed, and goateed, moving north and south under different names in the pay of two warring governments and one or more cotton rings, John Harrison Surratt was a consummate triple agent.

His alias in Canada was "Charley Armstrong." He was the presumed trustworthy courier whom Beverley Tucker, probably on Watson's advice, had selected to carry his report of the meat-for-cotton arrangement south from Montreal. Papers were stuffed into secret pockets sewn within Surratt's reinforced breeches, so that when he rode horseback, they were firmly held between his thigh and the saddle. He stopped off at Washington, and his sealed package was delivered to the War Department, where it stayed overnight, as did Surratt.

The following morning, November 6, Secretary of War Stanton examined its contents. Inside each of four envelopes addressed to Richmond was a letter dated November 2. One was from Clement Clay to his wife, Virginia: "My Dear Ginny, I am mortified and depressed at receiving no mail. . . ." Another was from "Jake" (Thompson), telling his family he intended to stay in Canada until spring, unless officially ordered home. The third was from Beverley Tucker to his wife: "I cannot bear the thought of staying here until spring without you." Another was to his brother: "I have sent a personal enquiring can I return at once or let my wife come to me." And finally, there was Tucker's full report to Richmond of the St. Lawrence Hall business transaction.

In due course all these items were lodged in federal archives, except Tucker's, whose report is excerpted, key names omitted, and headed: "Extract from the proposal of ——— sent forward and relates to a proposal of a party in the United States to furnish provisions for the rebel army."

Stanton read the material at home. It was a Sunday morning. According to his assistant secretary of war, Charles A. Dana, he said, "This is serious. Go over to the White House and ask the President to come here." Stanton might have carried the papers there, but he pleaded having a cold that kept him indoors. An immediate question was what to do about the dispatch bearer. His deliberate Washington stopover must not be known, in case it ended his continued service as a Union agent. The solution was to arrange his "arrest" and, after a brief period in the Old Capitol Prison, his "escape," each event being widely publicized.

The plan went ahead with a guise of official formality. General Christopher Augur, in command of Washington defenses, telegraphed Colonel Henry H. Wells, provost marshal general of federal troops south of the Potomac, that word had reached the War Department of a Confederate agent carrying important papers and expected to stop near an Alexandria tavern at 9 P.M. Friday, the 11th. He was to be arrested but in no way harmed.

At the appointed hour the courier from Canada, now calling himself George Peterson, was seized while watering his horse at a trough. Loudly praising the Confederacy while denouncing the North, he was borne off to the War Department, where, in the presence of Augur, Wells, Dana, and Stanton, he was stripped and his burden "discovered." Unaware that the material had already been found on him and replaced in the trousers, the army men signed a form as witnesses to its discovery. Throughout these proceedings, Dana recalled, the "courier"'s bearing was "that of an incomparable actor. He was one of the cleverest creatures I ever saw."

That same night he was handed over to William Patrick Wood, superintendent of the Old Capitol Prison, and committed "by order of the President," a distinction given few, if any, other names on current prison records. "George Peterson"'s escape was even more meticulously performed than had been his capture. It involved crossing a prison yard, forcing locks with a chisel conveniently left by a gas fitter, creeping along a passage near the women's department, and entering the front office, whereupon "he made his way into the street."

This was all given extraordinary publicity, newspapers carrying the War Department's announcement of a $2,000 reward for "Peterson"'s capture. That it was never claimed is hardly surprising. The escapee's description, from the same official source, revealed little other than his approximate height and weight, "sound white teeth," and a "peculiarly positive utterance in his conversation."

When Stanton's urgent summons reached the White House, the president and Mary were preparing to attend services at the New York Avenue Presbyterian Church. Instead of worship, Lincoln had found himself at Stanton's house, reading Tucker's claim to have "seen old Abe's signature," authorizing a lifting of the naval blockade to allow food into the Confederacy.

He knew Stanton's views on trading with the enemy. At cabinet meetings the secretary had opposed the very idea of it. His words that Sunday morning, and Lincoln's, can be only imagined.

The president's hope of using cotton to pay for the war was no big secret, nor was his encouragement of deals with Southerners in order to secure it. Not so well known was that he had sanctioned partial payment in the form of supplies. He had already begun signing the passes that protected a two-way traffic of food and cotton. But the Montreal plan was an illegality he dared not appear to be even aware of. Not with the election two days off.

Later, he would tell a Union army officer that rebels had forged his signature to fool Admiral Farragut into raising the blockade. What became a matter of record is that immediately after the confrontation with Stanton, Lincoln headed for the War Department telegraph room, where he dictated a message. It was tapped out to the military commander in New Orleans, for instant relay to Admiral David Farragut in Mobile Bay: "Do not on any account or on any showing of authority whatever, from whomsoever purporting to come, allow the blockade to be violated."

The telegram was mysteriously delayed in transit. Farragut thought it long overdue anyway. The admiral had an old salt's disdain for nuances and saw issues in black and white. A foe was a foe and to trade with him was treason. During the previous summer, Farragut had bluntly told the secretary of the navy that he was prepared to defy even the White House should it order him to lift the blockade of Mobile for the benefit of war profiteers. But by the time Lincoln's latest telegram reached Farragut's flagship, the token cargo of pork, as agreed on by the Montreal conferees, was safely past Union ships and off Pensacola.

At that rebel-held Floridean port stood General Dabney Maury. On December 10, he telegraphed his superiors in Richmond that "A. T. Stewart under contract with Messrs. Thompson and Clay has brought cargo meat into Pensacola to exchange for cotton pound for pound." The coded message added: "He will purchase all of the blockaded ships with cargoes of cotton on them." It concluded with word that the Union admiral's assurance of protection for them was hourly expected. That, however, was as far as things were allowed to go. Acting at once on Lincoln's order not to be taken in by false permits, Admiral Farragut alerted the captains of his battle-scarred ironclads and wooden walls. And the cotton ships at Mobile remained bottled up.

The bloodletting continued. Sheridan's legions spread destruction through the Shenandoah Valley, with savage retaliation in their wake. When captured Confederate guerrillas were summarily hanged, their leader, Colonel Mosby, ordered the execution of a batch of Union prisoners. Mosby was next out of the picture, said to be in a mountain hideout, recovering from wounds. When he reappeared, he sent his partisans to kidnap a Union general. And in that first week of November, when Northerners were casting their votes, Mosby's admirers in Richmond told each other that capturing high-ranking officers was a warmup for the main event—that the North's commander in chief would be next.

CHAPTER 8

Deepening Peril

From the war's beginning, the possibility of physical harm to Lincoln had often been discussed in the North. The villains would, of course, be rebels. It stood to reason that others, as well as Mosby, who operated mainly in northern Virginia, had tried to work up steam for kidnapping Lincoln. Newspapers north and south ran "disclosures" of kidnap plots in the making. Some appropriate reprisal against the North had been expected, following the Dahlgren affair, with its widely published "orders" to slay Jeff Davis.

Death threats abounded. A letter said to have been found on a Washington street contained details of a bomb mechanism to be attached to Lincoln's carriage, which would automatically explode when the wheels turned. A note mailed to the White House early in 1864 and signed "Joseph" declared the president "weighed in the balance, found wanting, and a dead man in six months." With the election campaign in full swing, a western editor who thrived on "red-hot journalism" branded Lincoln a tyrant and called for "some bold hand [to] pierce his heart with a dagger point."

Washington's metropolitan police force was new and inexperienced, and there was no government bureau exclusively responsible for the president's protection. Company K of the 150th Pennsylvania Infantry manned the White House grounds but served chiefly for ceremonial parades. The Lincolns spent each summer at Soldiers' Home, a cluster of buildings on a hill three miles beyond the capital's northern boundary, at which times the Union Light Guard, about a hundred men picked from the 7th Independent Company of the Ohio Volunteer Cavalry, was at their disposal. Even then, Lincoln often rode in his carriage, unescorted. Whatever walking he did in the vicinity of the White House was usually to and from the War

Department, a hundred yards west of his front door, along a path bordered by trees and a brick fence. During these strolls, he could glimpse through the intervening trees a somber edifice known locally as the old Van Ness place.

An austere example of Benjamin Latrobe's residential architecture, the mansion stood north of Tiber Creek, a city-polluted branch of the Potomac. In earlier years when the creek was clean enough for American presidents to swim in, its owner, General John Van Ness, enriched its commodious interior with marble mantels, paneled walls, and floors ornamented with mosaic. A society showplace during Van Ness's lifetime and silent and shuttered for years thereafter, it had come alive again under Thomas Green's ownership. Green was a Virginia lawyer and a devout Confederate. When war broke out, the glittering parties he had thrown for Washington's elite came to an abrupt end. Two of his sons fought for the South. Green was married to the sister of a rebel cavalry officer, Lindsay Lunsford Lomax. Early in the war, she and another Lomax girl were briefly jailed on disloyalty charges. For a time after their release, the Van Ness mansion was under watch by federal detectives, who suspected the Greens of providing food and shelter for rebel spies and couriers.

What they did not know then was that the Van Ness building had a hidden staircase that led to an extensively renovated wine cellar. The entire basement level had been partitioned and contained five cells, each furnished with a bunk, straw tick, and blankets. The doors were of oak and from the walls hung chains and shackles. At first glance, the scene may have appeared to be a row of slave pens or dungeons. Yet new brick fortified the fireplace, wall fixtures were free of rust, and the walls were freshly whitewashed, with trivets in place for candles. Ceilings were lathed as if awaiting plaster, but burlap bags had been stuffed above the lathes for soundproofing. In the rear of the basement, another door opened on a tunnel sloping east to join a storm sewer that paralleled Seventeenth Street and emptied into Tiber Creek. It was thus possible to pass unseen between the tree-cloaked house and the Potomac River.

Well known to Colonel Mosby, the old mansion's possibilities had also occurred to John Wilkes Booth. The notion of making a personal move against the North's leader had seldom left his mind since the aborted attempt to burn Richmond and, he was convinced, to slay the Confederacy's leaders. After attending the St. Lawrence Hall business meeting with Will Browning, he buttonholed Clay and Thompson at the Donegana Hotel and tried to interest them in a plot to abduct Lincoln. That pair had tasted enough of misfired, harebrained stunts and turned down the actor's proposal.

Even so, Booth had begun active planning. Before leaving Montreal, he drew funds from a Canadian bank and had his theatrical wardrobe loaded on the *Marie Victoria,* bound for the Bahamas. In New York he arranged for the transfer to his family of investments made in the Pennsylvania oilfields. From Water Street he received an accounting of his contraband business. He caught a train to Baltimore and checked into Barnum's Hotel, where he mulled over the next step to take toward successfully kidnapping Abraham Lincoln. Then Booth was on the move again.

Washington was tranquil the day the North went to the polls. Politics were at a standstill. A steady rain fell. Visitors to Stanton's home on K Street were turned away with word that the secretary had taken to his room, unwell. The secretary of the treasury had left for New York to discuss with leading capitalists the problems of raising money to finance the war. Other members of the cabinet had gone home to vote. A visitor who braved the weather to call at the executive mansion found the president seated quietly alone.

Late that evening Lincoln made for the War Department's telegraph room. As the returns came in over the wire, his delight was obvious, try as he might to conceal the emotion behind his characteristic mask of folksiness. By midnight he knew that he had won.

Near two o'clock in the morning, while still at the War Department, Lincoln heard that crowds were assembling at the White House gates. He walked out into the sodden night to greet them, and in an improvised little speech he said, "If I know my heart, my gratitude is free from any taint of personal triumph." But triumph it was, and daybreak brought out still larger throngs. Flags unfurled in the damp air. A lengthy parade with bands and lanterns filed through the capital's muddy streets and by late afternoon had surged along Pennsylvania Avenue and passed the National Hotel, where Booth had just checked in.

Citizens converged on the homes of government officials, applauding them and their families as they emerged. Only Stanton's door remained closed. He was said to be still out of sorts. The celebration of Lincoln's victory lasted until dusk. Cannons thundered from the White House grounds. The reverberations rolled across eight hundred yards of swampy turf called President's Park, to shake wet leaves from the trees around the old Van Ness place and rattle the chains and shackles that hung in the underground cells, waiting.

PART II

The Politicians

CHAPTER 9

The Fatal Rationale

Admiral Farragut had effectively stalled the meat-for-cotton super-deal so skillfully finalized in Montreal. But the president continued to endorse dozens of less elaborate deals, signing cotton permits as fast as Treasury agent Hanson Risley could dispatch them to the White House. Reviewing contracts, Risley knew that the quantities of cotton pledged in some of the agreements to which he had bound his government were set absurdly high. Far from being able to honor their signatures, few of the contracting parties had acquired legal control over a single bale. Cotton, for which speculators paid the planters cheap rates in the belief they were on to a good thing, was in many instances beyond reach of either, the cotton cut off by battle lines or stacked at inaccessible sites in forests and swamps. Aware that some documents that he processed were quite unrealistic, Risley didn't hesitate, when expediency demanded, to alter them without Lincoln's knowledge, even though they bore Lincoln's signature.

Northern merchants rushing to trade with the South found the War Department to be a stumbling block. Lincoln's endorsement of the Treasury regulations stipulated safe passage through military lines for cotton coming north and supplies flowing south. But to be effective, it required appropriate orders from Secretary Stanton to his officers in the field. D. Randolph Martin, president of the Ocean Bank in New York, wrote William P. Dole, commissioner of Indian affairs, "No goods can or will go to the rebels until Stanton gives his order. My arrangements are big ones and predicated on the parties bringing in cotton getting one-third return in goods." Accompanying Martin's name on his cotton papers were those of two partners who were not only busy speculators but who had also dabbled in treason and espionage. Lincoln signed their safe conduct passes in all innocence.

The fatal rationale was at work. He had signaled his readiness, in the public interest, to approve cotton deals that lined the pockets of Northern moneymakers. He had not declared himself willing to enrich spies and subversives. But neither could he be expected to know the background of every profiteer who took advantage of the situation.

No time was wasted on what a later generation would call loyalty checks. This had some incredible results. One speculator for whom Lincoln signed cotton permits was a Confederate agent named Maddox who had warned Lee of Grant's plan to blow up the Petersburg defenses. Another recipient of the president's well-intentioned largesse was David Preston Parr, a Confederate courier, whose relatives owned the Van Ness mansion, with its wine cellar now prison quarters, ready for Lincoln as captive. Whenever Jeff Davis's Canada-based "commissioners" desired a change in venue from Montreal, they moved to a summer retreat in southern Ontario. It was placed at their disposal by Robert E. Coxe, an Alabama-born financier living in Poughkeepsie, New York. Lincoln signed cotton passes for him as well, authorizing Union army protection for his fifty thousand bales. So far, radical Republicans in Washington were not fully aware of what was going on in the cotton business. Otherwise, they might have had a field day arranging Lincoln's impeachment.

On November 25, 1864, the Winter Garden Theatre in New York was filled to capacity for a gala performance of *Julius Caesar.* It was a fundraising affair for building a monument to William Shakespeare in Central Park. The cast was headed by Edwin, Junius Brutus Jr., and John Wilkes Booth, the three most illustrious brothers on the American stage. Just before the show, John Wilkes asked Samuel Chester, a bit player in the company, if he knew a good costumer, as Booth's wardrobe was either in Canada or somewhere on the high seas. Booth was unaware that the schooner *Marie Victoria* had, in fact, sailed no more than three hundred miles down the St. Lawrence River before foundering in a storm. But what Booth really wanted from Chester, a chum of his early days, when the two read plays for pennies in Baltimore hotel basements, was not just advice on where best to shop for a Roman toga. He spoke of having a "big speculation" on hand and wanted Chester's help in it.

The Booth brothers came onstage before the first act, to loud acclaim from a sellout audience in $20 seats and $100 boxes, in one of which sat the proud mother. The cast shone. Junius Brutus Jr. played Cassius to the best of his modest abilities. The often-erratic Edwin was this time in full command of his role. And the young Mark Antony was a critic's delight. He had evidently benefited from a long idleness. His voice had regained its strength, and once more on display was that "elan and fire which fairly electrifies the audience and whirls them along with him." Ignored were the bells clanging outside during the second act, for scattered fires had broken out across the city. These were quickly extinguished and later reported as financed by the rebel commissioners in Canada.

At Edwin's home the morning after the Winter Garden triumph, John Wilkes reverted to his familiar offstage role as advocate for the South. Those fires, if rebel-set, were no more than tit-for-tat—attempted retaliation for the Kilpatrick-Dahlgren raid and Sheridan's cruelties in the Shenandoah Valley. So Wilkes fumed about vengeance against the North, until his brother silenced him by announcing that he had voted for Lincoln.

The next day Booth went after Chester again on Broadway, where friends of both were twitting Booth regarding the mysterious "speculation" he rambled on about. It was only oil, they scoffed. Minutes later, alone with Chester, Booth said that nobody would laugh once people really knew of his speculation. He withheld details, and more than a month would elapse before the two next met.

Booth was money-hungry. His correspondence about Pennsylvania oil wells would show this. But he wanted the world to know that when the time came, capturing Abraham Lincoln would be sublimity itself and not the work of a hired knave. So he composed a lengthy statement of self-vindication, punctuated by slanted digressions into history and couched in the rhetoric of a born actor, reading his own lines. On his way from New York to Washington, he stopped off at the Philadelphia home of John Sleeper Clarke, a comedian married to his sister Asia. He sealed the lengthy missive and left it in Clarke's custody, with directions that no one open it. Not yet.

The letter began, "God judge me, not man," and continued, "the very nomination of Abraham Lincoln spoke plainly of war upon Southern rights and institutions. . . . This country was formed for the white, not the black." But the South was no crueler to blacks than was the North. "No one would be more willing to do more for the Negro race than I. . . . But Lincoln's policy is only preparing a way for their total annihilation." Though never on a battlefield, he had seen the effects of "this horrid war" and must "pray the Almighty to dry up this sea of blood. Alas, poor country . . . How I loved the old flag can never now be known. . . . My love is for the South alone. Nor do I deem it a dishonor in attempting to make for her a prisoner of this man, to whom she owes so much of her misery."

Booth caught the train to Baltimore. He left pistols and handcuffs with O'Laughlen and Arnold. His plans advanced fitfully, without a hint of federal intervention. The NDP spy Rob Rover's telegram to Lafayette Baker from Montreal had warned that Booth should be watched. Watched he may have been, but no action followed. Factors ranging from his imperfect leadership to the impassability of country roads in wintry weather compounded the odds against his taking serious steps. But there were no signs that he had anything to fear from War Department initiative.

The year 1864 ended with military action frozen to a near halt. In Washington there arose a strange rash of alarms and portents. John Nicolay, one of Lincoln's private secretaries, was told of "much talk in the city respecting the defenseless condition of the President's house and person now that rebel assassins and incendiaries are abroad." It was suggested that "a squad of experienced detectives be organized for the protection of the President and the White House, [their] duty to be constantly in the mansion in adequate force, or more or less near the President."

About the middle of December, the chief executive himself received a warning letter from Ward H. Lamon, scolding him for his failure to "appreciate what I have repeatedly said to you in regard to the proper police arrangements connected with your household and your own personal safety. You are in danger. Tonight, as you have done on previous occasions, you went unattended to the theatre. And you know, or ought to know, that your life is sought after and will be taken unless you and your friends are cautious; for you have many enemies within our lines."

A burly giant with a swashbuckling gait and the fussiness of a nursemaid, Ward Lamon had assumed presidential security as his special duty. On occasion, he rolled himself in a blanket and slept at Lincoln's door, surrounded by pistols and bowie knives. Two weeks after his warning letter to the president, he wrote again, this time to one of Lincoln's aides. He said that he might be overdoing it in worrying so much about Mr. Lincoln, "but I think I have good reason for my uneasiness. See that he don't [sic] go out alone, either in the day or night time."

Ward Lamon's latest warnings to the White House were issued not from his U.S. Marshal's office in Washington but from the Fifth Avenue Hotel in New York, a popular Manhattan haunt for the money men. A busy lobbyist for cotton gamblers, Lamon was in New York, waiting with other anxious fortune hunters for word about whether the War Department had at last fallen into line, that the order had been issued for army commanders to cooperate with Treasury agents and protect the transport of cotton north and supplies south. It came finally as a Christmas present.

Officers in the field reacted angrily. "For God's sake, get the law repealed," Major-General Cadwallader Washburn beseeched his congressman brother, Elihu B. Washburne. "There is not to exceed one honest man in the Mississippi Valley." Another commander, Edward R. Canby, wounded in action, swore before a congressional committee that agents of the cotton gamblers had even arranged the concealment of stacked bales in the path of the Union advance by feeding the enemy restricted information on planned troop movements. This officer blasted cotton-hungry profiteers as parasites. They "follow in the track of the army, traffic in its blood, and betray the cause for which it fought with all the baseness of Judas Iscariot, but without his remorse."

Protests were unheeded. When Sherman captured Savannah at the close of the year, the president named Simeon Draper special cotton agent at the occupied port, to arrange the movement of cotton stacked in the warehouses that Sherman had padlocked in the face of clamorous claims to ownership. Draper was customs collector for the Port of New York, a toady of that city's commercial interests, also an active fundraiser for Lincoln's debt-ridden wife. Secretary of the Navy Gideon Welles deplored Draper's appointment as "a swindle," bound to attract greedy cotton rings. General Sherman complained that Lincoln's cotton policies encouraged only "sharks and rascals." But as Oakes Ames, whose congressional career would founder in the Credit Mobiliere scandal, privately exulted, "The President is determined to have the cotton come."

CHAPTER 10

"Deem Myself a Coward"

Booth spent Christmas of 1864 with Edwin and their mother in New York. While there, he again pestered his fellow actor Samuel Chester with talk of engaging in a mysterious speculation. He called at Chester's home, 45 Grove Street, and together they walked to the House of Lords Saloon on Houston Street. Booth had written to Chester since their last meeting but without saying much more about his speculation. Now, over oysters and brandy, he was more informative. On the way back to Grove Street they avoided Broadway, Booth saying it was too crowded. In a secluded square off Bleeker Street he continued his earnest importuning. He was in a large conspiracy, numbering up to a hundred people, to capture the North's heads of state, Lincoln included, and to carry them off to Richmond. All that Chester would have to do was open the back door of Ford's Theatre in Washington at a set moment. He would be well rewarded. Chester declined, saying that the scheme was unthinkable and he had a family to consider. A disappointed Booth bade him goodnight.

Booth's next stop was again Philadelphia, at the home of his brother-in-law, where he signed the statement he had left there in November. This time, before resealing it, he inserted a letter to his mother, expressing his love for her, telling her that he would rather die than give her pain, and praying that God would "soften the blow of my departure." He professed that for four years, living in the North, he could not speak freely, even while in his own home, "constantly hearing every principle dear to my heart denounced as treasonable." Silently, he had "cursed my wilful [sic] idleness, and begin to deem myself a coward and to despise my own existence."

He had borne it for her sake. "But it runs that uncontrollable fate, moving me for its own ends, takes me from you, dear mother, to do what work I can for a poor oppressed people. Should I meet the worst I can say, 'God's will be done.'" His next call was on his collaborators in Baltimore, Samuel Arnold and Michael O'Laughlen. He directed them to load a trunk with provisions and kidnap gear and to make sure that it got safely to Washington. He then caught a train for the capital, where he arrived in the middle of a furor caused by the radical Ben Wade's latest speech in the Senate.

The North expected victory when the snows melted. But if the collapse of the rebellion was that close at hand, so, too, was the decisive round of the war within a war, the power struggle between Lincoln and his political foes. Lately, they had lost too many points. Their autumn of discontent was severe enough when derived from fears of a premature armistice and peace terms colored by Lincolnian clemency. Next, they were enraged by an unexpected turnabout on the president's part, an apparent disposition to let bygones be bygones. Addressing the new Congress in December, Lincoln had praised the radicals' antislavery program, forcing them to applaud while inwardly they fumed.

Although the radicals recognized the motive for these concessions—an unsubtle effort of Lincoln's to disarm them—they were at a loss for ways to checkmate him. And the more he behaved in a conciliatory fashion, the greater their private wrath, as they recoiled from that outstretched hand.

After the Christmas recess, they revised their Reconstruction Bill so drastically that not even in his newly accommodating guise could the president have embraced it. So the tug of war was on again. From the Senate floor on January 9, Wade questioned the president's sincerity. The Baltimore convention had nominated him on a platform dedicated to abolishing slavery. Was he now backing out, telling the rebels that all would be forgiven, so long as they laid down their arms? If so, it was too late for him to think he could get away with it. The war must go on until slavery was no more. "That is the platform on which we put Lincoln and he said he assented to it." If he dared retreat from that holy commitment, "so much the worse for the President."

As they had during the tense hours of summer, the ultras mapped plans in private caucas. A meeting at Senator Zachariah Chandler's home, five days after Wade's violent speech, lasted from sunrise until dusk. The next day they presented their Reconstruction Bill before Congress. It was defeated by a coalition of Republican Party moderates and the Democratic minority.

For Chandler, Wade, and their cohorts, it was the handwriting on the wall. They had aborted Lincoln's recent moves in the direction of political compromise. At the same time they had failed to halt the growth within their party of a majority that welcomed Lincoln's new approach. This fresh Republican faction, reinforced by Democrats, would be able to crush every measure they introduced. Their activism and resolve had hitherto outmatched the ardor of every other political class, secured for them an influence out of all proportion to their numbers. Now the situation had changed. Far from grasping the nation's helm during the crucial period of conversion from war to peace, the ultras might have to consider themselves lucky if they retained enough hold to steer the ship of state even marginally along their ideological course.

Booth was doing his limited best to complete plans for the president's abduction. George Alfred Townsend, a Washington newspaperman whose admiration for Chief Detective Lafayette Baker was rewarded with tidbits of privileged information, later wrote that after the rebel commissioners Clay and Thompson in Canada spurned Booth's invitation to help kidnap Lincoln, he had cast about for recruits, and "all those who presented themselves were military men." This was largely the result of Booth's appeal to Colonel Mosby for aid.

Confederate officers experienced in undercover activity, agents posing as deserters or turncoats, handpicked scouts from Colonel Mosby's command—these were the "military men" drawn into the plot. In the closing months of 1864 there was a pattern of movement that, in the light of later developments, could be envisaged as a sort of pocket mobilization.

One of the military men was Ringgold Browning, contrabandist, Confederate cavalryman, partisan scout—Will Browning's brother.

Union army pickets had arrested him as he seemingly lost his way and strayed into Union lines near Washington. He was registered at the Old Capitol Prison as "lieutenant and adjutant to Colonel Mosby." His brother composed a request for his release that Vice President–elect Andrew Johnson signed. At the White House it was endorsed by President Lincoln, who added that Browning could remain at large, "so long as he does not misbehave." Within a week Ringgold Browning, paroled with the president's innocent approval, was among those plotting the president's abduction.

Another of the military men was Captain James William Boyd, 6th Tennessee Infantry. A Kentucky miller's son orphaned in infancy, he was one of the three rebels captured by Union troops at Jackson, Tennessee, in the summer of 1863. This was the trio that included R. D. Watson's brother James and a fellow courier named Harry D'Arcy. They had been the object of a detectives' manhunt that reached from Chesapeake Bay to the Southern states. The pursuit had been by train, steamboat, and horseback, a long-distance chase that the hunted trio turned into a cat-and-mouse game, availing themselves of crafty ruses, thunderstorms, and rail service interrupted by the Battle of Gettysburg.

James Watson and D'Arcy were hanged. The third prisoner, Boyd, was too valuable to his captors. He was an ace Confederate spy and a scout, a battle-hardened veteran who before the war had been a deputy sheriff, a telegrapher, and a railroad detective. Boyd had studied law under a friendly Tennessean judge, yet he adhered to a retributive code of his own, inherited from grandparents who had reared him. As a sheriff's deputy, he had shot dead a horse thief who resisted arrest. He killed a man who tried to rape his daughter at a party. In the war, scouting behind Union lines, he was surprised by a Pennsylvania infantryman who fired at him, knocking him from his mount. Although grounded and bleeding, he quickly pulled around, reaching for his gun, and shot dead his approaching enemy. He suffered a wound in his right leg, however, that never healed.

Following his capture, he was sent to the Union stockade at Johnson's Island, Ohio, where NDP men expert at getting captives to change sides worked on him. They failed to "turn him around" but promised that if he supplied them with information gathered from other inmates, they would send cash to his consumptive wife and seven children. What Boyd gave the detectives was piecemeal and often meaningless. The arrangement ended.

At age forty-one, Boyd blamed himself for the destitute state of his partly scattered family. Weary of scouting and espionage, he was genuinely disposed to change sides, but only in return for an unconditional parole that would allow him to return home and provide for the children he feared would soon be motherless. "You and the kids come first," he wrote from prison to his wife, Caroline, showing a pathetic concern for his family that would trap the tall Confederate captain, aging adventurer, and ill-starred war spy into the plot against Abraham Lincoln.

Stanton ordered prisoner-of-war Boyd transferred to Washington, for questioning on what he knew about the alleged treachery of Union officers two years earlier at Holly Springs, Mississippi, which had resulted in a humiliating defeat for the North. Boyd's arrival in Washington under tight guard was duly noted in *The Evening Star,* October 31, 1864, which also reported that he was lodged in solitary confinement at the Old Capitol Prison.

Such newspaper announcements were not a usual press feature. This one was for public consumption. Though supposedly locked up, Boyd was occasionally at large on some assignment or other. Nothing would survive to precisely spell out whose interests he was serving or thought to be serving. So ambiguous was the nature of his allegiance that Lafayette Baker attached a "control" to him, a William B. Earle, who specialized in liaison with turncoats.

During those same late fall weeks, Booth had arrived in southern Maryland. He wanted to find horses and boats and get the bearings of local byways. Also, he intended to employ what smuggling facilities he still managed for the captive's passage through the region and across the Potomac into Virginia, where Mosby's men would take over, providing a military escort for the final triumphant leg of the journey to Richmond. Before the end of the year, Mosby transferred half of his command from northern Virginia to the uppermost of the three necks of the state created by the James, York,

Rappahannock, and Potomac Rivers. As for the Van Ness mansion in Washington, with its revamped basement and tunnel, Booth decided to use it only if city outlets to southern Maryland were blocked.

As the guest of a local doctor the weekend following Lincoln's reelection, Booth attended church near Bryantown, and after the service he met another physician, Samuel A. Mudd. In 1863 Doctor Mudd and his neighbors had faced charges of harboring Confederate officers, secreting arms, and rounding up ex-slaves for Confederate service. Now Mudd wished to find Booth good horses, not an easy task because the best animals had been commandeered for Union service. Booth paid $80 for a one-eyed bay, doing better with his purchase of a sturdy mare to pull his buggy. In it, he set out to get the lay of the countryside.

Booth was consumed with the idea of seizing Lincoln in a theater, preferably Ford's, where he knew every nook and cranny. Some members of his group didn't think much of this, especially Arnold and O'Laughlen, who argued that there was less risk in pulling things off outdoors. "We have studied Old Abe's comings and goings," said Arnold, "while taking care not to arouse the suspicions of detectives and spies." Booth brushed their objections aside. He had already rented a frame shack in the alley behind Ford's Theatre, paying a stage carpenter and a scene-shifter to fit it out as a stable.

The president was at Ford's that January. The formidable Edwin Forrest had arrived in town for a month's engagement. On the 4th, Lincoln saw him play the cardinal-duke in Edward Bulwer Lytton's *Richelieu; or, The Conspiracy.* One week later at the White House, with cotton lobbyist and bodyguard Ward Lamon at his elbow, Lincoln signed the papers that gave R. D. Watson and partners "free and unmolested passage" of the cotton they undertook to secure through the Union's military lines.

CHAPTER 11

The Kidnap Plot

Setbacks to the Montreal deal were accumulating. Cotton should have been moving north, with meat from the Watson Provision Company already reaching Lee's hungry troops. But after Beverley Tucker's dispatch fell into Union hands, the naval blockade tightened. Moreover, despite Secretary Stanton's official conformity with Treasury regulations, his officers in territory bordering the Ohio and Mississippi Rivers continued to harass wagon trains and to intercept river steamboats. James V. Barnes and Will Browning journeyed north and south, trying to break logjams and to clear bottlenecks. Most important, however, was that although the president had been obliged that uncomfortable Sunday in November to disavow the use of his name by the Henry Stewart Company, in its attempt to lift Farragut's blockade, he had by no means wavered in his pursuit of the South's cotton.

That same January a Northern newspaper reported turbulence in the marketplace, brought about by the opening of Savannah to general trade: "Mercantile men are anxious to try adventures in that quarter." There was a rush of applicants for trade permits. "If thirty thousand bales of cotton could be thrown onto the market it would greatly reduce the price of gold." Orville H. Browning wrote of contracts for $7 million worth of cotton, which would "make us rich if we could only get it out." As drawn up by the Treasury factotum Hanson Risley and approved by President Lincoln, the contracts for R. D. Watson covered a total of 20 million pounds of the staple. It was certified as located at sites in eight Southern states, to be delivered within four months.

The other commodity in the great exchange then began to move. Less than a week after Lincoln signed Watson's cotton permits, a consignment of five hundred barrels of pork on Watson steamboats went down the Tennessee River from Paducah, Kentucky, reaching the Confederates at Guntersville, Alabama. During the next few weeks, along different routes, meat shipments in excess of six thousand barrels would enter the Confederacy.

Plans to abduct Lincoln grew erratically. John Surratt left his mother's boardinghouse in Washington and crossed into Maryland to Port Tobacco. Before the war, inroads of silt had choked off the commercial livelihood of this small Potomac River harbor. With its sheltered location and inhabitants of strongly secessionist stock, Port Tobacco was a safe entry and rendezvous for Confederate agents and the ideal choice as a ferrying point along the presidential kidnap route. To oversee the preparations, Surratt set up temporary headquarters at the Brawner House, the town's principle hotel. He bought a flat-bottomed boat, big enough for fifteen passengers, and ordered it hidden in a creek until required.

Almost overnight, the moribund little port became as lively as a beehive. Rumors flew. An important party was expected down from Washington within a week or two. The regular crossings had been suspended to make way for it. The party might number twenty, perhaps Confederate officers, sprung from the Old Capitol Prison. A minority of residents guessed the truth behind the local hustle and bustle. Members of the Confederate "signal corps" had it all figured out, though. Abraham Lincoln was going to be kidnapped.

The "signal corps" was a web of communication posts, mail caches, and dependable havens of hospitality or medical aid for Confederate spies and scouts shuttling between Canada, New York, Baltimore, Washington, and Richmond. The network was composed of about 350 agents and over 100 "camps," or signal stations, secreted on farmsteads and estates.

On the Maryland side, where the war had ruined the aristocracy by lifting its slaves out of bondage, agents received help from locals whose homes overlooked fertile meadows no longer tilled. On the Virginia shore, in counties where resistance to outside authority was a tradition rooted in colonial pride, the war had sown a special hatred. Few had forgotten the house-burning and pillage wrought by General Kilpatrick's maddened troops after the death of Ulric Dahlgren and the alleged desecration of his body. Few would have withheld succor from the kidnappers of Abraham Lincoln when the cavalcade rode through. And they were buoyed by the arrival of some five hundred of Colonel Mosby's warriors, deployed to meet the kidnap party, with its valuable prize, and to hurry it on to Richmond.

The kidnappers were braced for action—all but John Wilkes Booth. The great actor Edwin Forrest was in town, and a critic bedazzled by his Lear wrote, "There is no denying the fact, Mr. Edwin Forrest is the greatest living actor. America should be proud of such a son. He towers above them all." That insulted the Booths. Edwin Booth's rivalry with Forrest was legendary. But John Wilkes Booth, even as he competed with his brother for their father's crown, more than once had taken on that other Edwin. Now their paths had crossed again. Booth was not in town for professional engagements. He had a tyrant to get rid of. But that public appraisal of Forrest as "the greatest" was a challenge impossible to ignore, even if it meant deferring fulfillment of an obsessive dream.

Booth wrote to his brother Junius about the discomfort he had felt living with Edwin in New York. "I am sure he thinks I live upon him." Only for his mother's sake had he stayed there at all. And what was he doing in Washington? "Well, a thousand things. My business at present calls me here." He did not elaborate. In fact, his abduction plans were suspended. As announced in the press, he had volunteered "to give his splendid representation of Romeo to the Juliet of Miss Avonia Jones in a benefit performance at Grover's National Theatre."

Not that anyone could have kidnapped Lincoln at a theater that week. On the two successive nights when Forrest played *Jack Cade,* the president confounded expectations by staying home at the White House. And on January 20, as Booth set hearts aflutter at Grover's, down the kidnap trail to Port Tobacco and across the Potomac in Virginia the relays of horses, the hostlers and the boatmen, the secessionist doctors, and four companies of John Mosby's bushwhackers north and south of the Union capital, all waited in vain.

On the day when some had expected him at Ford's Theatre, President Lincoln received a letter from Jefferson Davis in Richmond. It proposed that the North and the South appoint commissioners to "secure peace between the two countries." Lincoln sidestepped the trap in Davis's phrasing and replied that he would meet with any representative from Richmond on the subject of "securing peace to our one common country."

The Confederate leader let it go at that. Near the end of the month, he sent a three-man delegation across the lines with a white flag. The emissaries got as far as General Grant's headquarters at City Point. Their written request for an interview with Lincoln missed the general, who was inspecting troops elsewhere, and missed the White House as well, landing on the desk of the secretary of war. Stanton notified the president, who at once wrote an order to give the men from Richmond safe passage.

"Armistice would be death to our cause." So wrote one of Stanton's intimates to a fellow radical. "*No armistice* was one of the distinct points on which Mr. Lincoln was re-elected." Stanton needed no such reminder. To keep the guns firing, Mr. Lincoln had to be watched, controlled—if necessary, circumvented. The secretary sent Major Thomas T. Eckert south with Lincoln's response. But Eckert, chief of the War Department telegraph, was no mere messenger. He was told by Stanton to confer privately with the Confederate visitors before Lincoln got there. (The absent Grant afterward complained that he had been deliberately side-tracked.)

Not until Grant told him did the president learn that the Richmond trio was agreeable to his talks, based on the preconception of "our one common country." Lincoln then set out for Hampton Roads and talked with the three Confederates on the Union steamer *River Queen.* The meeting lasted four hours and got nowhere. Lincoln would not yield from his position that peace was attainable through national reunion, that slavery must go and the South's armed forces demobilize.

In Washington, radicals had begun attacking the president for even talking with rebels. "All tenderness towards the foe is treason," was the opinion of Indiana congressman George Julian. When Lincoln returned from Hampton Roads, the radicals forced a resolution through Congress, demanding a full accounting. Dutifully, Lincoln obliged. And again, his political critics felt outmaneuvered. As fellow Republicans applauded, relieved and delighted by Lincoln's unwavering insistence on the principle of "one common country," they had to join in the cheering or sit on their hands with silent Democrats.

Lincoln's popularity had reached full crest. War-weary thousands, convinced that he was indeed for peace, equally appreciated his determination to forfeit no honor in exchange for it. Lincoln's heart was in the right place. Moderate Republicans acclaimed him for his stand on the Thirteenth Amendment, outlawing slavery. Addressing a Boston audience, a prominent abolitionist praised him as most responsible for the passage of that historic measure. "The humble rail-splitter of Illinois . . . the Presidential chain-breaker for millions of the oppressed . . . Abraham Lincoln!"

Republican radicals had always considered themselves the champions in the struggle against slavery. Now they saw the credit going to the man they had so often to push in their direction. As for "the humble rail-splitter," it was a triumphant beginning to the final month before he again took the oath of office. In a mood to relax, he invited General Grant, in Washington just then, to a night out at Ford's Theatre.

Topping the bill was *A Comedy Carnival,* featuring John "Sleeper Clarke," a star laugh-maker. It was a bizarre twist, of which the audience had no inkling. Clarke was himself unaware, as his buffoonery drew smiles from the state box, that the sealed document left in his charge by his brother-in-law was a passionate declaration of intent to carry Lincoln off. That was a piece of madness beyond Sleeper Clarke's repertoire, an exclusive joke for demons.

February 1865 was a treacherous month in Washington. Mild weather of the first weeks lured blossoms to appear on Capitol Hill, while ladies strolled Pennsylvania Avenue in spring finery. Then winter swung back with gales and sleet. Storms of a different sort shook Capitol Hill. In Congress the radicals saw their Reconstruction proposals topple before the new coalition of Democrats and moderate Republicans.

Setbacks like these foreshadowed Lincoln's supremacy after a cease-fire that extremists, swearing to prolong the war "thirty years if necessary," felt to be alarmingly close. It was all very well for the president, sure of another four years in office, to try to free himself of their influence. "He must accept our views," one of them told the Russian minister in Washington, "or we will find some means to ruin him."

The public was on Lincoln's side. So were a majority of the national legislators. He could travel his own political road, no more submissive to the Republican Party's extremist fringe than in any further need to compromise with it. In any event, Congress would be adjourned until the end of the year, and Lincoln, ruling the roost, was free to indulge his all-too-magnanimous soul. In the absence of watchful radicals, he was sure to let the South off lightly. Neither would Edwin Stanton be in a position to stop him. An end to armed conflict would remove the secretary's restraining hand. What price, then, the radicals' hopes of seeing insurgent leaders, General Lee included, marched to the scaffold and rebeldom turned into a richly deserved purgatory under Union martial law? Instead, when Congress regathered, the rebels would be right there in Washington, claiming seats as official representatives. "If they come to the door of the House they will cross the threshold," warned Henry Winter Davis, and for this dire prognosis, "there is no remedy except to change the President." Outvoted in Congress, aware of power slipping away and time running short, the political radicals of the North had become, by the dawn of 1865, an uncommonly desperate force, thus more than ever determined and dangerous.

Ben Wade, the extremists' pugnacious spokesman, insisted that Congress had "full power to carry out the mandate of the people independent of the President." Should a chief magistrate persist in vaunting his will over the wishes of the legislature, then he must go. Prospects for constitutionally displacing Lincoln had been scattered by Union guns in August, then by November's avalanche of votes. Initiating impeachment proceedings now would be like trying to shift the Rock of Gibralter from one end of the Mediterranean to the other. And if that left prayer the radicals' only recourse, it would have to be the prewar invocation of abolitionist Owen Lovejoy, one that Congressman Julian now recalled: "O God, show the President the error of his ways and if Thou find this too great a task, do Thou remove him."

Booth was hardly fitted to play a role in any such divine plan, although still obsessed with dreams of abduction. He had first canvassed for recruits from among his Chesapeake Bay smugglers. That contraband service had lately declined, and most of the men had returned to their humdrum lives as farmhands and fishermen. Booth might not have bothered with them at all had he seen a picture of them taken in 1863 at St. Michaels, on the eastern shore of Chesapeake Bay. Some two dozen had gathered to face the camera of a couple of Lafayette Baker's most resourceful operatives, posing as itinerant photographers. St. Michaels was a contrabandist base, where medicines earmarked for the Confederacy were stored in a small warehouse, their odor lost in the smell of fish. The photograph, subsequently an item in NDP files, shows most of the smugglers gazing stonily ahead as if striving for dignity. It was a special occasion; many in the group had never been photographed. But the overall impression was hardly one of a team capable of kidnapping the highest official in the land. Booth had known few, if any, of his smuggling hirelings, and he didn't see the St. Michaels picture. The NDP was able to identify everyone in the photo.

So Booth had failed to organize an efficient gang. His impracticable ideas scared off recruits. He had done something about horses; the light bay had been stabled with the one-eyed animal at Howard's Livery on G Street, opposite the rear of Mary Surratt's rooming house, where his occasional visits quickened the heartbeat of her daughter Anna. But his ego was under assault. Mosby's men, assigned to help him, were becoming impatient, "unwilling to be subordinate to a civilian and mere play actor."

He grew ill at ease. The change in him was noticed not only by such co-conspirators as Arnold and O'Laughlen. Some of his acquaintances, including fellow actors, business associates, and lady friends, wondered what had come over him. After receiving an odd letter from him, Joseph Simonds, a Boston bank clerk turned business agent who counted Booth among his oil-speculating clients, replied, "I hardly know what to make of you this winter. Have you lost your ambition or what is the matter?" And Booth wrote to Sam Chester that his kidnap plan was close to collapse because others in it were backing out.

Ella Turner may have been on Booth's mind. Her real name was Starr. She dreamed of a stage career and lived on Ohio Avenue in Washington, where her sister ran the house as a brothel. She was among Booth's lovers and in February had sent him a desperate note:

> My darling Baby
> Please call
> this evening or as soon as you
> receive this note. I will not
> detain you five minutes—for
> gods sake come
> Yours truly
> E. T.
>
> If you will not come
> write a note the reason why
> Washington Feb 7th
> 1865

Perhaps she wished to inform him personally of her pregnancy and his responsibility.

That same month Booth paused in his restless itinerary to give money and directions to his closest accomplices, Sam Arnold and Michael O'Laughlen. This pair, equipped with weapons, handcuffs, and other kidnap gear, had taken a room at 420 D Street in Washington. But even they were beginning to show disinterest, their attitude giving Booth cause to sense that he was losing command.

The War Department in Richmond had promised General Robert E. Lee that food was on the way. The biggest exchange for cotton was to be that which Beverley Tucker had supposedly arranged in Montreal. But his superiors were beginning to suspect the whole project was nothing but Yankee trickery. Tucker was still in Canada, congratulating himself on a job well done, when he heard of wrangling in Richmond over who was to blame for Lee's food shortage. After the tireless negotiating, the false moves and fresh starts, resulting at last in signed contracts, it would be just like quarrelsome bureaucrats to mess things up. Tucker registered exasperation. Unless some reliable businessmen got into the act, "it will be botched at home."

Tucker was unaware that his Montreal report had been read en route to Richmond by President Lincoln and Secretary Stanton. Nor could he know that Lincoln had warned Admiral Farragut against a display of his purported signature. Meanwhile, Lincoln had continued to sign cotton passes, and for reasons of his own Stanton remained silent about the Montreal deal. Stanton, in turn, had no idea that the craftiest official in his own department was well informed of it.

In the great venal mania for reaping fortunes out of cotton permits, Lafayette Charles Baker was an unsuspected figure, going about the game with tactics and advantages peculiarly his own. Baker had fallen out of favor with Stanton since the middle of 1863, when the secretary of war discovered that Baker's NDP, at its Tenth Street command post in Washington, was tapping military telegraph lines. Yet, perhaps because he knew too much, Baker remained head of the War Department's detective bureau. And while privy to political mischief, Baker also fished in commercial waters.

As the Department's grand inquisitor, upon whose word hundreds of innocents languished in the Old Capitol Prison, Baker was ridiculed and hated and would be physically harmed and probably murdered. But never was he investigated. Had one of his own sleuths been rash enough to make the attempt and sought the source of the cotton he was selling through Demill and Company, the trail would have led to his earlier title of War Department provost marshal. This status had given Baker control over Confederate cargoes intercepted at sea.

The prize vessels were usually brought up the Potomac and unloaded at a government wharf in Alexandria, Virginia. Fruit, dairy products, and other perishables were conveyed to the federal commissary. The storage or disposal of nonperishable material was left to Lafayette Baker. And it included cotton. With one stroke of his pen, the chief detective could have padlocked 178½ Water Street, New York, for the duration. Instead, he did quiet business there.

Mercantile operators at that address who still used the old name Chaffey and Chaffey kept ledger books, one of which, covering the closing months of 1864, recorded payments totaling $150,000 for thousands of bales of cotton "from the stock of L. C. Baker." Confident of his unique power and influence, all that Lafayette Baker needed to fear was a recurrence of his epilepsy.

Baker had got wind of Beverley Tucker's mission to Montreal almost from the start. Much of his information came from indefatigable NDP spies covering the preliminaries at Nashville, as well as the main event in Canada. Baker had already tried to muscle in on the cotton rings. He had once cornered Hanson Risley at the Astor House in New York, but the Treasury official had brushed him off. Risley should have known better. Baker was soon leaking some of his knowledge of the racket in presidential cotton permits to Elihu Washburne, chairman of the House Committee on Commerce.

Speculators profited by selling cotton they often did not own but claimed to "control." The scheme had developed in the wake of the president's executive order of September 1864, which was not made public until December, when the *New York Herald* broke the story. "During that long interval," Baker wrote, "Hanson Risley made contracts." Baker charged that the original schemers were New York bankers in league with Thurlow Weed, Ward Lamon, Leonard Swett, Simeon Draper, and William P. Dole, all but one of whom were Lincoln's old associates. Congressman Washburne lost no time in preparing an investigation. And bribery was in the air. The same day as Baker's letter, Thurlow Weed at the Astor House was writing one to Hanson Risley, warning him that thanks to Baker, a "wicked falsehood" was in circulation to the effect that he, Weed, had been seen paying Risley $5,000 for a cotton permit. Risley replied that he had heard the same story and treated it with contempt. The cotton traffic he directed from his office in the Treasury building was entirely on the level. It must have pained Risley that not all of his clients were safely discreet. One of them, urging prompt action "to retrieve our imperiled fortune and contribute incidentally to the national prosperity," promised Risley that when next in Washington, he would "make suitable recognition of your labor."

Elihu B. Washburne launched his hearings in February. The probers dug deep and scrutinized the transactions of sundry rings, the spotlight frequently falling on Lincoln's friends, Ward H. Lamon included. Hanson Risley was in the witness chair three days, defending his methods and motives. "I am," he bitterly declared, "to a certain extent, myself on trial. I was made a sort of backwater to the cotton tide."

Had he actually erased entries and otherwise altered papers signed by President Lincoln? Risley admitted doing so. But, as he told the president privately, while the hearings were under way, he had only acted in conformity with his, Mr. Lincoln's, emphatic wish to swell and speed the flow of cotton into the North.

The committee subpoenaed Risley's records. He surrendered sixty-three contracts and related permits, reflecting ninety days' business through the end of January. Abraham Lincoln's signature numbered in the hundreds. But not included were Watson's papers, endorsed and signed at the White House on the 11th of that month. The deals probed by Congress, shocking enough to the probers, were at least legalized by that quiet executive order permitting one-third supplies in payment for the cotton. The Montreal deal involved pledges of massive amounts of cotton and pound-for-pound exchanges in meat. No hint of this emerged. Nothing was said of R. D. Watson, James V. Barnes, or Alexander T. Stewart's "Henry Stewart Company." That illegal superdeal remained under wraps.

CHAPTER 12

The Letter from Cape Girardeau

In mid-February 1865, John Wilkes Booth spent time with Harriet Alexander in Room 238 of the Metropolitan Hotel in New York City. Haughtily attractive, twelve years his senior, and a dominant lover, she was also an intimate of Vice President–elect Andrew Johnson, his private aide Will Browning, and several top radicals. She claimed to be one of the illegitimate daughters of Belgium's King Leopold I and thereby related to Queen Victoria. She called herself "Lola." In truth, she was born Harriet Stover in a remote corner of southwest Virginia, but when her family moved to South Bend, Indiana, she developed a close relationship with Schuyler Colfax, Speaker of the House of Representatives. Her Prussian-born husband, Julius, was a bounder, thrown out of two Union army regiments during the war's first year, and by its third, through the influence of his attractive and opportunistic wife, he had attained the rank of colonel. She had met Booth at a party. Now, only hours after his departure, she sent him a Valentine's Day card on which she had written, "It was so nice to see you tonight and I hope you will return soon. You are always welcome."

Booth's next significant stop was Belleville, Ontario, traveling by train via Buffalo, where he was joined by Martha Mills, his former wife's half-sister. There, the two checked in at the same hotel as did two men with whom Booth would spend a mortifying hour or more, hearing himself accused of not being up to the task of kidnapping Abraham Lincoln. One of the men was James V. Barnes, the other Captain James William Boyd, who had also been in New York that week, on business at 178½ Water Street.

Since his transfer to Washington four months earlier and supposedly in solitary confinement thereafter, Boyd had done undercover work, probably because of his expertise in telegraphy, for his captors. But in the meantime his wife, Caroline, had died, leaving seven children in Tennessee, virtually orphaned. On February 14, Boyd wrote a letter addressed to Secretary of War Stanton. Delivered by Colonel Wood, prison superintendent, this was no valentine but Boyd's request for a full pardon. In return, he offered to serve Stanton as a special detective.

He could supply the secretary with valuable information on the Holly Springs affair and also on the contraband traffic across battle lines. There would be risks. "If it was known," Boyd wrote, "that I was in your service, I could not wear my scalp very safely." He asked Stanton for a personal interview. Within twenty-four hours after his letter reached Stanton's desk, the register of the Old Capitol Prison showed "James W. Boyd, captain. Released on oath February 15th." A certificate of his release carried the name and address of his NDP control, William B. Earle, Park Hotel, New York.

Boyd now had an important secret assignment that, if successfully carried out, would be rewarded with freedom and a new life in Mexico, where the nationalist leader Benito Juarez offered land to men of either side in America's war if they helped him liberate his people from the grip of imperial France. At recruiting offices run by Juarista agents in the United States, paroled veterans were already signing up for two years in the "emigrant army." Boyd expected to organize and command its "secret service" division. More than ever, he was burdened by concern for his children. While in jail, he had heard that his stepdaughter Emma was about to marry a much older man to ensure security for herself and her younger siblings. He advised her not to. "I wish your mother was still with you." He went on to say that his leg was mostly healed. Not so. Boyd had been lucky enough to escape amputation. But the minie ball that had struck him earlier in the war had dealt its characteristic havoc of laceration and fracture, causing periodic festering and suppuration. He told Emma of signing up for "a two-year hitch in Mexico with the emigrant movement" and he proudly enclosed a photo of himself wearing his new "emigrant" uniform. Before Mexico, he must go to Canada. He did not say why but added, "I will send money as often as I can. Kiss the kids for me."

The day Boyd wrote to his stepdaughter, he appeared at 178½ Water Street, accompanied by his NDP control, Earle. The purpose of that visit may have been to obtain information on Confederate contraband activity. But if he did not already know of a plot to kidnap Lincoln, and of his role in it, he soon would. At any rate, Boyd's call was significant enough for Richard Demill to notify R. D. Watson at once. "We had a long talk. Our situation has become more complicated than anyone dreamed. But we now stand at the door of one of the largest business deals in history. There will be adequate profits for all."

After visiting the Demills in New York, Boyd entrained for Montreal. He still mourned his wife. "The heart went out of me," he wrote to a friend in Tennessee, "when Cary died. I still can't get used to it." He did not say why he was in Canada or for whom he was working. He ended this letter with, "I know there are thousands who will condemn me for what I am doing but they just can't know what I feel." And then Boyd was in Belleville.

James V. Barnes was born in Belleville and doubtless knew of the small town's most discreet hotel. The three men talked in one room. Martha Mills was next door and heard angry voices, her Wilkes loudly protesting to "someone called Virgul." She couldn't catch a third voice. But Boyd was there, witness to what was essentially a showdown between Barnes and Booth. "You don't realize how much money is involved!" Barnes shouted the words repeatedly.

He had been in touch with Northern politicians who wanted to usurp their president's authority. Even in private, Barnes knew that it was safer not to utter their names, and tell-tale papers of his were fated to go up in smoke. But he had secured their promise that with Lincoln off the scene, those who took his place would see to it that the Montreal deal, so frequently stalled, would be allowed to advance. Barnes knew, and he was one of many, that Booth was supposed to be working at an abduction scheme, but it had become apparent that the actor was not up to the task. He seemed unable to distinguish between acting and reality. Barnes told him so. It was better that he be replaced by someone experienced in military command and undercover work who could count on the obedience of

Mosby-type guerrillas. Such a replacement had been found in Captain James W. Boyd, formerly of the Confederate States Army.

In Martha's room later, Booth was "angry, livid, paced the floor." And when the two were at the Belleville railroad depot, waiting in freezing cold for the Buffalo train, "Wilkes was morose and said he was being squeezed out of the deal."

After that stormy confrontation in Canada, Barnes's destination was Cape Girardeau, a town on the Mississippi River at the heart of the fertile counties so much a part of the Watson livestock empire, and there it was his turn to be outraged. Local provost marshals had sealed Watson's smokehouses and impounded tons of pork valued at $2 million, awaiting shipment on Watson wagons and river craft. They had sequestered 1,300 barrels at Cape Girardeau and 800 at Shute's Landing, then pounced downriver at Hickman, Kentucky, with simultaneous raids at Paducah, Evansville, Owensboro, and Louisville.

Under the Montreal agreement, some Northern meat was reaching the South in spite of delays, military harassment, and winter weather. The quality was below that of the cuts supplied Union troops from Philip Armour's Chicago slaughterhouses, and one of the suppliers, R. D. Watson's brother-in-law, confessed to having packed more bones than hams and shoulders. Even so, what reached the South was an improvement over the notorious "Nassau bacon," often so putrid that groaning boys in gray suspected the Yankees of deliberately allowing it through their naval blockade to poison them.

As early as 1863, the military high command in Indiana had complained of contraband trading, involving parties in that state. In response to telegraphed appeals for help, Secretary Stanton sent six of Lafayette Baker's top detectives to the region, with authority for Indiana's governor Oliver Morton to issue them military commissions so that if caught by rebel soldiers, they would not be shot as spies. The NDP's two chief operatives were among them—Earl Potter, appointed colonel, and his brother Andrew, major.

No immediate action followed. In fact, a Midwest senator wrote, "So long as our [Union] prisoners are held in the squalor of rebel camps and prisoners will not be exchanged, it is the government's desire that sale of pork in limited quantities continue. The rebel government is doomed and cannot last more than the winter and a little pork is not going to change that." Six months later, the congressional hearings had made clear that more than "a little pork" was involved. Like his radical friends, Secretary Stanton opposed any kind of commerce with insurrectionary states. He was all for acquiring Confederate cotton but only through force of arms. What he had done when General Sherman captured Savannah showed how he felt. Tons of cotton had fallen into Union hands, and claimants to ownership clamored for their release. Stanton had himself hurried down to Savannah and personally ordered Sherman to destroy all cotton papers and rip the owners' name tags off every bale. Savannah cotton was soon at sea, bound for New York and sale at auction under federal auspices.

That had come about in the fall of 1864. By the year's end, thanks to the "arrest" of Beverley Tucker's chosen courier, Stanton was aware of the huge Montreal deal. Then had come the congressional investigation. Hanson Risley managed to survive it without mentioning the R. D. Watson permits, but Stanton knew of them. Upon his orders, the Midwest provost marshals had moved, and at the final count no less than 25 million pounds of pork destined for the Confederacy were in Union hands. Richmond's leaders had all but given up on Beverley Tucker's promises of forthcoming supplies. The soldiers' suffering worsened. An enlisted man's daily ration in General Lee's army hardly equaled one-sixth that of his Union counterpart. In the middle of February, Lee reported that units defending Petersburg had fought for seventy-two hours in sleet and snow without a mouthful of meat. Hunger and desertion decimated his ranks almost as much as did powder and steel.

On March 2, from Cape Girardeau—with endangered profits, not starving soldiers on his mind—Barnes relayed his grim news to R. D. Watson, just then in care of Demill and Company, New York. The meat seized had been stored in readiness for the great exchange, not to be sold to Union quartermasters "at army prices." So what was to be done? "It is essential that the President and Secretary not be harmed, but if they could be deposed for a fortnight the Congress, we are assured, could and would act in the manner of the

Executive. We are further advised that our contracts would be recognized in toto." Barnes did not name those who had assured and advised him.

And the "Secretary"? Here, Barnes meant the secretary of state. He had learned enough about American history to be aware of the anomalies clouding the issue of presidential succession. They had existed since the birth of the republic. Given the sudden departure of the chief executive through death or other causes, the vice president would inherit presidential duties and functions but not automatically become president. He would remain vice president until a national election that the secretary of state alone was constitutionally authorized to call. In the meantime, supreme power would belong to Congress, where, as believed by many lawmakers and most passionately by the radicals, it rightfully belonged anyway. And with the country in a state of war, full control would inevitably fall into the grasp of the Joint Committee on the Conduct of the War.

The money men Barnes represented were now more positively than hitherto at one with Lincoln's radical foes. All shared a vested interest in Abraham Lincoln's removal. And to ensure that the right men were in place to "act in the manner of the Executive," William H. Seward, as well as Abraham Lincoln, would have to go.

Barnes's letter continued in hard-headed businesslike tones. Unless more meat moved south under the contracts Beverley Tucker had worked so diligently to arrange, Northern investors would get no cotton, nor would its transatlantic flow resume. "Our friends in Liverpool," Barnes wrote, "are much upset by just this sort of thing on the part of the Lincoln-Seward administration and there is much speculation as to the effect this will have on the Crown's policy. It is certain that the loss of £250 Million [sterling] will not be taken lightly." The Liverpool "friends" were Brown Shipley, merchant bankers. The "Crown's policy" might shift again toward pro-Southern intervention in America's war. Barnes blamed President Lincoln, whose largesse with cotton permits he now conceived as a ruse to win reelection, through the campaign funding of influential beneficiaries.

Barnes reminded Watson that all the meat contracted for had to be delivered by June 1. There was a short-term solution. "Stringer has assured me he could have five million pounds of pork at Wilmington or Charleston by July first for transaction." Edgar P. Stringer, a British financier and shipowner with parliamentary backing, operated a transatlantic blockade-running fleet.

Contracts, of course, would have to be altered. That was a job for Ward Lamon. As for getting Lincoln off the scene: The Irish? Fenian groups training in the United States and Canada toyed with the idea of abducting U.S. heads of state and blaming the English. Barnes dismissed them as full of rum and bluster. The Confederacy? Too far gone for mounting bold enterprises. "Whatever is done must be done by us, directly or indirectly."

That might once have been left to John Wilkes Booth, had Barnes not grown impatient with the actor's unreliability. He told Watson of the Belleville encounter. Booth was incensed at being downgraded to a position under Captain Boyd. He had protested that "the plan was his and he should be allowed to carry it out." Barnes had retorted that the situation had changed, "it was no longer a question of what he *would do* but rather of what he was *able to do.*" The actor was unpredictable, as theatrical offstage as on. Barnes could scarcely have described for Watson how dangerously his scornful words had inflamed Booth's feelings. And assuming that Barnes knew of Lamon as Lincoln's bodyguard, the irony of his naming Lamon in near juxtaposition with the proposal to "depose" Lincoln might have escaped even his calculating mind.

CHAPTER 13

Desperate Elements

The letter left Cape Girardeau two days before Abraham Lincoln's second inauguration. Traveling through pouring rain, hundreds thronged into Washington by excursion train or stage. Army and municipal authorities, concerned about security, ordered special precautions against fires, riots, or even guerrilla uprisings in the capital itself on the festive day. Paroled Confederate soldiers, many still wearing the gray, strolled the muddy streets in groups. Deserters were among them, and nobody could be sure that rebel partisans, Mosby's in particular, had not infiltrated the city. A letter warned the War Department that Mr. Lincoln could be seized at any formal reception, "carried off by fifty determined men armed with bowie knives and revolvers, put into a market wagon guarded by a dozen horsemen and borne off. Look out for some such dash soon."

Louis Weichmann, a callow clerk at the War Department's commissary of prisoners in Washington, talked darkly of something big worked up at Mary Surratt's house, where he boarded. He hinted that he could have a part in it if he learned how to administer chloroform. No one paid him attention. But he was used to getting the same cold shoulder from his landlady's motley visitors. And though he could not know it, Weichmann's big moment was not far off, when lawyers and generals would listen and his wagging tongue would help send innocents to the gallows, his landlady included.

Andrew Johnson almost missed his own swearing-in. Ailing in Nashville, he was reported to be under doctor's orders against traveling. It took a pointed summons from President Lincoln to rouse him into catching the train for Washington. He put up at the Metropolitan Hotel. According to Johnson's military aide, who made the disclosure anonymously years later, the vice president–elect's callers the next day included his private secretary's chum John Wilkes Booth. But given the size of the actor's circle of social and political acquaintances, nothing sinister could have been read into an inauguration-eve visit by Booth to the man his deed would make president six weeks hence.

The congressional commerce committee, following its hearings on the cotton trade, had moved that the existing law be scrapped in favor of one halting the disgraceful scramble for wealth in time of war. The very idea of fighting a foe and trading with him at the same time was "a thing that never entered the brains of any other people in the world." Opponents of the proposed legislation claimed that 5 million bales of cotton were believed to be in enemy hands, and for the North to acquire just half of it for overseas trade would enrich the Treasury by some $300 million in gold, thus giving more value to the Union's paper currency and strengthening its economy.

Well into Friday night, March 3, the debate raged. The House of Representatives rang with impassioned argument.

> When General Canby said that permitting the trade to go on equaled the loss of fifty thousand [Union] soldiers he spoke the truth. . . . You cannot stop this traffic. . . . And hence we must increase it? I never could see the propriety of professing to carry on the war on one hand and trading with the other. . . . Cotton is King. We absolutely need cotton. . . . The only way it can be gotten is by fighting it out, never trading it out. . . . You say we must have cotton, it will sink the price of gold in the market. It may have that effect but it sinks your honor more.

On the other side of the Capitol rotunda, Lincoln sat quietly in the President's Room. Around midnight Edwin Stanton brought him a telegram from General Grant, reporting that General Lee had agreed to discuss a cease-fire. Lincoln rejoiced. He was ready, there and then, to authorize a battlefield truce on generous terms. But Stanton would have none of that. He intervened at once and sobered the president with stern words. The reply finally sent to Grant vetoed truce talks and directed him to "press, to the utmost of your ability, your military advantage."

By daybreak, the bill to restrict trade with the South appeared sure of passage. Lincoln was expected to have signed it before heading back to the White House for rest. The Washington correspondent of the *New York Times* cabled his head office accordingly. The news was public at midday, panicking cotton speculators, including R. D. Watson, who was still in New York and had yet to receive Barnes's letter from Cape Girardeau. The Thirty-eighth Congress, Watson read, had in its final throes revised the law governing commerce with insurrectionist states. "Permits are a thing of the past."

The presidential inauguration that same day was a mud-soaked gala, ennobled by Lincoln's oratory. The preliminary rites in the Senate chamber had been shamed by a flushed vice president stumbling drunkenly through his holy vows of office. Lincoln dignified the proceedings outside on the Capitol steps. In a well-timed burst of sunshine, he bade his fellow Americans to purge their hearts of malice and cultivate wholesale charity. Lincoln was asking the impossible and, in doing so, provoked some to anger. Others—the profiteers, the cotton gamblers—rejoiced when they read in the latest newspaper editions that earlier announcements were all wrong. Cotton passes were as viable as ever; Mr. Lincoln had not signed the new bill nor would he.

Congressman Washburne, chairman of the committee that had exposed the scandal of the cotton passes, usually counted himself among the radicals. He was, however, no fire-eating war hawk. In fact, he considered himself one of Lincoln's loyal supporters, the only person to greet Lincoln at the railroad station on his first arrival in Washington. But as enraged by Lincoln's pocketing the new cotton bill as New York speculators were relieved, Washburne descended on the White House and told the president bluntly that he would make Grant countermand every Treasury permit that appeared before him. Lincoln replied that the general would not dare. The congressman snapped back that there was only one way to find out, and off he went on the first available steamboat to City Point, Grant's headquarters.

Lincoln signed more permits, but opposition to commerce with the tottering Confederacy was now at full tide. He knew that to ignore it entirely would be political folly. He sent Grant a message in cipher, saying that as regards those cotton permits, the general could act as he wished. Arriving at City Point after Lincoln's telegram, Congressman Washburne had little more to do than pin a medal on the general's broad chest.

In New York, fortune hunters' emotions fluctuated. Within a week after the inauguration, they were still exulting over Lincoln's veto of the modified trade bill when a report, via their private telegraph, wiped the smiles from their faces. Grant had responded to the nod from the White House by issuing a special order: Cotton dealing was forbidden in all areas of the occupied South except that under General Sherman's direct command at Savannah.

Lincoln's latest turnabout on commerce with the enemy had no ameliorative effect on his Republican foes. Following the commerce committee's revelations, they were more than ever determined that "his power shall be curtailed," telling each other that by issuing cotton permits in such a selective and underhanded manner, he had violated law. He had added insult to injury by stalling in his responses to the investigating panel and had capped everything by pocketing a bill that would have secured Confederate cotton for the North without enriching profiteers.

Reviewing events in his diary, Congressman George Julian of Indiana wrote that it had taken Washburne's wrathful intervention to procure "the order which stands in the way of Lincoln and his friends, who hope to make a large fortune out of the miseries of this war." Lincoln had broken the law by granting cotton permits and refusing the Senate's request for detailed information. "I feel it cannot go on much longer before the Congress will take some positive steps to bring Mr. Lincoln to an accounting, or possibly take action never before felt necessary in the history of our nation. There is talk of impeachment." But Julian knew it was too late for impeachment. Time had run out on constitutional remedies. With the war about to end, Congress had adjourned, leaving Abraham Lincoln firmly in the saddle.

Barnes's letter had reached Watson in New York. He read it with foreboding. He wrote two of his own, the first to his wife. "This whole affair has gotten so out of hand it frightens me." He worried about his investment, relatively small at the outset but grown to such proportions that failure would mean financial ruin. He wrote of feeling like a swimmer in a dream, who realizes that the river he is struggling to cross is widening at an equal pace. He hinted of certain people resorting to dangerous measures and intimated their identity in the same paragraph by alluding to Washington politicians at odds with Lincoln over treatment of the vanquished rebels. "It would be easy for me to do another's dirty work," Watson went on cryptically, "and that I do not intend to do." Watson's second letter was to John Surratt in Washington, summoning him to New York "on important business." Surratt was to immediately acknowledge its receipt by telegram to Watson in care of Demill and Company, at Water Street, New York.

The converted sail-loft was in use by kidnap plotters, as well as by seagoing contrabandists. It was possible to be both at once. The middle of March saw much coming and going. Spiriting Lincoln from a theater was still on the kidnappers' agenda, perhaps a concession to the displaced and smoldering Booth.

But what next? The Van Ness building was still ready to receive the captured president but was dangerously near his official home. The imminence of an all-out attack by General Grant against Richmond had removed that city from practical thought as an effective destination. There was Mexico. Its French puppet emperor was believed to favor the Confederate cause, and Mexico was already the choice of some Southerners as a base from which to renew the struggle against the North. It might equally serve the kidnappers' purpose.

A final decision was made: Lincoln would go to sea. The week following Lincoln's second inauguration as president, Thomas Caldwell wrote shipping instructions. A nattily dressed and neatly mustached doyen of 178½ Water Street, Caldwell was related through marriage to Lincoln's old friend Orville Hickman Browning. Age thirty-five and Kentucky-born, Caldwell had led an active life, from teen-aged mariner to man of wealth through sundry business connections.

His letter was to two former Chaffey and Chaffey shipmasters, one of whom was John Celestina, who had smuggled Barnes into the Confederacy. They were to sail their vessels, carrying planks and shingles, to Baltimore. There, further instructions would be waiting.

About April 12, depending on the tides and other circumstances, they would take on a special cargo at Benedict's. At the same time they were to familiarize themselves with Okahanikan Cove and the currents.

Benedict is a small harbor on the Patuxent River, which winds through southern Maryland to Chesapeake Bay. Okahanikan Cove is a feature of the sand-fringed sprawl of barren marshland in lower Chesapeake Bay known as Bloodsworth Island. Centuries of tides had hollowed a mile-wide inlet out of Bloodsworth's shoreline, and Native Americans in remote times had named it Okahanikan. The seas around the island could be deceptively still for long periods before rising to furious and unpredictable tempests. Precolonial explorers, whose ships were stripped of sails by storms or becalmed for months on end, grew to dread the region, and they christened it Limbo. In Civil War years seabirds, occasional fishermen, or contraband smugglers were mostly Bloodworth's only life. As conjured in the minds of the purposeful men of Water Street and elsewhere, the scene would be desolate but the operation businesslike and undisturbed: the two brigs maneuvering into the secluded shallows of Okahanikan Cove, with timber for hut building and their matchless human cargo quietly put ashore, to be kept for an indefinite time, with the world outside Limbo none the wiser.

In the middle of March, shortly before receiving Watson's letter summoning him to New York, John Surratt held a midnight meeting with Booth in a curtained side room of Gautier's on Pennsylvania Avenue. Other conspirators at the exclusive Washington restaurant included Sam Arnold and Michael O'Laughlen. Booth paid the waiter to make sure no one would disturb them, except to bring fresh drinks and oysters. Then he made clear that while still brooding over his demotion as head of the kidnap plot, he had no intention of taking a back seat.

He did most of the talking. He hadn't abandoned the notion of carrying Lincoln bodily from a box seat at a play. Barnes was on the mark when he told Watson in his letter from Cape Girardeau that "[to Booth] the only thing is the 'the scene.'" Beyond motives of financial payment, vengeance, or patriotism as he saw it, striking at the all-highest was to Booth pure theater, best performed with footlights and a spellbound audience. Lincoln would be taken at gunpoint, in the state box, tied up, and lowered to henchmen on the stage, who would then bundle him out the rear door to a waiting carriage. To his nonthespian listeners at Gautier's, much of what Booth said sounded crazy, and they told him as much. Jeers were tossed. Sam Arnold swore impatiently that he would walk out on the whole deal if another week passed without action. Booth silenced them with threats to shoot anyone who tried to quit.

"The plan was his and he should be allowed to carry it out," Barnes had written, describing Booth's mood. Title to the capture of Lincoln as a legitimate prize of war belonged to him alone. That was how Booth felt. He knew that Mosby's men and other would-be abductors looked to someone else for leadership; it was amounting to a rival conspiracy. But he counted on a loyal handful, and he was not content to brood. He felt a growing compulsion to beat interlopers to the punch.

Lincoln was just over a mild bout of influenza. On the Wednesday night, March 15, when the plotters gathered at Gautier's, ten blocks west at Grover's National Theatre the president watched a performance of *The Magic Flute*. Word spread the next day that he would attend another play, a matinee presentation of *Still Waters Run Deep* for the patients and staff at Campbell's Hospital out near Soldiers' Home, his favorite retreat in the capital's northern outskirts.

On Friday morning a determined Booth met Sam Arnold and told him that although he still preferred to seize Lincoln at the theater, there was now no more time to lose; they would intercept the president's carriage and hustle it with its occupants across the river into southern Maryland. Deciding to give Booth one last chance, Arnold and O'Laughlen accompanied him to a livery stable for horses, then rode out to a tavern at the foot of the hill up to Soldiers' Home. Here they were joined by John Surratt and two more, a boatman from Port Tobacco named George Atzerodt and a Mosby parolee, Lewis Powell.

They were unaware of a last-minute change in the president's schedule. That afternoon Lincoln was on the balcony of the National Hotel (where Booth had a room), presenting a Confederate flag to the governor of Indiana, whose soldiers had captured it. Booth rode up to the hospital and asked if the president was expected. He was told no. Returning to his companions at the tavern, he dismissed them and left, his mood black. Arnold and O'Laughlen rode off to Baltimore, deciding to withdraw from the conspiracy and seek honest employment. In a letter to Booth the following week, Arnold warned that it was obvious that the authorities knew something was in the wind. "The undertaking is becoming more complicated. Why not, for the present, desist? Time more propitious will arrive yet. Do not act rashly." An earlier suggestion should have been acted upon, to "go and see how it will be received in [Richmond]."

Others of the group had also dispersed. And Booth's compulsion to jump the gun on rival abductors may have paled in contrast to the terrifying force with which, at Ford's Theatre that same week, he played his familiar role of Pescara in *The Apostate*. Past reviews had appraised Booth's Pescara as "the epitome of villainy" and the play itself a ferment of "intensity, suffering and overcharged horror." Given his present temper, Booth as Pescara was perfect casting. This latest rendition, fated to be his last professional appearance, stunned Washington critics as a masterpiece of "satanic passion."

Then everyone seemed on the move. John Surratt took a buggy into southern Maryland, with weapons and a monkey wrench for opening and shutting manacles. He left them hidden in the crossroads tavern where his parents had managed the post office. On Monday he was back in Washington to receive Watson's letter from New York, which, after reading, he tucked behind a mirror in his bedroom. Surratt left on the night train, conferred with Watson at the Astor House, and was soon off south again, but now for Richmond. Booth left Washington for New York. Lola Alexander had written him: "If you can come to town as supposed, I will be crushed if you do not stop to see me. Please do." But once in town, Booth went to the Winter Garden Theatre, where he watched his brother's one hundredth consecutive performance as Hamlet. The ovation Edwin received was deafening proof that he alone of the Booth tragedians deserved to wear their father's crown.

President Lincoln was also out of Washington, visiting Grant at City Point. He had accepted the general's invitation from a wish to see his son Robert, an officer on Grant's staff. But there were other reasons for the trip. Navy Secretary Gideon Welles believed that Lincoln wanted to be in on the South's surrender, "to make the terms lenient to the conquered." Cotton was also on the agenda. Asked by a speculator if he would support General Grant's official curtailment of barter across the lines, Lincoln replied that "if Grant thought the bacon was of more importance to the enemy . . . than cotton to us, why, then we must do without cotton." But the presidential party on the boat for City Point included Hanson Risley, the Treasury Department's liberal disburser of cotton permits.

Farther up the James River, cotton was on the minds of officials in the beleaguered rebel capital. The Confederate Congress vowed to prosecute the war against the North "until that power shall desist efforts to subjugate and until independence of the Confederate states is established." The declaration reflected optimism in a situation where panic might have been appropriate. Jeff Davis himself had set the tone by prophesying that before high summer the Yankees, not rebel deputations, would be crossing the lines with white flags. Even the Northern press had noted: "Rebels are expecting very soon to startle the whole country and astonish the world."

The defiant spirit appeared to have reached the war front. When Grant launched his spring offensive, undernourished "Johnny Rebs" stood their ground with suicidal valor. But they could not hold out unless properly salaried and fed. On March 17 the Confederate Congress passed an act "to raise coin for the furnishing of supplies for the army." The government would try to borrow \$3 million within thirty days, offering as "collateral" fifty thousand bales of cotton at fifteen cents a pound, in effect securing funds for military sustenance through the sale of government cotton at rock-bottom prices. This was stopgap legislation to obtain the amount that George A. Trenholm, Confederate secretary of the treasury, had calculated was required to keep Lee's fighting men on their feet.

Within a week of the new bill's passage, Trenholm had struck a deal that would net him 10 percent of the amount he wanted—and the deal resulted from John Surratt's timely arrival in Richmond, pursuant to the instructions R. D. Watson had given him in New York.

Each time the South's cotton had come within reach of Watson and his coterie, something had intervened. Farragut's tightened naval blockade, the raids on the secret smokehouses, General Grant's special order—such frustrations had led to Watson's nightmare of swimming toward an ever-receding shore. Now he hoped to get that cotton through Benjamin Ficklin, and when John Surratt slipped into Richmond near the close of March, he made straight for Ficklin's rooms at the Spotswood Hotel.

Benjamin Ficklin was the personification of commercial enterprise wedded to frontier trailblazing. The son of a Virginia Baptist minister, he first roamed the Far West with an army expedition against the Mormons. As deputy marshal for the territory of Utah, he rode shotgun with wagon trains across Indian country and fought and bested hardheaded eastern tycoons for coveted stage and mail contracts. Ficklin was instrumental in setting up and managing the Pony Express service. He returned east when the war began, and with a major's commission in the Confederate army and an officially worded appearance of "a refined pirate," he crossed the Atlantic to serve as the Richmond government's top overseas purchasing agent. His procurement ranged from ships and guns to the Scots lithographers who printed and engraved the Confederacy's banknotes. But impatient with Richmond's creaking bureaucracy, Ficklin branched out on his own, and by 1864 his blockade-running steamers were calling regularly at Liverpool, Bermuda, the Bahamas, Havana, Halifax, Newfoundland, and ports of the South.

Ficklin had studied the scheme to profit from the dislocated cotton trade. Following the Montreal conference five months earlier, it was one of Ficklin's ships that carried a token cargo of meat into Confederate waters. His fleet of blockade-runners continued to enrich him until the North captured the last of the South's major ports. The survival of the Confederacy then hung in the balance, but not Ficklin's fortunes if he could help it. Within twenty-four hours of John Surratt's arrival in Richmond, the major's signature was on a contract with Secretary Trenholm's, pledging $300,000 to the Confederacy in exchange for 2 million pounds of cotton.

Ficklin and Surratt left Richmond together. They crossed the Potomac from the Northern Neck, in a contrabandist's boat. Ficklin carried a copy of his contract with the rebel government and letters of introduction to Brown Brothers, the New York merchant bankers. But he also had papers addressed to President Lincoln from Mary Lincoln's half-sister, Emily Todd Helm, who lived on secessionist soil and wanted permission to get six hundred bales of her cotton through Union lines. Ficklin hoped that the favor would buttress his chances with Lincoln for permits to bring out his own cotton.

Ficklin and Surratt caught the Washington stage at Port Tobacco, where Surratt learned that federal detectives were on the lookout for him. He could not figure why; his uncertainty was common to double agents and more so to a triple agent, which Surratt was. Probably, he was now less interested in kidnapping Lincoln than in securing a share of the cotton profits. At any rate the two men separated, Ficklin reaching Washington first. He hurried to the home of ex-senator Orville H. Browning, who was still immersed in profiteering schemes. Ficklin left the papers from Mary Lincoln's relative with Browning and asked that he use them and his personal clout at the White House to assist his, Ficklin's, cotton plans. Surratt, meanwhile, was at his mother's boardinghouse late Monday night. He woke a boarder to exchange greenbacks for gold. Next morning, unaware that he would never see his mother again, John Surratt left Washington on a northbound train.

CHAPTER 14

The Fall of Richmond

In the Confederate capital as March ended, Jeff Davis's plea for citizens to stand fast defied reality. No more than forty miles away at Hatcher's Run and Five Forks, his exhausted soldiers faced annihilation. The thin gray line broke into blood-red fragments before Grant's rolling blue tide. On Sunday, April 2, Davis was at worship when informed that his capital could be defended no longer. Fires enveloped entire blocks, government offices, and the arsenal.

The government fled, all but a few anguished officials. Municipal control snapped, anarchy threatened, and the arrival Monday morning of the first Union detachments (Grant's main force drove west in pursuit of Lee's broken units) was in the nature of a deliverance.

In Washington, upon the news of Richmond's capture, Secretary Stanton gave workers the day off and ordered candles lit in every window. Flags, wreaths, and lanterns decorated his home on K Street. But Stanton was too much a mystery man for anyone to construe his impromptu speeches before well-wishers and serenading groups as an accurate reflection of his feelings. Neither were those proud telegrams and patriotic addresses, the brass bands and gun salutes, the colorful bunting and transparencies solely a manifestation of triumph and relief. They also signaled a climax to the North's private struggle, the intraparty contest for political mastery.

Neither side could afford to lose initiative. Stanton sent an assistant secretary to occupied Richmond, with orders to keep him informed about activities, which meant in practice watching the president, whose only purpose at the front might be to make sure his generals would go easy on the beaten foe. Lincoln had indeed urged Sherman and Sheridan, also visiting Grant's headquarters, to abjure all thoughts of revenge and reprisal. In Washington, radicals, fearful that Lincoln was about to make some new proclamation of amnesty, prayed that Stanton's man would keep eyes and ears alert for whatever foolish step Mr. Lincoln's known disposition to spoon-feed the South might trap him into taking.

As soon as Ben Ficklin heard that Richmond had fallen, he left Washington by train for New York. Aware that federal detectives following John Surratt had also glued themselves to his trail, Ficklin boarded the train in priest's clothing, with two young women dressed as nuns. They were friends of the Surratts in Washington and had obtained the costumes at a Roman Catholic convent down the street from Mary Surratt's boardinghouse. In Ficklin's case, this failed to shake off National Detective Police operatives, but after shadowing him to the Wall Street offices of Brown Brothers, then to the conspiracy-ridden sail-loft on Water Street, they lost his trail in the vicinity of the Astor.

Ficklin's object in New York, beyond obtaining bank drafts from Brown Brothers in excess of $150,000, was to confer with Watson, Barnes, and Thomas Caldwell. He had a short wait in hiding because Watson had joined Surratt and gone to Montreal. Booth, in whose tinderbox brain each gust of war news fanned fresh rage, reached that Canadian city at about the same time. All checked in at the St. Lawrence Hall. But a few days earlier, on April 5, Booth had made another significant hotel stop—perhaps the most consequential.

On a quiet corner in Newport, Rhode Island, stood the Aquidneck House, a sedate stopping place conveniently located near the pier where Wickford Company steamboats regularly unloaded passengers from New York. The vessels docked in predawn gloom, a useful schedule for travelers who wished to avoid recognition, because they could make directly for the hotel where the guests, according to the advertising brochures, "are of a class that do not care to mingle in the bustle of large hotels." It was little frequented this early in the season. The steamboat from New York docking on that chilly Wednesday morning had brought only a few passengers, two of whom had passed through the pillared entrance of the Aquidneck House to register as "J. W. Booth and lady, Boston."

In Montreal, at the same time, Martha Mills was on an errand for Booth. She carried drafts from American banks to cash in British currency. Booth's further instructions were that she take the cash to a second Montreal bank and deposit it "in the name of John Wilkes, a British subject," then telegraph him that the business was done. But the first bank, in her later words, "refused to cash the draft because, they said, of conditions in the United States. So I had to wire him of the trouble. He had told me where he could be reached."

Booth could be reached at Newport with his companion Harriet "Lola" Alexander. The couple was assigned to Room No. 3, overlooking Narragansett Bay. Alfred Smith, the desk clerk, said afterward that the woman was veiled. The two strolled in the gardens, and when they returned, Smith thought that the lady had been crying. Although Booth seemed agitated, he ordered a lavish dinner, asking for room service because the lady was indisposed. But before the meals arrived, Booth received Martha's telegram from Montreal and almost immediately the couple checked out. The two took the train for Boston, where they separated.

Booth continued on to Montreal. At the St. Lawrence Hall he used a false name. R. D. Watson was there. So was John Surratt, among whose tasks was delivery of the last dispatches out of Richmond to the Canada-based Confederate commissioners. Much of whatever else went on in Montreal during those final days of America's war would remain undiscoverable. But besides Booth's, Watson's, and Surratt's, other intriguing names or aliases sprinkled the St. Lawrence Hall register, identifiable as belonging to people involved in the cotton scheming and its by now correlative plot to abduct Abraham Lincoln.

Booth's role in it was reduced to that of helpful guide around Washington's theater precincts. He fumed all the more because of his inability in Montreal to secure the funds he would need after the kidnapping. He planned to escape using the name under which he first appeared on the American stage: John B. Wilkes. (His middle name, Byron, was that of his father's firstborn, who died an infant in England.) In his anger, Booth believed that those who had frozen him out of the kidnap leadership also sought to freeze his funds. As Martha Mills recalled, "the money in those banks was payment for medicines and had nothing to do with the capture plan. The medicines had been delivered and paid for, payment being deposited in various [American] banks. Wilkes felt betrayed."

He left Montreal with R. D. Watson. In New York he headed for the Metropolitan Hotel, Room 238, and a quarrel with Lola Alexander. They argued as they had in Newport, over the Kilpatrick-Dahlgren affair, Booth attacking the federals' mission as a monstrous crime, the woman defending it as honorable. The memory of that misfired raid preyed on Booth's thoughts and was never so oppressive as now, when at every street turning he was met with banners and singing, the public celebrating the downfall of the Confederacy. And the loss of command in the abduction plot still stung his vanity. Had she known of these things or of the "strain of madness" with which Asia Booth wrote that her late father and brothers were afflicted, Lola still might have failed to hold her tongue. The words flew like barbs, piercing Booth's brain as if conditioning it for the final fatal goad she would fling at him before another week passed.

On Saturday evening, April 8, aboard the steamer *River Queen* off General Grant's headquarters, President Lincoln enjoyed the Marine band in a farewell concert before returning up the Potomac to Washington. That same day, Booth left New York by train for the capital where, in an acutely morbid state of mind, he took Room 228 at the National Hotel.

Watson was in New York. He had checked in at the Astor House, where Benjamin Ficklin anxiously awaited him. Ficklin was still in religious garb, not inappropriately, for the two got down to business on Palm Sunday. They had much to review. Discussion touched lightly, if at all, on the original idea of shipping meat into the Confederacy. As a bargaining element in commercial negotiation, food for General Lee's soldiers was now as obsolete as the plight of prisoners of war. Cotton remained the big prize, to be secured for the Montreal group by the deal Ficklin had signed on its behalf in Richmond. Events had yet again upset plans, Richmond falling even as Ficklin headed north. The Confederate government was scattered, the contract with Secretary Trenholm no longer worth the paper it was written on. But the goal remained the same, to lock control over as huge a quantity of cotton as possible and get it out before the prices fell. And ideas were now focused on Georgia.

Stanton had seen to it that most of the cotton found stacked in Savannah, when General Sherman's troops marched in, was borne off to New York. Its sale as a legitimate prize of war had enriched the federal government instead of private dealers, some of whom had actually tried to get the auction postponed to permit enough time to buttonhole Lincoln on his return from City Point and talk him into new arrangements, cutting them in for a share. They had failed.

But the Savannah cotton was only a fraction of the total throughout the state. Beyond the grasp or ken of the military, thousands of bales were buried deep in the swamps and forests of an upland corridor formed by the Savannah and Ogeechee Rivers. Transportable only by steamboat, flatbottom, or wagon, there it lay, cotton in abundance, waiting to be claimed and brought out on a "first come, first served" basis. It was this enormous hoard that the Northern businessmen were now after, those speculators with contracts and presidential permits procured for them by Hanson Risley but who had yet to bring forth a single bale.

The superdeal closed at Montreal the previous year had been repeatedly knocked askew. The latest attempt to save it, Ben Ficklin's agreement with the Richmond government, was nullified by the city's fall. The war might end at any moment, spelling disaster for the speculators. How big a disaster had been indicated in February by accounts of the meeting between Lincoln and rebel peace seekers. The American consul in Liverpool reported then that "no event since the war commenced has produced so much excitement as news of peace negotiations going on in Hampton Roads. It amounts to a panic on the cotton market." The price of gold had already started to slide. As a newspaper put it: "The collapse has begun. The speculators are catching it. . . . gold prices are falling" and the decline a "mere prelude to the grand crash."

But the dream of windfall profits that business entrepreneurs had first conjured out of the South's predicament gleamed all the more irresistibly on the eve of the South's defeat. And those bales in the Georgia hinterland offered the last chance to realize it. This was the burden of Watson's and Ficklin's private conference at the Astor that Palm Sunday: Georgia cotton and how to reach it, how to assert ownership, how to get it out as soon as possible through the war-ravaged port of Savannah.

So fresh plans took shape. Those papers drafted in January by Hanson Risley at the Treasury Department would have to be altered, stipulating Savannah as the new delivery point. New permits would have to be signed by the president. And there was no time to lose. Hazards to the scheme abounded. No one knew this better than R. D. Watson, his natural milieu the rich farmlands of the New Madrid bend and that displaced Kentucky "thumb" wedged forever into Missouri. Even Wall Street's atmosphere was alien to Watson, and for the double-dealing of Washington, however adaptable to business purposes, he had little taste or understanding. He had heard of Northern politicians who wanted Abraham Lincoln out of the way and felt no particular sympathy for him but had no intention of being maneuvered into involvement with another's "dirty work." Neither could he pin much faith in Barnes's guarantees that a congressional junta taking over from the deposed chief executive would honor existing commercial contracts. But risks had to be borne. The main task was to lock hold on the cotton in Georgia ahead of whatever palpitating event broke next, a sudden spurt by rival business rings, a general cease-fire on the battlefield, or a political coup d'etat in Washington.

The ball was now at Ben Ficklin's feet. This resourceful bachelor, not yet forty, still possessed the drive with which he had organized and managed freight and mail routes in the Far West and blockade-running fleets on the high seas. After meeting with Watson, he caught the train to Washington. His mission now was to secure new cotton permits from Lincoln. Still wary of those meddlesome detectives, he had once more donned holy disguise. Dressed as a priest, presumably uninterested in worldly affairs, he probably did not buy a newspaper at the New York depot. It might have attracted attention. On the train, however, Ficklin could have discreetly glanced at copies read by fellow passengers. The headlines were riveting. Over the weekend General Robert E. Lee had surrendered his entire army to Grant, at a county seat called Appomattox.

CHAPTER 15

Holy Week: "Something Never Dreamed Of"

The president arrived in Washington on Palm Sunday. From the steamboat that brought him up the Potomac, he hurried to the bedside of his secretary of state, William Seward, who had fallen from a runaway carriage, fracturing his shoulder and injuring his jaw so badly that doctors had attached ligatures to his teeth to hold it in place. After Lincoln departed, the Sewards were visited by the secretary of war, who brought the telegraphed reports of Lee's surrender at Appomattox. Seward's daughter, Fanny, noted in her diary that Mr. Stanton appeared less flintlike than usual.

Stanton's thoughts were far from benign. Telegrams in cipher from Charles Dana, his assistant secretary of war, whom he had stationed in the Richmond area to keep tabs on Lincoln, showed all too clearly how things would go were the president allowed to have his way. And that sabbath evening, while Stanton's colleagues and subordinates celebrated the Confederacy's surrender, he reprimanded General Godfrey Weitzel, commander of the occupying forces in Richmond, for failing to direct that the city's churchgoers pray for the Union president, although he believed that the real culprit was the nominal beneficiary of such prayers.

This was a foretaste of what would come of too much magnanimity, as Stanton saw it, and within forty-eight hours the most blatant example of that attitude would demand his prompt intervention. In secret, at what was formerly Jefferson Davis's mansion and had lately been appropriated as a Union command post, Lincoln had conferred with a Confederate official who remained in the city, a moderate Southerner with whom he had talked at Hampton Roads. Now Lincoln suggested to him that the prewar Virginia legislature be reassembled to restore order within the state. In exchange for recognition as a de facto government, this legislature must first declare Virginia part of the Union and order Virginia's troops to lay down their arms. The truce at Appomattox took care of the latter, as Lincoln himself had acknowledged in a congratulatory telegram to General Grant. So the call had gone forth from Richmond, inviting Confederate politicians back into their legislative posts.

A damp Monday, April 10, dawned in Washington to the roar of artillery salvoes loud enough to crack windows overlooking Lafayette Square. An impromptu procession from the Navy Yard dragged six howitzers across town. Bands paraded along muddy thoroughfares suddenly abloom with flags and lanterns. The celebration hid signs of an imminent political rumpus. At first, Lincoln's extraordinary move while in Richmond was only the stuff of rumor, leaked from the War Department. The tension mounted on Tuesday, when Lincoln spoke from a window above the White House lawn. At another window his youngest son, Tad, hoisted a captured rebel flag that Stanton had given him. The president himself seemed attractively groomed for once, thought an onlooker, as if he had waited for the war to end before sprucing himself up. He began with a call for humble thanksgiving and rededication to the principles of national unity. His next words, to radical ears, were more upsetting.

The only peace aims were restoration and preservation of the Union. The means to these ends were merciful forgiveness, with Christian charity toward the penitent flock returning to the fold and no hurry to enact such controversial measures as suffrage for former slaves. Did his critics fret that he had equivocated on the question of whether seceded states should be in or out of the Union? Then let them. "I have purposely forborne any public expression upon a merely pernicious abstraction." And he threw his listeners a cryptic promise, or threat, to make some new gesture to the people of the South.

It was an oratory of defiance. In conclusion, Lincoln declared the tune "Dixie" to be captured enemy property. The Marine Band performed it on cue, then blared "Yankee Doodle." But in the crowd on the White House lawn, few extremists could have felt like tapping their feet or applauding the president's words.

Lincoln had declared his adherence to a reconstruction program that, in Congressman George Julian's words, had already "stirred the ire of Wade and Winter Davis as an attempt of the Executive to usurp the power of Congress." Grave-faced and excited, the radicals dispersed into private groups, discussing what now must be done. That night the *New York Tribune* reporter in Washington wired his chief that "the bribe of unconditional forgiveness offered by Lincoln to the rebels has already established a split in our party—the opposition is forming hourly." And then it gained strength from the news that Lincoln had invited the rebel legislature to reassemble.

By placing rebels once more in power, Lincoln had committed the unforgivable. Already Confederate officials were returning to their former capital, protected moreover by Union military. A "very unhappy" radical Charles Sumner contacted the secretary of war and found him "most disconcerted in feeling that we might lose the fruits of our victories." Sumner professed himself afraid of Lincoln's policies. "What shall we do? What can be done?"

Senator Ben Wade had an impulsive answer. He had read the first headlined accounts of Lincoln's proposal to the Virginia legislature when halfway to Charleston, South Carolina, for celebration of the fourth anniversary of the attack on Fort Sumter. Shouting curses, Wade wheeled his party back for Washington, exclaiming that if Lincoln indeed contemplated putting Richmond's rebels again in control, "By God, the sooner he is assassinated the better."

In Washington a rush of protests forced the president to admit error. He tried to stave off consequences. "Is there any sign of the rebel legislature coming together?" he telegraphed anxiously to General Godfrey Weitzel. "If there is no such sign, you may as well withdraw the offer." Weitzel's response came in the evening. It was too late to undo the damage; passports had been issued and the legislators were hourly expected. At this, a coldly enraged Stanton lectured the president on the folly of his action, telling him that he had better send General Weitzel clear-cut orders. Lincoln drafted a message. The secretary pronounced it to be too weak, and at his dictation, the president drew up another. Too much had been presumed from his original suggestion. Grant's successful offensives had taken care of the "withdrawal" of Virginia's troops from the fighting. Moves toward reconvening the old state legislature must cease immediately. This draft met with Stanton's approval.

Things were humming on the commercial front. At a cabinet meeting Tuesday morning, April 11, Confederate cotton topped the agenda. Hugh McCulloch, new secretary of the treasury, appeared vague on the subject but knew where his interests lay. This former Indiana banker owed his cabinet post to speculators' influence and had applauded every effort to go after rebel cotton and bring it out. The way now seemed easier, for in another policy reversal General Grant agreed to Lincoln's revoking the order banning trade across the battle lines. But immediately following that cabinet session, the president sprang yet another surprise by imposing restrictions on foreign shipping at certain ports of entry, effectively closing Savannah and Wilmington to the export of cotton.

Presidential sanction alone could get the staple moving out of Georgia. This is why Major Ben Ficklin was back in Washington, fresh from his Palm Sunday conference with Watson in New York. Within hours of the White House proclamation sealing Southern ports, some of the busiest manipulators, including Ficklin and William A. Browning, still the personal secretary of Vice President Johnson, met in a private room of the Kirkwood Hotel on Pennsylvania Avenue. The burden of the meeting was reflected in a scrap of paper picked up later and ultimately lodged in a federal file on Ficklin as a suspect in Lincoln's murder. Addressed to "F" and signed "W" and written in a hand resembling Ward Lamon's, it stressed, "the permits, we must get the permits. I can have them endorsed by the secretary of war."

Ward Lamon, said to be ill with rheumatism, had been out of sight for three weeks. On Wednesday, April 12, he called at the White House, where he obtained a presidential passport to go South. Lamon's destination was Richmond. Once again, Lincoln's bodyguard left the side of his precious charge. Haunted years later by the very calamity that his presence in Washington was universally supposed might have prevented, Lamon would write in a self-extenuating vein. His mission south was connected with Mr. Lincoln's program for postwar reconstruction. Before his departure, he had told the president to exercise caution and, above all, to stay away from the theater. As usual, the president had brushed the warning aside as if humoring a fussy nurse. Lamon argued in those later years that it was hardly fair to blame a faithful guardian if his ward persistently refused to take his exhortations seriously.

James W. Boyd had returned from Canada. The Confederate secret service officer was using Annie Lomax Green's fabled Van Ness mansion in Washington as a relay point for communication with Mosby's command post and with her no-surrender brother, General Lunsford Lomax, in the Shenandoah Valley. Each was located less than half a day's ride west of the capital. Headquartered in one of the lower Maryland counties, Boyd had organized smugglers and rebel "deserters" into a motley cavalry unit. When the right time came, they would take up position in Yankee uniform alongside Willard's Hotel in Washington. Nothing was allowed to interrupt Boyd's work. A friend's wife, living near Annapolis, complained that Captain Thomas A. Watkins, a Union provost marshal, had sexually harassed her. Boyd rode to the officer's home overlooking the Patuxent River and shot him to death. The ensuing manhunt was not for Boyd but for a nomadic rebel named John Boyle, who was known to have borne Watkins a murderous grudge and who had already tried to kill him. This was not a case of mistaken identity, in Boyd's opinion. In the work he was doing, he felt protected. As he wrote to a Tennessee friend the following week, "The government looked the other way."

By then, many of the kidnap band he had recruited and drilled in the forests and swamps between the Potomac and Patuxent Rivers were in place within Washington. Some had got there as rebel "deserters"; others had been freed after a stay in Wood's Old Capitol Prison. Confederate guerrillas and sympathizers who intended to clear a path for the kidnap party positioned themselves southeast of Washington. Colonel Mosby had two hundred men dressed in Union blues along the upper shores of the Potomac, ready to move in from the west. Others were stationed below the capital. Whistles blown by Mosby's officers would signal action.

Plans for carrying Lincoln off to Richmond had of necessity been abandoned. Abduction from a theater was still in the works, with an approximate date set. Lincoln had attended the theater four times that year. It was expected that some such night out would be on his calendar during victory celebrations. An hour for action was not difficult to pinpoint. When details were known, the word would be given. At the theater there would be no nonsense of lowering the captive to the stage. He would be lured outside, probably during intermission, through a message or a telegram delivered by someone from the War Department. Lincoln would be overpowered in his own carriage, his coachman having been enticed to a saloon and suitably replaced. The guerrillas in Union garb waiting near Willard's—tactically close to where Lincoln's regular cavalry escort customarily bivouacked—would gallop up and move into position, and off they would go.

The theater was John Wilkes Booth's professional habitat. But denied leadership, he would be on hand mainly to smooth movements and make sure nobody got lost. Moreover, he knew too much about the varied interests involved and was too dangerously volatile a character to be totally written out of the plot. After Lincoln was swept off by the bogus troop of cavalry, Booth would see to his own immediate flight, rejoining the main group across the Potomac. To assist the kidnap party through Washington and to avoid wrong turnings, more whistles would be blown. This was a signal system favored by Mosby—the partisan chief wore a pewter whistle on a ribbon around his neck. Something would be done about the public gaslights along Pennsylvania Avenue—at least, where they were concentrated in the vicinity of the Capitol building.

A password had been arranged for the kidnap cavalcade to cross the Navy Yard Bridge. Some fourteen miles farther on at the quaintly named village of T. B., the party would fork. Booth and an accomplice or two would gallop southwestward in the direction of Port Tobacco, where, off Balls Point on Nanjemoy Creek, Captain John Celestina's latest brig, *Indian Prince,* had tied up. By prearrangement, some of her crew had jumped ship. Booth and friends would take their place. The abducted president would be bundled eastward across Charles County to Benedict's Landing on the Patuxent River, where a second old Chaffey vessel, *Indian Queen,* was moored. With the captive safely aboard, the ship would sail into Chesapeake Bay for anchorage of an undetermined period at Bloodsworth Island, in the region of storms and doldrums that explorers of old had named Limbo.

At first, Lieutenant Dana had little more to go on than signs of simple horse thievery, but he sensed something bigger afoot. David Dana was brigade provost marshal, with jurisdiction over the region of Maryland flanked by the Potomac and the Patuxent. Lieutenant Dana had become sure that deep within the swampy forests and untilled farmland between Upper Marlborough and Port Tobacco, preparations were under way for an escapade of some sort against the national government. He had notified brigade headquarters, requesting reinforcements. They responded with 150 men to augment his patrol.

Other steps were also taken to tighten Washington security. Pickets were installed over a perimeter of five or six miles, linking the capital's southeastern line of army forts. Bridges were ordered closed to unauthorized civilians during the night hours. But these measures took effect the second week of April, too late to stem the influx of rebel "deserters," "refugees," and others of doubtful designation. And although Lieutenant Dana's pickets were deployed as directed across the intrigue-ridden counties of southern Maryland, orders from higher up on Thursday, April 13, made no mention of any rumored plot against Lincoln's government. They warned only of "lewd women and prostitutes" said to be enticing sentries from their posts.

Seventy miles from Washington, at the foot of the Blue Ridge Mountains, Colonel John Mosby had reunified his command. Richmond was gone, the Army of Northern Virginia broken and conquered, but the guerrilla chief had determined to fight on. Lee, in capitulation, did not speak for the entire South. Even as his infantrymen were throwing down their arms, politicians fleeing Richmond continued to voice hopes that before long the Union, not the Confederacy, would be forced to call it quits. Jeff Davis, somewhere in North Carolina, breathed defiance out of an apparent conviction that loyal cavalrymen would still save the day. He spun visions of a stubborn South refusing to lower her banners, of a Confederate government kept alive in Mexican exile as Maximilian's guests until he, Davis, returned north in triumph and reestablished his government in Virginia.

Dispirited rebel infantrymen footslogging home would have spat at the thought, but not so General Lomax's cavalry. He had regrouped his units, and they were riding back up the Shenandoah Valley to join forces with Mosby. By the middle of that holy week, Lomax estimated his strength at some three divisions. Colonel Mosby, meanwhile, had received an ultimatum from a Union field commander. His reply was to refuse surrender and to propose a cease-fire, "until I can obtain sufficient intelligence to determine my future actions." Mosby's staff was of a mind to seize the entire Union command at Richmond and flee with it to Mexico. But this would have been in the nature of a consolation prize, to be pursued only if the troopers Mosby had within Washington and those closing on it failed to get hold of the supreme hostage—word of whose capture Mosby awaited as he stalled for time in the thaw-sodden foothills of the Blue Ridge.

A French observer noted that the political storm clouds had massed on Tuesday, after Lincoln spoke from the White House window. His informal address reflected a forgiving spirit toward the South, and for the next twenty-four hours he was the target of "a veritable campaign." His words, in one newspaper's opinion, were more than enough to fuel his perennial conflict with radicals who wanted "more blood, confiscation, extermination, subjugation, annihilation and no quarter." They had seldom wanted for reasons to oppose him. Now their opposition was all the more dangerous. If it was possible for them to forgive his recently exposed tolerance of commercial graft, his deception of Congress on the issuance of cotton passes, or even his provocative remarks of that week, beyond all redemption was his move, no matter how quickly retracted, to reconvene Virginia's rebel legislature.

When dusk fell Thursday, the city sparkled as never before. The Capitol glowed with gaslight from the basement to the newly finished tholus. Sixty candles burned in each of Washington City Hall's windows; six thousand candles turned the Patent Office into a block-long sheet of light. A semicircle of gas jets framed Willard's main entrance with the word UNION, and the gas-jet pattern of a clothing store on Pennsylvania Avenue inquired tauntingly, HOW ARE YOU, LEE? Above F Street, where the new horse-drawn cars ran perilously along timbered track between stretches of sunken roadway, multicolored lanterns hung from ropes. Public and commercial buildings, playhouses, restaurants, and homes glittered and gleamed. The spectacle was heightened by the variety of flags and the novel brilliance of transparencies.

At the Stanton home on K Street, musicians played on the sidewalk, and every window danced with candlelight. Inside, the secretary and his wife held a reception for General and Mrs. Grant. The atmosphere was strained. That afternoon Mrs. Lincoln had asked the general to join her and the president on a drive through the illuminated streets. The invitation failed to include Grant's wife, who did not get along well with Mary Lincoln, and he had politely turned it down. Then Lincoln had suggested that all of them, wives included, share a box at the theater the following evening. Ford's would present Tom Taylor's farce *Our American Cousin,* and Grover's National would round off its play with fireworks, patriotic poems, and music. But at the reception Julia Grant told Stanton's wife that she planned to visit her children at school in New Jersey and would most likely leave town with her husband on Friday afternoon. Ellen Stanton thereupon decided that neither would she join the Lincolns' theater party.

Earlier that evening Booth had called at Grover's National and asked the manager if he intended to invite the president for tomorrow's special show. The manager said yes. All afternoon and into the night, Booth had prowled feverishly about the jubilating people. *Union . . . Liberty . . . Victory . . . Grant . . .* wherever he turned, the hated words met him in a blaze of light and color. He plunged in and out of taverns, yet part of him remained sober and coldly deliberate. He bought a box seat at Grover's, then went upstairs for more drinks in Jack Deery's saloon and billiard parlor, over the theater. Booth was also seen that day hovering about the commissary of prisoners, where the latest batch of captives paraded for registration. They included high-ranking Confederate officers who seemed not a bit crestfallen, who instead talked knowingly of tables about to be turned, of a dramatic event now imminent, "something never dreamed of." Booth, his own tongue loosened by drink, was overheard to say that he had a big undertaking on his hands and there was plenty of money in it.

While Washington celebrated, so did New York City but with less fire and pageantry. Wall Street was anxious and a pall of gloom had descended upon 178½ Water Street. The expected market collapse had begun. Press columnists predicted disaster for "all those factitious fortunes which have been heaped up in stocks and speculative enterprises." Schuyler Colfax, speaker of the House of Representatives, might have mentioned the worsening business situation Wednesday night at the Metropolitan Hotel while visiting his intimate friend Lola Alexander.

Colfax left the next day for Washington, after promising Lola that he would call on Treasury Secretary McCulloch and put in a good word for her husband, Julius, who was seeking a government job. She had just written McCulloch to this effect. Colfax may have favored her by carrying the letter with him personally. Since the Speaker of the House usually boarded at the National Hotel when in Washington, he was a convenient choice to double the favor, taking a second letter that Lola had written and sealed that same day. It was penned with scathing emotion and addressed to John Wilkes Booth.

PART III

The Assassin

CHAPTER 16

Good Friday: April 14, 1865

The day began mild and cloudy, with a damp breeze. After a night of celebration, Washington awoke with a hangover. All over town shopkeepers and servants were up early, scraping tallow from countless windowpanes. Christians prepared themselves for church to commemorate the anniversary of their Savior's crucifixion. Before twenty-four hours had elapsed, they and their fellow Americans would mourn another martyr.

At the executive mansion the president had breakfast with Mrs. Lincoln and their son Robert, fresh from a silenced battlefield. All morning people arrived at the White House and left. Schuyler Colfax was an early visitor, to discuss a planned tour of the western lands. If fate had staged a special grotesquerie to begin this day, which would be full of them, Colfax was not only the bearer of Lola Alexander's latest letter for Booth, it was in his pocket as he paid his respects to President Lincoln.

At eleven, Lincoln's cabinet met at the White House. Grant was an honored guest. Before the meeting adjourned, Lincoln had removed any doubt that he intended to be the whip-hand in the Reconstruction process. He did so with a deceptive gentleness, appearing to his secretary of the interior as being "full of charity to all." Attorney General James Speed, a friend of the young Lincoln but lately sympathetic to radicals, thought that the president "never seemed so near our own views."

Secretary Stanton urged continuance of a Union military rule in the South. Secretary of the Navy Welles objected. Lincoln refrained from directly attacking Stanton's proposition but suggested that it needed modifying. And when, finally, the president spoke of Congress out of the way throughout the summer, he made clear that nothing would induce him to recall it in special session. Ben Wade's Joint Committee on the Conduct of the War, shortly to designate itself the Committee on Reconstruction or "Committee of Fifteen," had ensured its remaining in Washington for eventualities by voting itself a ninety-day extension beyond the date of congressional adjournment. Lincoln appeared undisturbed, and his Good Friday cabinet meeting ended in a spirit of outward geniality.

Ten blocks east of the White House, John Wilkes Booth was the last person for breakfast in the National Hotel's dining room. Close to noon, he walked around the corner to Pumphrey's Livery Stable and hired a smart saddle horse, leaving word that he would call for it about three o'clock. He was next seen on Tenth Street, where Harry Clay Ford, youngest of the three brothers who owned and managed the theater, told him that the Lincolns and General Grant would be in tonight's audience to see *Our American Cousin.* Unaware yet that Grant would not be in the party, Ford had sent appropriate notices to the local newspapers. Their latest editions, as well as extra playbills rushed into print, were on the festooned and mistily sunlit streets before the middle of the afternoon. Meanwhile, Booth read his mail.

Nothing had developed to cool his ignitable emotions. The cause he had championed everywhere but on the battlefield was dead, and in the last bold enterprise that might alone quicken it to life, he had lost the stellar role. As noted later by an informed journalist, "The mortified bravo found himself compelled to sink to a petty role in the plot." Supplying medicines for the South had been a necessarily covert service and long past. The curtain was descending on the sanguinary national drama without Booth's having once occupied the spotlight. He had neither shed nor drawn blood. Stage props, costume, and greasepaint—these had been the accoutrements of Booth's combat experience.

To still any pangs of regret that he had promised his mother to shun military service, he savored the thought of leading a gang to carry off the North's supreme warlord. Lincoln still had to go, for the good of the North, as well as of the South. Booth's own words would at least imply that his masters in the plot to remove Lincoln were of the North, not the South. At any rate the moment had arrived. Tonight Lincoln would be at the theater, exposed to capture, with Booth a mere accessory in his own original program. The minutes ticked by. Time, against which politicians and profiteers raced, was also running out on Booth. In so doing, it stoked his impulse to leap ahead of rivals by a daring *coup de main.* The mind of the "mortified bravo," poised near the center of the five arched doorways of Ford's Tenth Street facade, had become a powderkeg. He read a letter from his brother Junius that reminded him quite needlessly that Richmond had fallen, Lee had capitulated, and the South lost. John Wilkes had habitually scoffed at the Union's war propaganda. He could do so no longer. His brother's words only shortened the fuse.

Another letter dated April 12 supplied the spark. Lola Alexander had written haughtily, mocking and scolding: "You, sir, were rude to me!! I do not like it nor will I condone it. You do not *own* me, not even a little. I saw in you a side I did not dream existed." Her pen had run on to prick at the old wound. "How can you be jealous of the dead?" This was a reference to Ulric Dahlgren. "And [Dahlgren] was a good soldier." Did Booth not understand this quality? "I have it from the best authority that he *was* following the order of his commander-in-chief."

When Booth first believed rebel charges that Colonel Dahlgren had ordered his men to burn and kill at Richmond, Browning persuaded Booth that it was not so; the stories were false, concocted by war-hawks of the Confederacy. That explanation had in turn crumbled, with Browning conceding that Dahlgren might have had wholesale assassination in mind but was a young glory-seeker acting on his own. Now Lola's letter said exactly the opposite. Her words confirmed what Booth had preferred to believe all along. The Kilpatrick-Dahlgren raid had really been Lincoln's work. And there could be no disputing that "best authority." Lola was not only a Union army colonel's wife but, more intimately, the confidante of men of power, including Johnson's private secretary, the quondam friend whom Booth, in a renewed fit of self-torment, now concluded had shamefully betrayed him.

The closing sentences of Lola's letter were the most inflammatory. "You seemed to forget that [Dahlgren] paid with his life for what he believed good and necessary. When you have served your cause with half the dedication and loyalty he showed, then perhaps you may have earned the right to criticize. But I doubt that this will happen." A fellow actor approaching Booth outside Ford's saw him finish reading his mail and, thrusting it into his pocket, curse an unnamed woman.

Will Browning had spent part of the afternoon at the Capitol with the vice president. When he returned to the Kirkwood Hotel, where both men boarded, Booth was waiting. He saw Browning come in and kept out of sight, then sent up a signed card: "Are you at home?" The card was brought back down, with word that he was not. Booth left the card in Browning's box at the hotel desk, convinced, as he was shortly to write, "that you were not at home to *me*."

At Pumphrey's Livery Stable, he collected his rented horse, a black-maned bay mare with a small white star on her forehead. She was, James Pumphrey warned, a sensitive animal best not hitched; someone should hold her. In late afternoon Booth called briefly at Mary Surratt's place on H Street. He cantered his frisky bay down Tenth, pausing at the Star Saloon next to Ford's for a drink. In Baptist Alley, behind the theater, he was seen in agitated conversation with a girl wearing a black silk coat and white collar. Almost certainly, she was Ella Turner, who adored him and was pregnant with his child. (His other lovers just then included Kate Scott, a Pennsylvania ex-army nurse whom he had also left pregnant. Gossip, hastily denied, would also link him to one of the daughters of New Hampshire senator John P. Hale.)

Between five and six that Friday night, Booth and his temperamental mare were in Baptist Alley at his makeshift stable. Someone heard Booth call the horse a bad little bitch. Saddle-gall bothered the animal, and Booth had to arrange his shawl under the saddle, giving additional thickness to the saddlecloth that Pumphrey's had provided. Booth sometimes used a blanket for the same purpose, which when properly folded served also as a hiding place for papers, and to this end he had tucked Lola Alexander's letters into its recesses.

A couple of stagehands who looked to the actor for liquor money saw to his horse and stabled her. Booth pocketed the key, took the stagehands next door to the Star, and left them well catered for. He entered the theater and checked Boxes 7 and 8, converted into a single space and specially furnished for the presidential party, which, Booth had learned by now, would not include General Grant.

What Will Browning had escaped hearing from him in a confrontation at the Kirkwood, Booth poured into a letter that, ever the performer, he wrote as if to be read with emotion before an audience. "Tis true, the last cup from the bottle bears the bitter dregs. . . . how bitter it is to be deceived by such a trusted compatriot, one whose cause was mine in summer's heat and barren cold of winter." When Browning needed his assistance in the meat-for-cotton deal, Booth had gladly responded, had virtually abandoned his profession, "followed you like a modern-day Christus in search for an end to this madness." Browning had offered glib excuses for Dahlgren's conduct at Richmond. "But oh my friend (if ever you really were) why have you thought to deceive me? Expediency—or shame? Have you too been deceived? If so, why have you avoided me?" But the real perfidy was in the olive-branch approach to the Confederacy that concealed a devilish intent, and the devil "Him who promised with the right hand—while secretly rescinding with the left, holding the lure high and handsome while fondling a dagger under his cloak"—in plain English, Lincoln offering amnesty one moment and the next authorizing that atrocious raid against Richmond. In a final Shakespearean burst, Booth identified himself as the chosen instrument of retribution. "We still have judgement here . . . being taught, return to plague the inventor." The Union cavalry may have blundered at Richmond, but its failure was beside the point. "The design condemns us all."

Washingtonians were still in a mood to celebrate. With President Lincoln expected any moment, the lower blocks of Tenth Street were especially lively. Barrels with tar torches lined the sidewalks. Touts hired by the Fords passed out handbills and bellowed of the night's featured attraction. Under the large gas lamp in front of the theater's vaulted entrances, parties alighted from carriages drawing up, one after another, at the wooden curbside platform. Here, too, a handful of the president's would-be kidnappers had begun to assemble.

Lincoln had managed an hour or so outdoors that afternoon, riding with Mary in an unescorted barouche. They returned before dinner, with minutes left for him to amuse guests with excerpts read from the latest book of a favorite humorist. The Lincolns dined between six and seven. Crowds gathered at the White House gates. Upstairs in the president's private office waited Orville H. Browning, who wanted to set up a meeting between Ben Ficklin and Lincoln, with a view to getting cotton permits. But it was after eight; the president did not go upstairs again before leaving and Browning had to settle for a promise that Mr. Lincoln would see him first thing the next morning. Callers would have detained the president all night if he had let them. Disengaging himself, he shepherded Mary into the waiting carriage. A torchlight parade of civilians, soldiers, and bandsmen approached from the city arsenal. The Lincolns could hear the strains of "The Battle Hymn of the Republic" as their carriage moved off from the White House and turned north. It made a detour of four blocks in order to pick up Senator Ira Harris's daughter Clara and Major Henry Rathbone, a betrothed couple whom Mrs. Lincoln had invited to join the theater party to replace the Grants.

The Lincolns arrived late at the theater. The curtain had been up half an hour when their carriage rolled to a halt at the alighting platform outside Ford's. The president entered through the center door and crossed the front lobby, acknowledging a salute from the doorkeeper. With the rest of his group, including one of the four policemen assigned as a security detail for the White House, he climbed the stairway to the 420-seat dress circle. They filed along the south aisle to a small vestibule that led through two doorways into the converted single box. Within the box, set against walls that were papered a dark red, stood three velvet-covered armchairs, a sofa and six cane chairs, and a walnut rocker for the president. The six glass globes of the chandelier suspended near the top of the widened box cast only a dim glow upon the honored interior, and yellow satin drapes that overhung lace curtains gave additional privacy.

Onstage, Tom Taylor's comedy had reached the scene where Lord Dundreary explains to Flora Trenchard why a dog wags its tail. Lincoln and his party entered through the door of Box 8. He settled himself quietly, to avoid distracting attention from the players. Only a portion of the slightly less-than-capacity audience in the white- and gold-trimmed auditorium was visible to him. He, in turn, could be seen by comparatively few. Scattered handclaps marked his arrival. Behind him, the box door closed. After a while, the special policeman sitting by it left his post and wandered out of the theater. He was a former carpenter, with a blemished record since joining the police force. Outside Ford's, the president's coachman moved his vehicle half a dozen yards beyond the alighting platform. The policeman and a White House messenger who did footman's chores for Mr. Lincoln persuaded the coachman to join them for a drink in the Star Saloon. Twenty minutes later the coachman was back on his perch, feeling drowsy.

Plotters within and beyond the city were in various states of expectancy. The hour had arrived. The apparatus for abducting Abraham Lincoln was as perfected and ready as it ever would be. Horses and vessels were in place, kingpins and cat's paws more or less geared for action. And it all came to naught, suddenly and rapidly, in less time than the torchlight procession from the Washington arsenal required to complete its glittering circle around Lafayette Square.

Why did the kidnap plan collapse? The shipmaster John Celestina, whose *Indian Prince* moored on standby awaiting the kidnappers, lingered in Washington. Celestina had fed Lafayette Baker's NDP morsels of information. His only allegiance was to money. His version was that the assignment that had brought his brigs to Chesapeake Bay was postponed for a fortnight. The "cavalry escort" in Washington had got drunk and wandered off. When the night unleashed its frightfulness, Celestina fled town. Along the chain of command, such as it was, someone got cold feet. Mosby's explanation was that a last-minute message from Lunsford Lomax, somewhere in the Shenandoah Valley that Good Friday afternoon, warned that since the Confederacy had lost, nothing should be done to stain its reputation. "My feelings exactly," Mosby recalled, and he had disbanded his command.

Whatever the reason for the plot's failure, it had a harrowing effect on Booth. A few of his gang fretted on the sidewalk in front of the theater. They were confused, unable to decide what to do. It was Booth's opportunity. Far from calling everything off, he would see to it that something was done tonight. His mind had been in a combustible state even before Lola Alexander's letter. On top of that incendiary missive, Will Browning had refused to see him. It was time to wrest atonement for Lincoln's "bloody demeanors." The original plan had involved no bloodshed. In Booth's words, "For six months we had worked to capture." But the conspiracy had evaporated, and for once, his dilly-dallying could not be blamed. What had been his idea all along was about to be betrayed by those who would not "strike for their country with heart." He alone must act, compelled by divine force. "God simply made me the instrument of his punishment." No less irresistible than heavenly will was the new situation as pure drama. Confusing fantasy with reality is not uncommon among the greatest thespians, and Booth came from a stock with a feared strain of madness besides the seed of genius.

Our American Cousin neared the end of the second act. Booth stole around to Baptist Alley. He unlocked his stable and let out the rented bay. The owner had been right; the horse jibbed at being tied. Booth wanted her untethered anyway for a prompt departure, and he called for someone to hold her. It was a bad time to seek help from Ford's stagehands. The property man had problems connected with the wine cellar scene in the next act. The scene shifter would also be busy on stage left, pushing his flats around to stay abreast of as many as seven scenes in Laura Keene's production of the farce. Booth wanted his horse held fifteen minutes or so, too long for either stagehand to be off the job. But another man was available for holding the bay, a stage-doorkeeper called Peanut John, from the days when he had pushed a barrow along Tenth Street.

Intermission brought the Star Saloon its usual parched swarm. Booth entered last. He had scarcely drained his glass when the play resumed with Act Three. After Booth left the Star, Ford's doorkeeper out front saw him twice in the lobby. Booth asked the time, and the doorkeeper pointed at the clock hanging over the center door. Close to ten. Booth passed through the entrance to the parquette. Reappearing in the lobby, he took the stairway to the dress circle and walked quietly behind the rear rows of Sections A and B. He paused with his back to a pair of doors that led into a lounge, and he studied the progress of the play. Act Three, Scene Two. He knew that the moment approached when the stage would be empty but for a single character. Booth had decided that he would then strike and jump. The jump was nothing, child's play to a gymnastic actor who had astonished audiences with his spectacular plunge into the witch scene in *Macbeth*. He advanced another yard or so, soft-footed, disturbing no one in the audience. Again Booth halted. From where he now stood, the front of the state box and its sublime occupant were blocked from view. The policeman had not returned to the vestibule behind the box; no one stood between Booth and the target. He reached the door of the vestibule. He had the important details memorized. He knew the position of the president's rocking chair, knew the distance of the drop from the velvet-layered balustrade to the green baize carpeting of the proscenium. What John Wilkes Booth did not know was that he had been upstaged again. Someone else had just taken the diabolic privilege of initiating the night's horror.

CHAPTER 17

Unholy Night

The house where the Sewards lived was a thirty-room mansion overlooking Lafayette Square. It was built with a U.S. Navy commodore's prize money from the War of 1812. After the officer's death, it became notorious as a private club for men about town, deteriorating physically as well as in repute. When Lincoln's secretary of state bought the house, he had it renovated, but, outwardly at least, it retained a brooding aspect. Nearby stood a partly gutted building that had been the military headquarters of the District of Columbia. On the night of Saturday, April 1, much of it and a row of frame houses nearby caught fire, reportedly as the result of a defective flue. The army staff was relocated across town. Thus, the secretary of state was deprived of the protection afforded by proximity to a military hub.

The Sewards were burdened with domestic secrets that they strove to keep, at all cost, within the family. Seward's wife was an overprotective mother, driven almost mad by a prolonged struggle with her husband over the upbringing of Augustus, their diffident firstborn. When Seward decided to let the army have Augustus, she wrote to the War Department in an effort to prevent the youth's graduation from West Point. But she had lost him, first to the Mexican war, then to western frontier service, until 1861, when he was brought back east by his father's apparent wish to steer him into Civil War firing lines. This time, the mother's intervention secured her boy the safe job of Washington paymaster. Almost forty and never to marry, ungainly and progressively withdrawn, Major Augustus Seward was so unlike his brothers Fred and William as to seem somewhat of a family misfit. Inner resentments that he harbored against his father were brought violently to the surface by bouts of heavy drinking.

Since the street accident, Seward was immobilized in his bed. Someone was always at his side, usually his daughter Fanny. William was away with his regiment. Fred was at home. Also in the house was Seward's wife, who had broken a self-imposed seclusion at the family home in Auburn, New York. She occupied a room next to that of her bedridden husband. Two male nurses had been assigned to the secretary, and two State Department messengers, each armed with a Colt revolver, were working shifts as Seward's bodyguard.

That Good Friday evening one of the messengers, Emerick Hansell, reached Seward's home shortly after nine in the evening. He was hefty, a former wrestler in his native Pennsylvania. After a meal in the kitchen, he settled himself in an alcove on the third floor, where most of the family bedrooms were located. The secretary's was in the southwest corner. All doors were closed and the hall landing was quiet, until Major Augustus Seward charged from his room in his underclothes, waving a cane and shouting commands. Hansell had handled such outbursts before. Solemnly saluting, he took the major's arm and led him back to bed.

Shortly before ten Seward's doctor, Tulio Suzzara Verdi, called briefly to check on his condition. Then silence again filled the house. Seward's right arm, fractured at the shoulder, extended beyond the edge of his mattress. That evening he felt more alert and had listened to the music of the parade through his opened window and watched the reflection of fireworks on the ceiling. His teeth were still wired to keep the right jaw in place. Now he slept. Fanny Seward sat on one side of the bed, reading in the glow of a lowered gas jet. On the other side sat Private George F. Robinson, a convalescent Maine soldier appointed the previous day as male nurse.

Three weeks would pass before Fanny wrote her impressions of the horror that followed, and during that interval she was never questioned. She would recall opening the door and seeing her brother Fred with "a very tall young man in a light hat and long light overcoat. The man seemed impatient. Fred shut the door quickly." What followed, Fanny remembered as "an interval of quiet." Then she heard "the sound of blows, as many as half a dozen, sharp and heavy, with lighter ones between. I did not fully connect this with the person I had seen."

Robinson heard the blows as well and thought they were "made with a cane." The door swung open and in rushed a strapping figure "with light sandy hair, whiskers and moustache," who knocked the soldier flying. Fred Seward lay crumpled near the entry, his face bloodied. In the gaslit gloom Robinson struggled to his feet and saw the intruder thrust Fanny aside and leap at the prone secretary. A knife glimmered in the attacker's hand. Pressing down with the other on Seward's chest, the figure stabbed at him. Seward tried to roll his head clear. Two or three thrusts slashed the bedsheets before the blade found its mark, cutting Seward from his upper right cheekbone diagonally almost to his nostril, then back to the lower jaw, then forward again to just beneath the chin.

This was no assassin's work. Seward's body was otherwise unscathed. The knife struck nowhere near the heart or any other vital organ. It was not aimed at the windpipe. It targeted Seward's face—in particular, his ligatured jaw.

Robinson pounced on the attacker and wrenched him off Seward's bed. The man struck backward at him, and Robinson felt the knife. Bleeding from his shoulder, he wrestled the man to the door. Then another figure plunged into the room. It wasn't Fred. He had already staggered to his bedroom, beaten nearly senseless. The new arrival was Emerick Hansell. After leading the dazed Major Seward back to his room that night, Hansell had settled himself in the hall, reading a newspaper. When he had heard violent sounds from outside the secretary's room, he supposed the major was up again and making a delirious attack on his father. Hansell found the two men struggling there. He heard Robinson cry, "Hansey, help me." The hall light was dim, but Hansell instinctively took Robinson's attacker to be the major. He and Robinson dragged the man to the hall bannister, intending to heave him over it. A fist rammed into Robinson's stomach. A knife cut Hansell. The attacker broke away and rushed downstairs.

Outside, the sky had grown pleasant with pale moon and clearing sky. Strollers in Lafayette Square heard shouts from the mansion close by the charred former military headquarters. The Sewards' black houseboy ran for a doctor two blocks away.

The savagery at the Sewards' had lasted brief minutes. Six blocks across town, the hands of the clock in Ford's lobby crept past the hour of ten. The play was going well. On the stage Mrs. Mountchessington flung scornful words at Asa Trenchard, the uncouth rogue who had confounded her schemes by proving no wealthy catch. Unseen behind the decorated section of the theater, overlooking stage left, Booth reached for the knob of the door to the presidential box.

With a pompous shrug, Mrs. Mountchessington flounced into the wings. The door behind Abraham Lincoln's rocking chair edged open. Alone onstage, Asa Trenchard capped the lady's haughty departure with a comically withering retort: "Don't know the manners of good society, eh? Well, I guess I know enough to turn you inside out, old gal—you sockdologising old man-trap." The audience roared, as Booth knew it would, and at that instant he stepped into the box with a single-shot derringer pistol.

The .44 caliber bullet that entered the president's head cracked the frontal skull bone and buried itself in brain tissue half an inch behind the right eye. Pulling the trigger, Booth shouted, "Sic semper tyrannis!" (Ever thus to tyrants!) But in the echoing mirth at the solitary comic onstage, not every member of the audience heard him. Booth darted between chairs and reached the front of the box when Major Rathbone sprang forward and grabbed him. The derringer fell, but a knife flashed in Booth's hand. Rathbone's left arm took the slash. At the center post of the double box, Booth swung his legs over the balustrade and lunged into midair. Accident marked the bravura. His boots knocked askew a gilt-framed portrait of George Washington, and his right spur caught in the Treasury Guard's regimental colors. Booth tumbled and hit the stage aslant. He twisted upright, and amazement froze Harry Hawk, playing Asa Trenchard, as his well-known fellow actor hobbled toward him with bloody knife raised. Hawk shrank aside, Booth dodging awkwardly around him—a weird pas de deux behind twenty-seven gaslit footlights that brought the audience to its feet as Booth made an inelegant exit, stage right.

From there to the rear of the theater ran a narrow corridor formed by the star's dressing room and a row of props and scene flats. Costumed players stood awaiting their cue. The corridor had to be kept clear always. Some of the twenty or so performers involved in the production saw Booth half hop through the corridor, knife in hand. The conductor, stumbling across his path, was knifed and elbowed aside. Booth made for the back door opening on Baptist Alley. In the dark court, Peanut John leaned against a carpenter's bench, holding Booth's horse. He felt the bridle wrenched from his grasp. A push and a kick sent him sprawling. The bay pawed and tossed as Booth hauled himself into the saddle.

Inside the theater, some of the audience panicked and fought for the exits. Others strove to reach the dress circle, if not the box itself, from which came shouts for medical aid. Mary Lincoln screamed. A mob choked the carpeted stairways and lobby, spilling outside to form shocked clusters on the Tenth Street sidewalk. A local resident familiar with every outlet from Baptist Alley had the presence of mind to speed friends in opposite directions—to the lane that opened on F Street, to another egress at E Street, and to a private passageway alongside a grocery on Ninth. They were too late. The assassin had vanished, and no one knew for sure in which direction.

Residents along F Street heard hoofbeats passing eastward. But this was off Booth's course and had other drawbacks, an extended slope upward and deep furrows plowed in the unpaved clay by traffic crowded to one side since the installation of the streetcar railway. To prevent pedestrians from tumbling into the muddy channels, the city corporation had erected fencing along the edge of the sidewalk. This formed another barrier to anyone in a hurry along the lane from Baptist Alley into F Street. But someone was heard fleeing east on horseback over the timbered rails. Wrongly believed thereafter to have been John Wilkes Booth, it was Edwin Hynson, a pint-sized guerrilla scout for the South who had smuggled medicines for Booth, joined the actor's conspiracy, and was to prove his most devoted subordinate. Hynson appears in the NDP's photo of assembled smugglers.

Hynson was one of a few conspirators who had shown up at Ford's Theatre. Between ten and half past ten, from curtained windows on F Street, his roan horse was seen tethered at a gap left in the pedestrians' fence by removal of a board earlier in the day. Hynson rented the roan that afternoon at Nailor's Stable, with the assistance of Will Browning's Mosbyite brother Ringgold. And during those electrifying moments in the theater, Hynson had lurked in a vacant lot that stretched from Ford's greenroom to F Street. If Hynson had not known by then that Booth meant to kill, he at least expected him to bring the president outside, a captive at gunpoint. Hynson waited for Booth in the shadow of the greenroom. When he knew the actor had emerged through the back door at Baptist Alley and was making off on horseback, he, too, had moved. Occupants of the alley, tenements, and back rooms at F Street heard him clamber over a six-foot fence bordering the vacant lot. To reach his horse, Hynson had to squeeze through the gap in the second fence, the protective paling along the curb. The rutted clay was unsafe, so Hynson rode off at a gallop along the streetcar planking.

Neighborhood dwellers, hearing the rapid hoofbeats on timber, were also puzzled by a series of shrill whistles—the Mosby touch. They were not the only odd phenomena that night. Someone had shut off the power to the commercial telegraph. For three hours the only communication out of Washington would be over military lines. And within the same thirty minutes after the shooting at Ford's, someone at the gasworks on Maryland Avenue shut off the gas that fed the lights around the Capitol and westward along Pennsylvania Avenue. This was about the time Booth spurred his horse eastward along the same stretch.

Hardly less peculiar were certain individual reactions to news of the shooting. Salmon P. Chase, an aspirant to the White House until Lincoln appointed him to the Supreme Court, had huddled with Republican hard-liners in Baltimore the previous day for some undisclosed reason. As Chase himself wrote, when aroused from bed in his Washington home and told that his president had been shot scarcely four blocks away, "reflecting that I could not be of service, I decided to wait until morning." He returned to his bed.

On Pennsylvania Avenue, at the Kirkwood Hotel, a friend of Andrew Johnson's who had sped there from Tenth Street found the vice president's door locked and the room dark. Assuming Johnson to be in bed, he hammered on the door until it opened. On hearing the news, Johnson evinced that same curious lack of compulsion to reach the fallen leader before he breathed his last. He lamented fully half an hour, then sent his friend back alone. Finally, Johnson ventured forth and went to the house of a Scandinavian-born carpenter named William Petersen. Lincoln had been carried there from Ford's across Tenth Street. In a back room on the ground floor, Johnson joined the gathering of politicans, generals, and priests. By the light of a single hissing gas jet, four doctors worked on the stripped and mustard-poulticed body stretched diagonally across a six-foot-long four-poster bed. Mary Lincoln, when not at the bedside, sobbed hysterically in the narrow hallway. Vice President Johnson stayed but a few minutes.

Edwin Stanton was in his bedroom. The doorbell rang and his son answered. Two War Department clerks who had rushed to the secretary's home gave a breathless account of what had just happened at the theater. They named John Wilkes Booth as the gunman. Stanton was quickly in his carriage, headed not for Tenth Street but in the opposite direction, toward the Sewards' home.

Major Thomas Eckert was shaving. An assistant from his War Department telegraph room arrived at 10:30 P.M. to blurt out that the actor Booth had shot the president. Eckert made a beeline for Stanton's, where he learned that Stanton had left for Seward's house.

Gideon Welles, secretary of the navy and a neighbor of the Sewards, was at their home when Stanton, then Eckert arrived. Eckert advised against riding to Ford's Theatre; the streets, he said, were full of dangerous characters. Welles bundled Stanton into a carriage. He later hinted that except for his firm grip, Stanton would have jumped back out.

With a nine o'clock curfew imposed on unofficial crossings, the Navy Yard Bridge was guarded by a sergeant and a detail of the 3rd Heavy Artillery, Maine Volunteers. Earlier that evening, the sergeant had told his men that a password, "TB," would be used for crossing, with the countersign "TB Road." The soldier who revealed this thought it curious that "until then we had never had orders to use such a password." He was stationed on the Maryland side of the bridge.

Between ten and eleven, he heard through the blockhouse door a horse coming over from Washington at a gallop. The soldier and his corporal sprang outside and demanded of the rider where he was bound. "TB" was the response. TB what? "TB Road." The corporal ordered the gate opened and the horseman rode off. Another soon followed, using the same password. He, too, was allowed through. Said one of the soldiers, "It is funny what's going on tonight."

CHAPTER 18

The Incredible Hours

A hush descended on the throng keeping vigil along Tenth Street. Notables crowding the Petersen home had closed their eyes in final prayer or from hours-long weariness. The silver porcelain-tipped probe searching for the bullet through feebly pulsating brain tissue was withdrawn for the last time. Meanwhile, an unprecedented coverup was already under way.

From his temporary headquarters at the Petersen home, the secretary of war issued orders, dispatched telegrams, and supervised the interrogation of witnesses. The full cast of *Our American Cousin* was held for questioning. Harry Hawk, on center stage when Booth leaped, joined the theater's ticket taker and others in vouching for the assassin's identity. A wounded young veteran, acting as War Department clerk, recorded the interviews in shorthand. By midnight, he had taken what he calculated was enough testimony to put the noose around Booth's neck.

Stanton also knew that Booth had fired the fatal shot. He had said as much to Gideon Welles. His close aide Eckert knew the assassin's name within thirty minutes of the deed. Almarin C. Richards, Washington's police superintendent, wrote later that it was well and certainly known before midnight that Booth was the assassin. But none of Stanton's first messages named the killer. His bulletins to the national press and directions to army commanders kept mounted couriers shuttling all night between Tenth Street and the War Department telegraph room. His first dispatches described Lincoln's condition as beyond recovery. The violence at Seward's he declared officially to be the further work of an assassin. No agency, however, not subject to the secretary's control could transmit Booth's name by telegraph until after twelve, when the commercial system would resume operation, and no agency under his control did. In Booth's room on the fourth floor of the National Hotel, War Department detectives ransacked his trunk, soberly inventorying theatrical costumes as criminal disguises. Press reporters allowed into the room later found little more than embroidered slippers and black cashmere pantaloons, tobacco, hair oil, and old play programs. The War Department announced that the trunk contained a Confederate cipher key and a gimlet used to make a peephole in the door to the state box at Ford's. Nothing was proffered to explain how this conclusion was reached. The letter Sam Arnold had written to Booth in March, advising a halt to kidnap plans pending knowledge of Richmond's views, was made public.

Other items taken from Booth's room were not made public. These included a printed map with the route of the would-be abductors and a woman's photograph, which was promptly slipped into Lafayette Baker's National Detective Police photo files with "Lola Alexander" scribbled on the back. Also found was an empty envelope bearing James V. Barnes's name and address and a roughly sketched map, showing the confluence of the great rivers that marked the location of R. D. Watson's smokehouses. No hunt was ordered for Barnes.

After they crossed the Navy Yard Bridge, Booth and Hynson rode eastward along the Washington–Marlborough turnpike. Under an almost full moon blurred by thin clouds, they stopped a traveler to confirm their route. It would be said, and perpetuated with seldom a challenge, that the pair then headed due south to Surrattsville (now Clinton, Maryland), where stood the tavern, also formerly a post office, owned by Mary Surratt and leased to a habitual drunkard named John Lloyd ("Whisky makes me forget a great many things"). A confession dragged out of Lloyd by a gas fitter-turned-"special officer" to assist Washington's military provost marshal described a visit by Mary Surratt on Good Friday afternoon and the supply of a carbine to Booth at midnight.

In fact, Booth and Hynson swung off the turnpike on a roughly southeasterly course. They were making for the Patuxent River. The original plan was for the kidnap party coming down from Washington to divide where the road forked below the hamlet called T.B. Booth would have raced southwest to the Potomac and boarded the *Indian Prince.* The ship lay in a Potomac inlet called Nanjemoy Creek. At Benedict's on the Patuxent, a second vessel, the *Indian Queen,* awaited the special cargo destined for Bloodsworth Island.

There was now no kidnap party for those old Chaffey craft to accommodate, only a fleeing assassin who had decided that it was safer for him not to head for Nanjemoy Creek but to fork southeast. Bryantown was a convenient last stop for the abductors and their prize before reaching Benedict's. Now it was all the more important to Booth, for whom flight was an agony. That jump from the stage box had wrenched his left leg. Near Bryantown lived Doctor Samuel Mudd, whose cooperation in the kidnap venture had been secured and whose services as a physician, Booth hoped, would be as generously available.

Mudd recognized the injured man half carried across his threshold at four o'clock Saturday morning, but he was unaware of the carnage in Washington. Neither did he know the little fellow who had arrived with Booth and who gave his name as "Henston." Mudd cut off Booth's left riding boot to inspect the swollen ankle and diagnosed the trouble as a straight fracture of the tibia two inches above the ankle. He improvised splints. After resting in the Mudds' bedroom, Booth shaved off his mustache.

Bells tolled thirty miles away in Washington. The president's life had ceased shortly after seven. Later in the forenoon Andrew Johnson was sworn in as president. The ceremony was conducted with haste in his rooms at the Kirkwood Hotel. During the same hour, in the guest room on the second floor of the White House, doctors held a postmortem of the remains of his predecessor.

From the War Department, public pronouncements directly implicated the South. A bulletin over Stanton's signature shortly before 5 A.M. declared that two assassins had struck: Booth at Ford's Theatre and a co-conspirator at Lafayette Square. Misquoting Sam Arnold's letter to Booth, Stanton affirmed it as proof that the crimes had been plotted well in advance by Richmond's political leaders.

That rain-sodden Saturday morning the secretary of war had scarcely paused to rest. Once he had seen to the removal of Lincoln's body from Tenth Street to the White House, he raced to his office and composed letters and telegrams whose tone and phrasing prefigured the official version of events. To saddle the South with responsibility for the crimes and dispel any embarrassing curiosity over why Lincoln and Seward alone were victims, it had to be shown that others, especially the supremely anti-rebel secretary of war, had been in the assassins' sights. Recalling General Grant to the capital, Stanton warned of a threat to the government from "the large number of rebel officers and privates, prisoners of war and rebel refugees and deserters that are coming among us."

For no known reason, Stanton hired Britton A. Hill as unofficial private investigator. Hill was a politically radical attorney who had left his practice in St. Louis to lobby in Washington for business. As a lawyer, he had successfully handled insurance and railroad cases. His service to Stanton was confined to perfunctory questions in the servants' quarters of Seward's home and a brief scavenge for gossip in the taverns along Tenth Street and Pennsylvania Avenue. He was soon apologizing for having publicly charged while drunk that Lincoln had only got what he deserved for consorting with pro-rebel profiteers. Hill was quickly on the train back to St. Louis, but the "findings" he left with Stanton were precisely to the secretary's taste. "All the circumstances," ran a typical note, "signify a plot laid in Richmond before the city's capture. You were to have been killed also."

Newspapers were handed stories of a muffled man crouching at Stanton's doorway Friday night and making off at the arrival of the two War Department clerks from Ford's Theatre. Stanton himself told of one or more prowlers hiding behind a treebox outside his home, and it was said that a defective doorbell saved his life by frustrating a sinister caller who intended to gain entrance. Years later, the surviving of the two clerks emphatically denied that he or his companion had seen any lurking men and recalled that the Stantons' doorbell had rung as it should have.

But Stanton was in full command during those crucial hours. Publicly alert to what he insisted was a continuing danger, a plot to destroy the whole Union leadership, he ordered every cabinet member's home surrounded by military platoons, a precaution that Gideon Welles privately ridiculed. Reporting to overseas United States diplomats on events of the preceding night, Stanton claimed to have acquired absolute proof that the attacks were ordered by Confederates desperate in defeat. His telegraphed report to General Sherman contained the imaginative touch that the murderer—Stanton still did not name him—had shouted "Virginia is avenged," as well as "Sic semper tyrannis." And Sherman was to consider himself among the assassins' targets, thus should be "more heedful than Mr. Lincoln was of such knowledge."

Through private and public channels, as fast as rail, steamboats, and the telegraph could spread the news, Stanton induced the world to believe in a preconceived insurrectionist attack upon the United States government, in which the vice president and the secretary of war were spared by providence or pure luck and the bedridden secretary of state had been in no position to resist, and to which the president, God rest his soul, had fallen victim through his own stubborn folly.

Radical Republicans were quick to amplify and embellish the theme. The Confederacy's proven guilt for those terrible deeds exposed the futility of that "tender and forgiving spirit"—Secretary Stanton's words—that the chief executive had displayed to the end, the fatal namby-pambyism from which an assassin's bullet had rescued the country. "It is well that [the murder] happened," wrote Francis Lieber, prominent among those who favored punishing the South. "Lincoln could not die a more glorious death." Some detected the hand of God in the crime. Divine will had kept Lincoln in power only until he could be replaced by a better man. This was the opinion of Charles Sumner, one of Mary Lincoln's favorite social escorts, who wrote of feeling sorry for the late president's family but consoled himself with a belief that "his death will do more for the cause than any human life."

And the new president would surely toe the line. He was a former member of the Joint Committee on the Conduct of the War and had attacked the insurrection in one fiery speech after another. Close study of Johnson's past oratory would have disclosed more of ingrained prejudice against the slave-holding aristocracy than of retributive

Northern dogma and the principles of black suffrage. But few radicals were in a mood for second thoughts. Entranced by visions of political revival after months of steadily corroded influence, the Committee of Fifteen welcomed Johnson's presidency, confident that compared with its efforts to control Lincoln, keeping his successor on the right track would be smooth sailing.

Within twenty-four hours of Lincoln's death, half a dozen of them gathered in Senator Zachariah Chandler's room at the National Hotel to make their choices for the new administration. Disrespectful allusions to the late president's alleged shortcomings turned the caucus into an ugly wake. Even George Julian of Indiana, who had become convinced that Lincoln's removal from power was necessary, recoiled from Ben Wade's coarse oaths. But he shared the spirit that ignited them, writing afterward that everyone at the radicals' meeting regarded Lincoln's assassination as "a godsend to our cause."

That same morning, upon hearing of Booth's crime, his pathetic little blue-eyed lover, Ella Turner, tried to kill herself with chloroform. She was saved by a doctor hurriedly brought to her sister's brothel.

The man who had left her pregnant rested at Samuel Mudd's. The doctor had gone to Bryantown, ostensibly to buy calico for making bandages. He was actually seeking a carriage for his lame guest and what information he could pick up of Union troops in the vicinity. From townsfolk and federal soldiers, he learned for the first time that someone had shot Lincoln. He also heard it said that the assassin was believed to be a man called Boyd.

When Mudd returned home, without a carriage, he found his visitors on the point of leaving. They asked his advice on easterly roads. Booth was helped to the saddle. He and Hynson rode toward the Patuxent River. "The murderers have, it is believed, gone southeast and will perhaps attempt to board some vessel waiting to take them to sea." Those words, from Quartermaster General Montgomery C. Meigs of Baltimore, were the closest any official statement came to describing Booth's intended course.

Having themselves stayed too long at Doctor Mudd's, Booth and Hynson now had Lieutenant Dana's patrols to contend with.

Beating a path through bog and pine groves, they were met by a farmhand who warned of soldiers at Benedict's Landing. They wheeled northward and crossed Black Swamp Creek, hoping to strike the river further upstream. But again they were headed off, by troops riding into Horse Head village, and for the second time they were forced to change direction. As Saturday night fell, they rode westward, bound now for the Potomac River, part of their journey through a dense man-made fen called Zekiah Swamp.

Police Chief Almarin Richards acted on a tavernkeeper's tip that Booth's recent associates included John Surratt. Richards sent officers to the house on H Street. While Mary Surratt frowned from an upstairs window, her young boarder Louis Weichmann furnished the callers with names of the conspiratorial guild to which he had been a frustrated aspirant.

With this information and what he had picked up elsewhere, Superintendent Richards decided to scout those Maryland counties that the War Department appeared to have neglected. Relying on the department for horses, he requested some from "the thousands in corrals." At least eight valuable hours passed before any arrived for him. At the city's army headquarters, relocated since its fire, General Christopher Augur, military commander of the District of Columbia, did his best with only scraps of information to coordinate a manhunt for Lincoln's attacker and "the would-be assassin of Secretary Seward." Near dawn, bewildered by conflicting reports, Augur concluded that "the murderers are still in the city." Only then were orders issued blocking the southeast exits from Washington.

Thanks to Louis Weichmann's story of what went on at Mary Surratt's boardinghouse, suspicion fell upon her son and two minor figures as among Booth's chief accomplices. Surratt was believed to be in Canada. The other two were not expected to get far. One, George Atzerodt, was a Port Tobacco boat builder recruited by Booth through his knowledge of boats and country byroads. A shambling eyesore to all but the mistress he kept on the Potomac shore, Atzerodt was described in the first War Department dispatches as Secretary Seward's assailant. Soldiers were on the lookout for him. The other man,

David E. Herold, was not the cloddish young delinquent portrayed thereafter by writers ignorant of his three years' schooling at Georgetown University, although he drank and talked altogether too much for his own safety.

Herold had kept just one steady job, that of apothecary's clerk in Washington. The only son in a houseful of girls, he liked to wander off to hunt quail in the lower Maryland counties, where his acquaintances included rebel blockade-runners and secret agents. He had seen Booth a few times and was vaguely stagestruck, honored to have drawn a minor role in Booth's original production. Herold was among the group of unsuspecting smugglers who were photographed in 1863 by NDP agents posing as itinerant cameramen, at St. Michaels. That same sheepish tableau on glass plate also included the stocky little figure of Booth's fellow fugitive, Edwin Hynson.

In Washington, behind the panoply of official mourning, a process of concealment continued: a systematic recourse to doctored statements, suppressed testimony, and planted evidence. In Room 126 at the Kirkwood Hotel, one floor above Andrew Johnson's quarters (the new president had not yet moved into the White House), items allegedly found were touted as evidence of a criminal liaison between Atzerodt, Herold, and Booth. The room was registered as Atzerodt's but had not been slept in. The Kirkwood's day clerk, who had entered Room 126 earlier that morning, found nothing there and said so. His testimony was ignored. Publicity was given only to discoveries and statements, genuine or otherwise, that pointed to a bloody plot hatched in Richmond and directed at a broad array of the Union government.

CHAPTER 19

The Eager Connection

At 4 A.M. Saturday, the 15th, Colonel Lafayette Baker received a telegraphed summons in New York from Edwin Stanton: "Come here immediately and see if you can find the murderer of the President." Baker had been conducting a publicized campaign against "bounty brokers who used the military recruitment system to defraud the government," and this business was not so important that he could not have taken a train to Washington that morning. But Baker also had other business at hand, business of a distinctly private nature. Awaiting its outcome, he was still in New York on Saturday night, at the Astor House.

Elsewhere in the Astor House, Robert Daniel Watson sat alone in a darkened room. Watson knew John Surratt not only as a sometime agent for cotton speculators but now as a fugitive, wanted in connection with Lincoln's murder. Watson was mortally afraid that Surratt might have failed to destroy the letter he had written in March, summoning Surratt to Water Street on important business.

Watson did not know that federal detectives had found it tucked behind a mirror at Mary Surratt's house. Nor did he know that Washington hotels were checked for the man he and his associates had engaged to secure the cotton. Benjamin Ficklin was quickly under lock and key, his papers confiscated, including a letter addressed to a London businessman, saying, "When all this is over, I will go south and get my cotton." Thanks to Orville Hickman Browning's intervention, Ficklin was soon a free man. Browning had emphasized the lack of evidence linking Ficklin with the assassination and explained his presence in Washington as connected with legitimate trade and a wish to discuss it personally with the president.

Watson's letter or a copy was soon in Lafayette Baker's hands. Watson could hardly have been more on edge than he already was when someone knocked on his door at midnight. It was no federal lawman with an arrest warrant but a caller conveying the same threat and intent upon relieving Watson of meat-for-cotton contracts. When the visit ended, signatures were blotted on new agreements and Watson quietly packed for home.

What he had done was to sign over the majority of his investment to a firm that called itself the Henry J. Eager Company, which used the familiar Water Street address. Two of its three partners, John McGinnis and Roswell E. Goodell, had held government meat contracts and were as opportunistic a pair of fortune hunters as had ever wheeled and dealed. Originally from Chicago, sons-in-law of a former Illinois governor whose career had succumbed to scandal, these two were perpetually alert for profit and employed the political services in Washington of Orville H. Browning and his fellow influence peddler Ward H. Lamon. Browning, Lamon, McGinnis, and Goodell—all four had numbered themselves among Abraham Lincoln's friends during his early years as lawyer and state congressman. All four had repeatedly sought to strike a bonanza from that friendship while he was in the White House. His sudden death had not put the brake to their efforts, even though the covert trade deal from which they anticipated fat rewards had become interwoven with a plan to have Lincoln, in James V. Barnes's words, "deposed for a fortnight."

McGinnis and Goodell were two members of a three-man company, hastily fabricated to seize the lion's share of Georgia cotton. Its senior partner, "Henry J. Eager," was the inveterate schemer likely to have known every link between the Water Street clique and the bloodless kidnap plot aborted by murder. That third man was Lafayette C. Baker.

Shouldering into control of a business enterprise thrown into disarray by recent events had been easy for this operator. While R. D. Watson was in one room of the Astor that night, Baker (as Eager) was waiting in another. He had learned of the meat-for-cotton deal from his NDP agents in Nashville, New York, and Montreal. Until

Lincoln's murder, no opportunity had arisen for him to move in on it. But now he was armed with Watson's letter to John Surratt, a hunted assassination suspect. Any connection with Lincoln's murder was the last thing Watson could want.

The blackmail worked. John McGinnis, Watson's midnight visitor, brought word back to Baker that the transfer of 75 percent of Watson's interests in the cotton deal to the Henry J. Eager Company had been duly signed. Only then did Baker revert to his official role as War Department special agent and obey Stanton's summons to see if he could find the man who had killed President Lincoln.

Baker was in Washington Sunday morning, with no reception from the U.S. Army. He had cultivated not only a public image of an aggressive patriot, but also that of a moral crusader. Earlier in the war, he had gone after Washington's gambling saloons and whorehouses with axe-wielding posses. This, as much as his high-handed attitude toward regular army officers, had made Baker an execrable figure in military eyes, and in the manhunt under way the army neither offered him its cooperation nor invited his.

Baker did not care. The last thing he wanted was a close liaison with soldiers. Secretary Stanton had appointed a panel of three officers under Joseph Holt, military judge advocate general, and given it the task of "developing the theory of conspiracy." All law enforcement and investigative bureaus were instructed to hand over their findings to Holt's Bureau of Military Justice, the new name for the judge advocate general's office. Baker, as usual, had other ideas. The band of detectives who had served him in the NDP's formative days had been assigned no particular role in the hunt for Booth. But those agents—"my entire force," Baker called them at the time—were no more capable of sitting out events than their wily chief was. Reconnoitering among lower Chesapeake Bay smuggling haunts, of which the army knew nothing, on Sunday morning they picked up a drink-dazed David Herold.

He was already a target for suspicion. Louis Weichmann, a willing informer savoring revenge for his humiliations at Mary Surratt's boardinghouse, had told Police Superintendent Richards of Herold's visits there with John Wilkes Booth and co-conspirators. Also at police headquarters, the stableman from Nailor's had named Herold as having hired a horse for Booth on Good Friday. But Edwin Hynson had also hired a horse and was seen by the stableman, and that night it was Hynson, not Herold, whom the stableman saw racing out of town. The next morning policemen arrived at Herold's home. They were told that he had been out all night. This "looked very suspicious," they reported to Richards, "and confirmed our impressions that we were on the track of at least one of the guilty persons."

Besides his physical resemblance to Edwin Hynson, it was hardly to Herold's advantage that in a sister's words, "Davy is a loose-tongued, scatterbrained, lovable little boy who made up stories just for the fun of hearing himself talk." Nor did it help that in the war years, he had sought adventure down Chesapeake Bay with rebel smugglers. But what could not have been worse for the errant Georgetown University youth was that his companion in and out of Washington the day Lincoln was shot happened to be a neighboring blacksmith's son named Johnny Booth.

Without fanfare, the NDP brought Herold into Washington, drunk and manacled. He had worked peripherally in the kidnap plot, and although the Booth he had caroused with on Good Friday was unrelated to the assassin, Lafayette Baker figured that Herold might be a useful guide in his private manhunt. Herold was photographed at NDP headquarters and hustled back out of town into the Maryland countryside.

His picture was sent with *cartes de visite* of Booth and John Surratt to the Army Medical Museum, staffed in part by hospital stewards who photographed and classified surgical specimens taken from the war's dead and wounded. When Lincoln was shot, the stewards were given the immediate task of working on pictures of suspects. The pictures were intended for reward purposes. The photo of Herold already in handcuffs puzzled at least one hospital steward, but, he later recalled, at that time it was wisest to ask no questions. For a reward poster, with Herold's picture, soon issued, the manacles were cropped.

On Monday the 17th, detectives were moving among the deceptively serene hamlets between the Potomac and Patuxent Rivers, pushing Herold on ahead as bait to trap secessionist locals into betraying clues to Booth's whereabouts. They halted at a crumbling plantation hut between Piscataway and Surrattsville that served as hideout or command post for the paroled Confederate secret agent James W. Boyd, of whom they knew little, other than that he had ostensibly cast his lot with the North. They called him out and attached him to their group.

Boyd had performed his kidnap duties more or less without interruption. In exchange for "secret service" to the Union secretary of war, he had been freed and promised a new life in Mexico. Once the American emigrant legion had helped Juarez expel the French from that land, he would settle down as a colonist there and send for his children. This had been Boyd's optimistic vision—shattered like so much else by an assassin's bullet. Boyd now had cause for great fear. In the wake of Lincoln's murder, that original plot was fast unraveling. The conspiracy's nameless higher ups may have already decided on a safer means of securing the silence of hirelings than the promised gift of Mexican acreage. After Booth's mad act, which had caught everyone off guard, the need was all the greater to obliterate cogs in the kidnap apparatus.

The party stopped at isolated farmsteads, questioning sullen landowners and "free darkies." Early on Wednesday, they had crossed into Charles County and before sunrise were resting between Bryantown and the eastern edge of Zekiah Swamp. The detectives appeared to be asleep. But if it all looked too easy and stirred Boyd's apprehensions of some elaborate setup, he would take that chance. Quietly, he collected one of the detectives' carbines and three pistols, then stole away, with David Herold at his side. From that moment, not one but two pairs of fugitives were at large. At daybreak, a couple of detectives plunged into Zekiah Swamp after Boyd and Herold. Their colleagues clung to the trail of John Wilkes Booth and by sundown were not far behind him.

The southeastern reaches of Zekiah Swamp oozed into a Potomac inlet near the village of Allen's Fresh. Here among the pines huddled Booth and his solitary companion. Hynson was a dumpling of a youth who had lost some of his rebel zealotry and now prayed. A mulatto guide had brought them safely through the marshy maze to the baronial estate of a planter named Samuel Cox, one of the local recruits in Booth's kidnap plan. The collapse of the Confederacy and Lincoln's assassination were reasons enough for Cox to now stay clear of trouble. But also, he had applied for a Union pass to attend the bedside of a son dying of war wounds.

Booth and Hynson appeared at his door early Sunday morning. Cox turned them away. He sent a servant after them with blankets, and to avoid recognition of their horses, he ordered the animals taken into a swamp and shot. But he transferred further responsibility for the pair's survival to a foster brother, Thomas Jones, the Confederacy's chief signal agent on the Maryland side of the Potomac. Jones steered them deeper into the forest.

Bad weather persisted. Pain tore through Booth's left leg. But the Potomac was only three miles away, and a further five miles west across a bight, the river backed up into Nanjemoy Creek. Somewhere within this broad inlet lay John Celestina's *Indian Prince,* her name obliterated from the stern, as had been the *Indian*'s twelve months earlier when the same shipmaster brought that vessel up the Atlantic coast with James V. Barnes on board.

Captain Boyd also knew of the disposition of those weather-beaten Chaffey brigs, knew that one stood by to take Booth aboard. The ship could just as well be Boyd's own means of escape. In any event, he intended to embark on a journey of his own, Mexico-bound. While they led their horses splashing through Zekiah Swamp, he invited Herold to Mexico with him, where they could "learn the language, make a fortune." The pair approached Nanjemoy Creek, Boyd's progress, like Booth's, hampered by a game leg. Crossing the swamp on foot had caused his right ankle to swell, the old minie ball wound suppurating.

At Nanjemoy Creek a locally prominent family with whom Herold had lodged while on hunting trips provided him and Boyd with food. The masts of the *Indian Prince* were visible above the tall reeds—and it was the closest the two were ever to come to her. Federal parties had learned of the vessel moored in the backwater. Twice on Tuesday night a Union cavalry lieutenant and detectives from a steam tug waiting downstream had drawn alongside and gone aboard. They found only the first mate, who told them that the crew had jumped ship. A rainstorm prevented further investigation—the boarding party had its own work cut out getting back to the tug—and on the next favorable tide the *Indian Prince* stole down the Potomac and out to sea. Boyd and Herold, meanwhile, found an old bateau with a broken oar. They crossed the river under cover of fog, landing on the Virginia shore just west of Mathias Point.

Still on the Maryland side, Booth and Hynson had not moved from the pines near Allen's Fresh. Shivering under a blanket, Booth wrote notes in an out-of-date pocket diary. On one of its pages he sketched a current calendar. Under the date April 18, he had scrawled the word *ship*. But the *Indian Prince* was beyond reach, and that left Booth with no safe alternative. He had counted first on escape down Chesapeake Bay, only to be cut off at the Patuxent exit. Now he faced the Potomac. To remain where he rested meant certain capture. He had to attempt a crossing of the river, unseen.

While awaiting a chance, Booth diarized his thoughts, backdating a first entry and awkwardly linking two dates as if unable to resist the theatrical analogy: "April 13, 14, Friday the Ides. Until today nothing was even thought of sacrificing to our country's wrongs. For six months we had worked to capture . . ." When the imminent defeat of their cause demanded "something decisive and great," none but he was strong-hearted enough to attempt it. "I struck boldly and not as the papers say. I walked with a firm step through a thousand of his friends."

On the same note of pride, Booth corrected another error he had seen in newspapers that Thomas Jones had brought to the swamp for him. "I shouted 'sic semper' before I fired"—and he boasted that although breaking his ankle in the leap from the state box, he had succeeded in dodging army pickets and that night "rode sixty miles . . . with the bone of my leg tearing the flesh at every jump." Killing was hateful, but "I cannot repent it. . . . our country owed all her trouble to him, and God simply made me the instrument of his punishment." Booth was on the point of discussing a "long article" he had left in Washington for publication when he heard the threshing of a nearby search party. He hobbled off with Hynson to another hiding spot in the pines, and once more he opened his red leather-bound booklet.

* * *

In Washington a funeral procession that had formed outside the White House moved off, turning at the Treasury Building, and tramped down Pennsylvania Avenue, slowly, with thirty bands, drums muffled, and a self-appointed honor guard of four thousand top-hatted blacks, white-gloved, hand in hand. Sunshine broke upon the crowded city, enriching the hues of green lawn and the fresh-blooming magnolia and flashing from the eight massive silver handles of the hallowed casket.

Waiting on the sidewalks for the cortege to pass, people read black-bordered newspaper columns describing the manhunt across Prince George's and Charles Counties. By all accounts, it was gathering momentum. Detectives had converged on Port Tobacco, ransacking George Atzerodt's workshop and harassing his paramour, while on the other side of Zekiah Swamp at Bryantown, suspicion had officially fastened on Doctor Samuel Mudd. More squads of the New York Cavalry had crossed from Washington into southern Maryland. From Point Lookout on Chesapeake Bay, units of an Illinois regiment fanned northward.

Their advance patrols brushed Allen's Fresh. Booth could have sensed the counties at his back filling with troops and detectives. He was still weak, his left leg throbbing. Out on the Potomac would be gunboats to dodge, but he could wait no longer. The rebel agent Thomas Jones brought a canoe around from the foot of the bluffs near Pope's Creek. And while Abraham Lincoln's body lay in state in the U.S. Capitol rotunda, receiving a final homage from the city that had known him four years, some thirty-five miles to the south the assassin prepared to take his chances on the river.

CHAPTER 20

Arrests and Confessions

During those hours of public mourning, forces were at work plugging leaks and blocking potentially embarrassing lines of inquiry. Almost immediately after his father's death, Robert Todd Lincoln had telegraphed an old family friend, Judge David Davis of Illinois, to come and take charge of personal affairs. Anxious lest certain documents fall into the wrong hands, young Lincoln wanted them transferred to Davis's home in Chicago for sifting, some to be preserved, others destroyed.

Superintendent Richards of the Washington police had not taken kindly to the War Department order that all evidence be handed over to the Bureau of Military Justice. Richards was prevented from investigating a report that more than fifty people, all of the North, had joined in plots against Lincoln. But he tried to do his duty—too thoroughly for comfort, in some quarters. Without Secretary Stanton's knowledge, he had sent men into Canada on John Surratt's trail. Mary Surratt's talkative boarder, Louis Weichmann, was taken with them. When Stanton learned of it, he had Richards immediately on the carpet, telling him to get the party back and all but calling the police chief an interfering meddler.

Richards discovered that Ringgold Browning, whom he suspected of involvement in the conspiracy, was sheltering with his parents in nearby Bladensburg. Richards asked the War Department for a horse, in order to ride out and arrest him. Browning's brother Will, the new president's cotton-dealing private secretary, may have heard of this, for no action followed the police chief's request. Detectives had identified a photograph found in Booth's hotel room as that of "Lola Alexander, New York." Superintendent Richards promptly telegraphed his counterpart in Baltimore to question "one Bishop, low comedian, as to Booth's woman." He meant Charles Bishop, a laughmaker drawing crowds that week to Ford's Theatre in Baltimore. Again, nothing resulted from the police chief's initiative, and the photograph was suppressed, with others, in War Department detective files, to be left undiscovered for more than a century. When telegrams from Newport, Rhode Island, advised the secretary of war of Booth's few hours at the Aquidneck House in early April with an unknown woman, no leads were traced to Lola. The letters she had written to the assassin, found tucked within his saddle blanket the morning after the murder, received the same treatment. "The claver was that Lola was the connecting link between Booth and conspirators in New York City who wanted Lincoln out of the way," a War Department detective wrote years later. The discovery of the letters "caused a bit of a stir for a short time. The marshal in New York was informed to look for Lola but nothing came of it."

Actually, it was not a Lola that New York's lawmen were told to look for. Under Secretary Stanton's system for centralizing the investigation, the Lola letters were, like everything else, turned in at the War Department. They gave no clue to the writer's full name or address. The War Department, via cipher telegram, sent New York police chasing throughout the city for eighteen hours, seeking an "Etta," who was supposed to have written Booth, egging him on to avenge the fall of Richmond by "doing something desperate." The New York police superintendent at once suspected a hoax. He telegraphed for additional details and finally got from the War Department what should have been told him in the first place, that the envelope containing "Etta"'s letter was postmarked April 19, five days after the assassination. With negative reports coming in from his footsore patrolmen—"The name of Etta is unknown among the sisterhood"—and infuriated by what appeared to be gullibility or worse in Washington, the New York police chief protested that the whole thing smelled "fishy," as if "a sell . . . to distract the attention of officers from points where their services would be useful."

There had grown a curious pattern of indictment and immunity. A Washington newspaperman wrote in connection with the assassination, "The arrest of several parties well known here who have been accumulating wealth and been the recipients of untold favors from the government will probably lead to important developments." There followed no such arrests or developments. Lafayette Baker's NDP knew of the March 19 letter from Watson to John Surratt, now a fugitive. Watson was never apprehended.

Thomas and Annie Lomax Green, owners of the old Van Ness mansion, were arrested for "disloyalty." Stanton's War Department accepted their story that the subterranean oddities exposed by inquisitive detectives were simply excavations for a storm sewer. Those cellars and the Greens' disloyalty were made to order for Stanton's efforts to blame the South for anti-Lincoln plotting. But he kept the Greens behind bars only until rumors of their complicity in Lincoln's murder had died down and the excavation was filled in. Then Stanton released them. The couple vanished into rustic obscurity.

Others were not so lucky. They include the scene shifter at Ford's. The discovery at his home of eighty feet of coiled rope, understandably of use backstage, but also ideal for tripping mounted pursuers, was all it took to land him in jail as one of Booth's cohorts. Michael O'Laughlen and Sam Arnold were arrested in Baltimore. Arnold talked freely. The plot against Lincoln was abduction, not murder. Widely published, this assertion conflicted with Stanton's scenario of a Richmond-based assassination plot. The secretary fired a volley of telegrams, threatening to penalize the Baltimore provost marshal unless he kept his prisoners muzzled.

Well and truly muzzled were prisoners below deck on the *Saugus*, a war-scarred armored monitor laid up for repair in the Washington Navy Yard. George Atzerodt was one. Another was a sturdy youth with an impassive, handsome face. On the night of Monday, April 17, he arrived at Mary Surratt's boardinghouse and walked straight into the grasp of five military detectives. He was roughly clad, shouldered a pick-axe, and said he had come to dig a ditch. A certificate of parole found on him claimed his identity as a Lewis Paine or Payne. Neither Mary nor her daughter could convincingly explain his visit.

Early on the 18th, within a few hours of the arrests at Mary Surratt's, a circular signed by Lafayette Baker offered $30,000 for information leading to the capture of John Wilkes Booth and "the person attempting to assassinate Secretary Seward." Booth's description was given in a scant three lines, that of Seward's alleged attacker ran to ten or more in weird detail. He was "six feet one inch tall, had a small mouth, protruding upper lip, soft hands with tapered fingers, spoke in a thin tenor voice, wore a double-breasted overcoat spotted pink and gray." And he was black-haired, red-faced, with "no beard or appearance of a beard."

While that circular was issued, the Sewards' black houseboy was hauled from bed to identify "Payne" as the intruder whom he said had gained entrance Good Friday night on a pretext of bringing medicine for the injured secretary. Even as the houseboy was speaking, and the odd description of Seward's alleged attacker circulated, a resourceful newspaperman dodged guards at Douglas Hospital to reach the bedside of George Robinson, the army nurse stabbed during the attack. Robinson recalled the attacker as tall, heavy-set, "with light sandy hair, whiskers and moustache."

Brigadier General William H. Seward, newly in town to be with his stricken father and brother, replied to a question regarding affidavits from the family, that none was taken, "merely the colored boy's statement." This left only that lad's widely distributed testimony and identification of a smooth-faced Payne, to settle the matter. It should hardly have done so. Given Private Robinson's first-hand impressions of a bewhiskered assailant, the man admitted to the Sewards' house with "medicine" and the knife-wielder on the third floor must have been two different persons.

Something had to be done to still that discordant note from Douglas Hospital. Robinson's description too aptly fitted Augustus Seward. With minor head wounds, unlike those suffered by his father and brother, the major hurried to Douglas Hospital for a talk with Robinson. When he emerged, he announced that the private's recollection now agreed with his: The attacker was clean-shaven, beardless—the prisoner Payne, no less. Robinson's earlier account had appeared in a single newspaper edition. It was never repeated.

Nothing conclusive would ever banish the mystery of what had happened at the Sewards' home minutes before Booth shot Lincoln at Ford's Theatre. Immediate testimony was lacking. Secretary Seward was in no condition to talk. His son Fred was barely conscious. The secretary's wife had caught only a vague glimpse of the struggle in the bedroom. Fanny's diary entry, written weeks after the event, was extensive. But of those few moments of horror in her father's bedroom, she wrote only "a fearful dream." Doctor Verdi took her to the *Saugus*. He later recorded that when the prisoner (Payne) stood before her, she "could not identify the man." Mrs. Seward died two months after the attack, Fanny following her in death ten months later. Her father recovered but would never speak publicly of what had happened that Good Friday night.

When Private George Robinson left Douglas Hospital, the War Department announced that he was taken to the *Saugus* and had identified Payne as the man who tried to kill Secretary Seward. A month later, in a courtroom with Payne before him, the soldier's testimony was less than forthright, ending with, "Yet I am not sure." In general, however, Robinson adhered to the War Department's version of events. Credited thereafter with having saved the secretary's life, he received a pension, he was promoted to lieutenant colonel upon his retirement, and in the centennial year of the attack at the Sewards' a ten-thousand-foot Alaskan mountain was named after him.

The Seward episode was further complicated by a coincidence. Within twenty-four hours of the Good Friday attack, newspapers reported that Emerick Hansell, the State Department messenger on protective duty at the Sewards' home and knifed on the third floor, had died of his wounds. The obituaries were all but correct. There were two men named Emerick Hansell. One had indeed succumbed in Washington, but he was a farrier at the Union cavalry depot at Giesboro at the edge of the city. His widow was informed that he was kicked in the head while shoeing a horse. He lingered a week, to die just eight hours after the stabbing of his namesake.

The farrier's death had the effect of stilling questions that only the other Hansell might have answered. Many years would pass before the State Department's messenger, then in pensioned retirement following a resumed career on the federal payroll, would give his story under strict guarantees of confidentiality. His recollection then was that he had been the third man on the landing, rushing to Private Robinson's aid, convinced that the man he and the soldier grappled with was Major Augustus Seward, the secretary's troubled son.

When he testified at both the conspiracy trial of 1865 and the Surratt trial in 1867, Augustus Seward claimed to have heard the attacker dash downstairs and out the door shouting, "I'm mad! I'm mad!" No one else testified to having heard such words. Seward died, age fifty, as a result, wrote his medical officer, of a "diseased condition of the brain."

As for his father's alleged attacker shackled on the *Saugus,* the enigmatic Payne was given a fresh identity, that of Lewis T. Powell, late of the Confederate army and of Mosby's band. "His name changes every day," complained a newspaper. It certainly appeared so. The *Philadelphia Inquirer* said, "A great mystery envelopes this man, a mystery that seems impenetrable." Solving the "mystery" was hampered by the scant opportunity that Colonel William E. Doster, the prisoners' counsel at the forthcoming conspiracy trial, was given to question him. Nothing much was extracted from him. He said that he had been given a bottle of medicine with which to gain access to Seward's house, but of what occurred therein, "he had only confused memories."

Already convicted in War Department press releases, Payne was effectively denied utterance. Eckert was the only person allowed to visit him at length in his ironclad prison. He promised Seward's son William a copy of Payne's confession of guilt, but Seward was to assert that he never received any. To doubly ensure Payne's silence, and that of George Atzerodt, Secretary Stanton directed that "for better security against conversation a canvas bag be put over the head of each [prisoner] and tied around the neck with a hole for proper breathing and eating but not seeing." In due course Michael O'Laughlen, Samuel Arnold, and David Herold would be similarly hooded and blinded. Arnold recalled that "daylight never lit upon the eye, they not even permitting the hood to be withdrawn for the purpose of washing the swollen, bloated and soiled visage."

* * *

The authorities, which in those immediate post-assassination days meant Edwin Stanton's War Department, seemed unsure what to do about John or Joas Celestina, Portuguese adventurer, kidnap tool, shipmaster, Confederate contrabandist, and sometime NDP informant. Two hours before the shooting at Ford's, he had left Washington for an unknown destination. The NDP considered that it would be safe for all concerned if Celestina be found and kept out of sight. A search began. He was arrested near Philadelphia and on April 18 brought to Washington. At first, Stanton ordered him locked up in the Old Capitol Prison as an assassination suspect. He was placed in solitary confinement. A week later he was transferred under heavy guard to the *Saugus* but within two hours was taken to the *Montauk*, another inactive monitor at the Navy Yard. Then he was moved again, back to the Old Capitol Prison.

Stanton prepared a military commission to try those who, "incited by Jefferson Davis," conspired to kill Abraham Lincoln, Andrew Johnson, General Grant, and William Seward, "whose duty it was by law upon the death of the president and vice-president to call an election for president . . . the conspirators intending to deprive the forces in the field of a commander-in-chief and to prevent a lawful election." The first mention of Grant as among the intended victims, and the reminder that only a secretary of state could call a presidential election, might have diverted curiosity as to the absence of the secretary of war from the rebel hit list. Stanton's directive, clearly a pretrial assumption of motive and guilt, named those who were to face trial. Celestina's name was there—for unknown reasons, heavily underlined.

CHAPTER 21

"We Have Booth's Diary"

Booth was foiled by Union river patrols in his first attempt to cross the Potomac. He and the faithful Hynson were guided back inland, to the lowest reaches of Zekiah Swamp, and left on the front porch of an elderly couple named Adams, whose tavern had been a rendezvous for the Confederate underground and members of the kidnap plot. They were offered food, but the Adamses stopped short of allowing strangers across their threshold. In the appropriate space of his penciled calendar, Booth noted where he and Hynson spent Friday, April 21, with a single depressing word: *Swamp*.

He poured forth his feelings onto the small pages, "hunted like a dog . . . chased by gunboats . . . wet, cold and starving . . . every man's hand against me . . . And why? For doing what Brutus was honored for. What made Tell a hero? And yet I, for striking down a greater tyrant than they ever knew, am looked upon as a common cutthroat." Ambition and revenge were the spurs for Brutus and the fabled Helvetian, but what *he* had done was a consecrated act, a stroke of immaculate patriotism. He had "struck for a country that groaned beneath the tyranny and prayed for this end, and yet behold the cold hands they extend to me."

Booth's choice of words reflected his addiction to allegory and self-dramatization. All the same, they more than hinted at the identity of his masters in the kidnap plot. Those "cold hands" were not of an ungrateful South: The Confederacy no longer existed. Booth had known that the North's political extremists were impatient for Lincoln's removal. When Booth wrote that his only wrongdoing had been service to "a degenerate people," he did not mean Southerners.

He charged that "the government [had suppressed] a long article" he left in Washington, containing "a little . . . a very little . . . to clear my name." Booth had given it to John Matthews, an actor who played a tipsy lawyer in *Our American Cousin.* Matthews was to have delivered it to the *National Intelligencer* the morning following Lincoln's murder. Years later, Matthews testified to having destroyed the letter at once and vouchsafed only a hazy recollection of its contents. What it said, Booth wrote in his diary, was that credit for removing Lincoln was due him and the Almighty. This was indeed "a very little," implying that he could tell more.

That much would not have sat well with Stanton. Any suggestion that the assassination was a unilateral act, heavenly inspired, ran counter to the picture produced by the secretary and his radical cohorts of a murder plot masterminded in Richmond, with Booth no lone wolf or divine instrument but a lackey of Jeff Davis and company.

In later years, too little attention would be paid to what Booth penciled while being pursued. The diary was belatedly made public with pages sliced or scissored out—eighteen, as Stanton first reported; half the booklet, as ultimately calculated. Even so, it might at least have been inferred that Booth's "degenerate people" were not conquered Southerners but Northern politicians so bent on Lincoln's removal as Reconstruction leader that they had "prayed for this end." At any rate, some of them now had reason to pray for Booth's silence. So had the profiteers who, while concerned that the president not be harmed, had enlisted Booth's aid to get him "deposed for a fortnight." What none had expected was bloodshed.

As for the violence at the Sewards' home, Booth disclaimed responsibility, writing, "I have only heard of what has been done (except what I did myself) and it fills me with horror." He had half a mind "to return to Washington and in a measure clear my name—which I feel I can do." But tonight, one week after he had shot Lincoln, Booth would try again to cross the river. He had not forgotten his companion. "As for this brave boy with me, who often prays (yes, before and since) with a true and sincere heart—was it crime with him? If so, why can he pray the same?" No mere ruminations to pass the time, Booth's diary jottings were designed as if for an audience, and he concluded with a valedictory flourish. "I do not wish to shed a drop of blood, but I must fight the course. . . . 'Tis all that's left me."

That Friday night was blustery, with a heavy sea running in Chesapeake Bay. Two ships stood down the Potomac and the steamer *Don,* flagship of the Potomac flotilla, failed to see their lights in time. Maneuvering to avoid one of the vessels, she collided with the other, which sank. During the confusion, a third ship came down and the *Don,* damaged in the bow, showed all lights and managed to fire four of her eight guns. The stranger continued to advance, passed the flagship, and disappeared south. The second of the Chaffey kidnap vessels had made her escape.

Through the gusty darkness, Thomas Jones led the way from Allen's Fresh, a silent Booth astride Jones's horse, Hynson stumbling alongside on foot. At Jones's farm, Huckleberry, they paused for a meal, then moved on, passing the public road to strike directly over fields to the bluffs above Pope's Creek. Daylight neared. The two put off in the boat Jones had provided. They touched the Virginia shore safely at Machodac Creek. Booth wrote "M.C." in his makeshift calendar. A federal gunboat lurked nearby. Booth saw another stream, Gambo Creek, where at a footbridge they tied the boat to a walnut tree and waited. A Confederate scout took over. He led them to Cleydael, the summer home of Doctor Richard Henry Stuart, probably King George County's wealthiest landowner. Stuart was related to General Robert E. Lee. His wife had knitted socks for Lee's soldiers. Twice, Stuart had served time in Union jails for disloyalty, but he continued as a reliable link in the Confederacy's intelligence network.

Unsigned statements attributed to Stuart, sundry locals, and stragglers from Colonel Mosby's command—all roped in by Lafayette Baker's detectives and summarily released—these constitute the only official record of what occurred that third weekend of April 1865 in the thickly wooded expanse between the Potomac shore and the banks of the Rappahannock River.

Testimony wildly conflicted. Stuart family tradition placed Booth in Cleydael, the doctor seeing to his fractured leg. Stuart's statement, as composed in Baker's intimidating shadow, said otherwise. One of

Stuart's ex-slaves described two men who stayed overnight in his cabin, one lame and rough, who addressed the other as "Dave." The next significant location was Port Royal, years earlier a busy tobacco outlet with a river ferry operable only at high tide. However extracted, testimony from witnesses at this crossing clearly indicates that two separate pairs of men were involved. Willie Jett, an ex-Mosby eighteen-year-old youth at the ferry, was so confused by the appearance of the second couple that he asked one of them for the name of his lame companion. The response came, "If he told you his name was Boyd, he told you right."

Two other former Mosby partisans were at the Rappahannock ferry, Absalom Bainbridge and Mortimer Ruggles. They were arrested and imprisoned. But testimony, if taken from them, was never disclosed. After a fortnight, they were hustled from Washington to a Union prison in far-off Ohio. A quarter-century later, their published accounts, "as told to" Prentiss Ingraham, a dime-story writer best known for mythologizing Buffalo Bill, contradict each other and defy plausibility.

The War Department publicly asked black Americans to help in the manhunt. The president's murder was defined as a sacrifice on their behalf. "Had he not been faithful to you and the great cause of human freedom he might have lived." Booth had held the pistol, but it was fired by the slavemasters. "Think of this and remember . . . this good man labored to break your chains." So they should keep their eyes and ears alert. Rewards had been posted, but no such mercenary stimulus should be required to hunt down "the assassin of your friend." This carefully tailored appeal did not circulate as far afield as King George County, which is where it might have done the most good. For there above Virginia's Northern Neck, a number of blacks had become privy to secrets about the flight of Booth that white America's history would be denied.

From the beginning of the Civil War, the North was bravely and loyally served by hundreds of Pamunky Indians, descendants of intermarriage between free blacks and members of the Pamunky tribe. They lived and operated largely in eastern Virginia and North Carolina. A Pamunky Indian scout, Whippet Nalgai, attached to a band of NDP operatives, could "stay in the saddle for days without stopping for food or rest. He carried parched Indian corn and nibbled at it constantly." These were the admiring words used by Detective Andrew Potter of the man who made a discovery of such potential that its suppression was inevitable. Early on Sunday, April 23, the detectives were scouring the Virginia side of the Potomac and had broken their search with a halt at King George Court House. Nalgai continued to scout on his own. Before midday, he was back with a collection of articles he had found in the grass near Gambo Creek: a blood-stained ulsterette, a pistol, a compass, and two near-empty brandy bottles, as well as a wallet containing $2,100 in Union currency, several letters of credit on Canadian and British banks, and a diary with a small map and six pictures of women tucked into its inside pocket.

The items were rushed to the Potomac River landing at Belle Plain and borne north to Washington on the NDP steamboat *Jennie Baker,* named for the chief detective's wife. Stanton's War Department made no announcement of the startling new find, but reference to the ulsterette believed to be Booth's appeared in Monday's early morning edition of the *New York Tribune.*

Obeying an urgent summons from the secretary of war, three political radicals were soon in his office, Congressman George Julian, Senator Zachariah Chandler, and John Conness, senator from Massachusetts. Stanton may have sent for others as well. The reaction in his office was as if a smoking bomb had landed there. Julian recorded the scene in his private journal. When a grim-faced Major Eckert had met him at the door, "I sensed something was amiss." He could not have chosen a truer understatement. "We have Booth's diary," said an obviously shaken secretary, "and he has recorded a lot in it." Chandler thumbed through the little red book, anxiously mumbling. Conness snatched it from him, scanned its pages, and moaned repeatedly, "Oh, my God. I am ruined if this ever gets out."

Julian felt that Conness was in a stew because he had "shared his bed and women" with the actor, an intimacy the diary might have revealed. The Indiana lawmaker himself shrank from it when Stanton proffered it for his study. He had never met Booth and was not named in the diary, so "I was better off not reading it." Stanton said, "It concerns you for we either stick together in this thing or we will all go down the river together." Each man nervously eyed the tell-tale booklet on the secretary's desk until Eckert whisked it away, under Stanton's order to secure it in his iron safe, for "We cannot let it out."

Still more convincing evidence that Booth's diary arrived in Washington three days before the body said to be his could have been found in the Army Medical Museum. Doctor Edward Curtis ran the photomicrographic department, which, in the museum's two years of existence, already housed thousands of photographs of human tissue salvaged from hospitals and battlefields. Five pictures of women found in Booth's diary were taken to the museum, where Curtis's job was to have his hospital stewards make prints of them for mounting on cardboard. A sixth picture, a tintype, vanished.

The three-inch by four-inch glass negatives were soon in NDP possession. Each was marked NDP E.C. 4-24-65. "E.C." were the doctor's initials. The date: April 24, 1865. These plates still exist, with two of the pictures wrongly identified by a visitor at the War Department, and the error perpetuated ever since. The women are Kate Scott and Izola Booth. But the most significant factor is the marginal markings, material proof that Booth's diary was in Washington on April 24, 1865, thanks to the diligence of the Pamunky Indian scout Whippet Nalgai.

CHAPTER 22

Body Snatching and Doctored Documents

Ill organized and meandering, the manhunt for Booth continued. On the Maryland side of the Potomac River, Colonel Henry H. Wells, provost marshal for army defenses south of Washington, had rounded up suspects: Samuel Cox, the Adamses, Thomas Jones, and other secessionists. He might have arrested more, but, he said, "their testimony is so conflicting that I find it impossible to come to any satisfactory conclusion." Reluctance to cooperate was doubtless a factor. But the more likely reason for the colonel's bafflement was that people he interrogated were talking of not one pair of fugitives but two. Officially, the climax to the pursuit of Abraham Lincoln's murderer was at Richard H. Garrett's farm, six miles south of the Rappahannock River. Two men were sheltered and fed by the Garretts, who believed one of them, pensive, a pipe-smoker, and lame, to be a wounded Confederate officer named James W. Boyd. The Garretts, a family of six, were also told that the men were bound for Mexico. On Tuesday night, April 25, a cavalry troop of twenty-six men commanded by Lieutenant Edward P. Doherty and two "special detectives" appointed by Lafayette Baker surrounded Garrett's tobacco barn, where the pair rested, and shouted for them to surrender. During a verbal give-and-take through the locked door, no names were uttered. Soldiers forced the Garretts to unlock it. David Herold emerged, hands raised. His captors insisted that the man inside was the assassin Booth. Herold argued, "He told me his name was Boyd."

Without the cavalry commander's knowledge or approval, Everton Conger, one of Baker's special detectives, stole to the rear of the barn and set it alight. As it burned, someone shot into it and the man inside fell. Soldiers dragged his body from the flames to the Garretts' front porch. No one had seen who fired. At first, Conger said that he thought the man had shot himself. The other detective, Luther Baker, a cousin of the NDP chief, had an immediate impression that the gunman was Conger. The credit finally went to a Sergeant Corbett, who had changed his given name from Thomas to Boston, after the city in which he claimed to have found religion.

Port Royal's resident physician was sent for. He was Charles Urquhart, aged seventy-one, the son of Scots immigrants. After private tutoring, he had studied medicine at the Medical College of Pennsylvania. Settled in Virginia, he was considered prim and portly but a good doctor. While in his fifties, he married a Port Royal girl less than half his age. They had a daughter, Finnella, who would have been about four when soldiers from Garrett's farm pounded on her father's door.

Upon reaching the man shot in Garrett's barn, Urquhart examined his wound and declared it fatal, gave him an hour to live, and rode away. No detailed account of the doctor's actions at the Garretts' ever appeared. If he wrote out a death certificate for John Wilkes Booth, it was never published nor is there one in official archives. Doctor Urquhart made no public or written statement, and he died fifteen months after his extraordinary house call.

Everton Conger rode off with what he had taken from the dying man's pocket. The contents included a small black book in which the Garretts had seen him writing. (Booth's diary is bound in red, its entries ending three days before what the Garretts saw.) Also found with the fugitive was a carbine, two pistols, and a bowie knife. Lieutenant Doherty prepared to leave the Garretts. His party consisted of soldiers, the special detectives, and two prisoners, Herold and the Mosby youth Willie Jett. Luther Baker took charge of the prisoners and the dead fugitive. They crossed the Rappahannock on a flat-bottom scow, nine men and horses at a time.

The morning grew warm. Baker moved on ahead uphill with a buggy, toward a tree-shaded ridge. An anxious Doherty had given him a sergeant as escort and he later described what ensued. "Baker sent the guard back under some pretense or other, with some frivolous message, and stole away with the body." Doherty ordered a search. Ten or twelve hours elapsed before Baker appeared at the Belle Plain landing with his grim burden and the prisoner Herold. He said that he had taken a wrong road and allowed Willie Jett to flee because he had cooperated with his captors. There was some grisly moonshine about a collapsing wagon and the body sliding off "as if in an effort to escape." Lieutenant Doherty sharply reprimanded Baker before the whole bizarre force boarded the waiting steamer *John S. Ide* for Washington.

When the party arrived near Washington before dawn on Thursday, it halted at the Potomac port of Alexandria, where Lafayette Baker took over. He immediately telegraphed Major Thomas Eckert at the War Department of "the assassin"'s capture and death. He asked Eckert to meet him across the river at the Washington Navy Yard. Here, the body was furtively placed on board the two-hundred-foot monitor *Montauk*. The vessel's captain, who happened to be onshore, was not notified. He protested later that what happened was "a most informal and unmilitary procedure which should have been nipped in the bud." Lieutenant Doherty had not suffered the last of his affronts. Upon arrival in Washington, he was met by Lafayette Baker, who told him to go to his barracks and keep his mouth shut. Baker added that he, Doherty, would be in line for reward and promotion.

On what became an unusually warm spring day, thirteen people were permitted to view the body. All but the war photographer Alexander Gardner, his assistant, and a hotel clerk were connected with the War Department. Joseph K. Barnes, army surgeon general, stood in charge. Booth's alleged conspirators were on the ironclad, shackled inside the windlass room. They could have been brought forth to identify the body, but they were not. Booth's fellow actors were in town, but none saw the dead man. Neither did any of his relatives, nor did any of his known friends. A newpaper briefed by the War Department explained, "So changed was the assassin's look that his stage or street acquaintances would hardly have recognized the corpse as that of John Wilkes Booth." Almost to a man, all who viewed the body and were afterward questioned in the pilot house atop the ironclad's turret parroted that they identified it as Booth's body, chiefly from "its general appearance."

As if aware that only believers in fairies and a flat earth could accept the goings-on aboard the USS *Montauk* as genuine identification, Lafayette Baker called personally upon John Frederick May to come to the Navy Yard and identify Booth. A Washington physician who had once operated on the back of the actor's neck to remove a tumor, May "deemed it most prudent to obey." His immediate words upon viewing the body that lay on a carpenter's bench, mercifully shaded by an awning, were "There is no resemblance in that corpse to Booth, nor can I believe it to be him."

Baker and Barnes stood at the doctor's side. May said that his surgery on Booth had left a particular scar. The body was turned over for closer examination. A scar was discovered. May then said that he thought the body was Booth's, although "His appearance is very much altered. . . . looks older . . . more freckled. I do not recall that he was freckled." Pressed for more detail, May spoke again of the scar, also "the features, which though much changed and altered, still have the same appearance. . . . I think I cannot be mistaken."

On the sunbaked monitor, nothing was said of a leg injury. Nothing recorded, that is. In his official autopsy report to Secretary Stanton, the surgeon general described it in some detail. The "left leg and foot were encased in an appliance of splints and bandages, upon the removal of which, a fracture of the fibula (small bone of the leg) three inches above the ankle joint, accompanied by considerable ecchymosis was discovered."

Shortly before his death in 1891, John May wrote a memoir that said that the "right limb was greatly contused, and perfectly black from a fracture of one of the long bones." A confused researcher in the 1920s questioned May's son, also a doctor, concerning the apparent conflict. His reply was that his father was a stickler for detail. If he said that the right leg was bruised and discolored, "that would undoubtedly mean that it was the right leg that was broken."

* * *

The cadaver from Garrett's farm had a proclivity for disappearing acts. The cavalry had lost it en route to the Potomac River, a macabre sleight of hand repeated at the Washington Navy Yard. It was spirited off the *Montauk* for subsequent burial in a storage room of the Washington Arsenal, the city's old penitentiary, under the supervision of Lafayette Baker and Major Eckert.

The Navy Yard's commandant was incensed. "The removal of the body was entirely without my knowledge, an unusual transaction." And the *Montauk*'s captain stated that the body's stealthy departure from his vessel was as improper as its arrival on board. He officially regretted that "I was not present at either time or I should have put a stop to it." A War Department detective accompanied Gardner into the darkroom, following orders to remain with him until he had developed a picture. Then the detective, as ordered, took the plate and a single print from it to Lafayette Baker's headquarters. On the way he stole a glance into the envelope. The photo looked not unlike the Booth he had seen on reward posters, except that the hair was longer and the mustache "ragged and dirty." The detective was unaware that the assassin had shaved off his mustache. After the picture was delivered, it disappeared.

Why all this apparent subterfuge? Asked this question forty years later, when he was a veteran executive in commercial telegraphy, Eckert had only a cryptic response: "No explanation on my part need be made at this late date. The exigencies of the case required quick action."

Two other dead bodies had been brought into Washington that Wednesday, in the belief that each was Booth's. Doctor Joseph J. Woodward had conducted an autopsy on one. A future pathologist and a pioneer in photomicrography, Woodward was assistant to Surgeon General Barnes on the *Montauk*. Barnes had removed the cervical vertebrae and the spinal cord from the dead man's neck. Woodward carried these specimens to the Army Medical Museum, where they were added to its collection. Aware that at least two bodies had arrived in Washington, each thought to be Booth's, Woodward slumped into a chair, buried his head in his hands, and, as if wondering when the ghastly comic opera would cease, he muttered, "How many more will there be?"

That same night, after at least three "Booth" bodies had been disposed of, the warm night when doctors shivered and printing presses labored on words to describe what the War Department had said were the assassin's last hours, Thomas Caldwell got off the train from New York with papers bearing Abraham Lincoln's signature. Caldwell was the Water Street operator who had signed the Bloodsworth Island "special cargo" shipping instructions. Not that Caldwell needed to feel apprehensive on that account. John Wilkes Booth was reported dead. What he might have told of a connection between cotton speculators and a plot to abduct the president had presumably died with him.

Though events had reshaped the commercial deal as composed in Montreal, it could still go through with maximum profit. Caldwell took a room at Willard's and the next morning walked around the corner to the Treasury Building for a private meeting with Hanson Risley. Along Pennsylvania Avenue, newspapers spread officialdom's account of how retribution, as managed by Colonel Lafayette Baker, had overtaken President Lincoln's assassin. Caldwell had brought R. D. Watson's cotton papers for necessary revision. Lincoln had endorsed their content and signed a permit for safe delivery of thirty thousand bales to Treasury agents in Nashville, Memphis, and New Orleans. That had been in January. Lincoln had since been slain, but his signatures remained intact: The papers must be altered. This was Hanson Risley's job. He would have to replace Watson's name on the documents with "Henry J. Eager" and change the delivery locations to Georgia. As if to further legitimize the process, Caldwell had also brought from New York a letter written by John McGinnis, one of the "Henry J. Eager" trio, containing the statement "This [presidential] permit was obtained for us by the Hon. Ward H. Lamon."

As the man from Water Street and the Treasury official Risley knew, "Henry J. Eager" was a fictitious name to cover a partnership formally registered five days after the president's murder. The January 11 "memorandum of agreement" between the contracting parties, the contracts themselves of that date, and the executive permits for safe passage, all necessary for the shipment of cotton from Southern territory through the blockade or the military line, were made out not to Henry J. Eager but to R. D. Watson Co.

Some slick paperwork in the Treasury Building that morning was required to change the date of delivery and the delivery locations so that the Georgia cotton could be more conveniently secured. But the Treasury official and his clerk got busy with neither delay nor compunction. First they amended the memorandum of agreement, retaining the same January date, to show that Henry J. Eager, not Watson, had pledged the cotton. In addition, the name of the original party, R. D. Watson, had been written twice on each of the three permits signed by Abraham Lincoln, but, again, no scruples slowed the action. Some vigorous abrasions with a scraper—and a total of nine spaces was provided for the new firm's name. (Little more than a century later, under National Archives auspices and using special chemical application, we restored to view the original "R. D. Watson" on each document. The documents can be seen at the National Archives with no sign to the naked eye of R. D. Watson's name.)

Stage-managed by Edwin Stanton, the trial of Booth's alleged co-conspirators began in May before a military commission, conducted by Judge Advocate General Joseph Holt. The accused were Doctor Mudd, Arnold, Payne, Herold, O'Laughlen, George Atzerodt, Mary Surratt, and Edward Spangler, the Ford Theatre's scene shifter. Although on Stanton's original list, John Celestina was not among them. The hearing took place in a makeshift courtroom on the third floor of the Washington Arsenal—not far from the *Montauk* body's unmarked grave.

Testimony, much of it perjured, focused largely on an alleged rebel assassination plan hatched in Richmond and plotted in Canada. The all-military court revealed little, if anything, of Booth's itinerary between the halt at Doctor Mudd's in Maryland and the crossing of the Rappahannock in Virginia. Nothing on record accounted for that significant span of fifty miles, save half a dozen affidavits composed under the guns and glare of Lafayette C. Baker. Lieutenant Doherty, already silenced by Baker when he brought the body from Garrett's farm, was refused admission of his testimony until he sharply reminded the court that he had been in charge of the military detachment.

A puzzled newsman covering the trial wrote of "an unrelated interval . . . a whole week unaccounted for." Benn Pitman, the stenographer given the task of compiling and editing the proceedings for publication, thought the forensic leap of eight days and so much distance mighty strange. From the Phonographic Institute in Cincinnati, he wrote to the War Department, wondering why "the testimony relates to Booth and Herold at Dr. Mudd's on the 15th and at the ferry on the Rappahannock on the 24th and contains no word relating to the flight of the conscience-stricken fugitives in the interval."

As the trial of the luckless eight dragged on into midsummer, others were released in bunches. Prison gates opened for the Garretts, whose slain visitor they had known as Captain Boyd; for Doctor Stuart; and for the Mosby men on the scene at Port Royal. Farmers who had fed Booth in Maryland were freed. But an ex-slave named James Owen, whose busy tongue had led to several arrests, as well as to his own, never emerged from the Old Capitol Prison alive. As those he had betrayed marched out of their cells, Owen abruptly died. Records on the cause of death are blank.

The defense of Doctor Samuel Mudd, one of the accused, was written for him by Orville H. Browning, one of the old friends of Lincoln who had so industriously used that friendship to advance business schemes designed, in his own words, to "make us rich." Browning had already helped to keep the names of Ben Ficklin and other cotton profiteers free of scandal, but he might have felt a qualm when R. D. Watson's name arose. The prosecuting judge, Joseph Holt, confronted Louis Weichmann with the letter Watson had written to John Surratt from Water Street a month before the assassination. Mary Surratt's talkative young lodger claimed to know Booth's handwriting. Was this letter written by him? Weichmann answered no.

Nothing more was said of that letter. R. D. Watson's name had come and gone, presumably as erased from the minds of the ten military men who comprised the court as it was from the cotton papers that, as the trial in Washington neared its conclusion, served to expedite the flow of bales from the interior of Georgia to Savannah's waterfront.

The other Browning, William, testified briefly. Booth's calling card left in his box at the Kirkwood? He had known the actor hardly more than a year and assumed that Booth merely wanted to pay a social call. The court accepted Browning's testimony, also conceding the possibility that the card was meant for Andrew Johnson and was placed in Browning's box in error. But these were nervous hours for Johnson's private secretary, and he probably appreciated the invitation that Lola Alexander had just sent him. Lola's husband had left New York for a distant government post that she had secured for him by lobbying among Washington's influential, the new president included. Really, Browning ought to come up, she pressed. New York was bright, Central Park abloom, and she had a parlor and bedroom at his disposal.

The military tribunal reached its verdict behind closed doors on Friday, June 30, the beginning of a weekend when President Johnson, Secretary Stanton, and Will Browning were reported "indisposed." All eight were found guilty: prison terms for four, including Doctor Mudd, and the gallows for David Herold, George Atzerodt, Lewis Payne, and Mary Surratt. The execution was set for July 7, 1865. But not until the last minute would the condemned be told of their fate. Neither were their counsels immediately notified of the sentences, certainly not of Mary Surratt's. All expected that she would be acquitted or, at most, sent to jail. No woman had yet been hanged in the United States. One of Mary's lawyers, John Clampitt, heard the news at five o'clock on the evening of July 6, through a newsboy's shouts. Astonished and angry, he hurried to the White House with Anna Surratt, who begged to see the president. They were turned away. Andrew Johnson had issued strict orders that he was not to be disturbed. Clampitt and Anna raced to Judge Advocate General

Joseph Holt's office, Anna pleading for at least a stay of execution. Holt was unable to do more than tell them that "the president has examined the commission's findings and sees no reason to change the date of execution."

A senior member of the defense team advised Clampitt to secure a writ of habeas corpus so that Mary could be released from military custody. Controversy still existed whether, the country now at peace, a military commission should have been assigned to conduct a trial of civilians. This and other points were made in the application for a writ. It took well after midnight to prepare. At two in the morning Clampitt rang Judge Andrew Wylie's doorbell. Wylie was a member of the District of Columbia Supreme Court. At four o'clock he sent a marshal to serve a writ of habeas corpus on Major General Winfield Scott Hancock, whose task was to complete the executions by two o'clock in the afternoon. Already the scaffold was erected and four graves dug, on the grounds of the old penitentiary, not far from the courtroom in which the condemned had been tried and from the undisclosed burial place of the man identified as their leading conspirator.

Along the manhunt trail from Washington to Garrett's farm, not one person, including the guard at the Navy Yard Bridge, Doctor Mudd, and Samuel Cox, had positively identified Herold as the assassin's companion, yet this, too, counted for nothing. The youth who had attended Georgetown to study the humanities was described as putty in the hands of a monster by his counsel Frederick Stone. Booth had forced him to act as guide. "This accounts for their companionship." And Atzerodt? A confession that his only involvement concerned abduction failed to save that pitiable figure.

The Reverend George Powell of Live Oak, Florida, uncertain whether the condemned "Payne" was his son, set out north, only to turn back sadly when convinced that he could not possibly reach Washington before the executions. Persistent doubts compelled the clergyman's family to send a daguerreotype of their soldier son to the War Department. No one there admitted to receiving it. But a photo of Lewis Powell, late of Mosby's Rangers and, before that, the 2nd Florida Infantry, lodged undisturbed in NDP files. It bore little resemblance to Lewis Payne.

The final word came from the White House. The president had overruled the writ of habeas corpus and had refused a recommendation for mercy. The afternoon had grown hot; a chair was provided for Mary Surratt. Except for the sound of a blow as soldiers knocked away the pin from beneath the trap and the continued echoes of Anna Surratt's sobs, the four were hanged in silence on Tuesday, July 7, 1865.

Watson's name had come briefly before Stanton's military court because of his letter to the still-missing agent John Surratt, who was not informed of his mother's execution until after it had been carried out. He had been hiding in Canada since early April, sheltered by Catholic priests. Surratt would later flee to Europe, giving his name as "Watson," and would finally be traced in the improbable role of a member of the Papal Guard in Rome. The United States government did not return him to face trial as Booth's accomplice until its apparent reluctance to do so excited international curiosity. In Washington, the jury weighing his fate failed to agree. Surratt was set loose. Except for a controversial lecture and a couple of vague newspaper interviews, he thereafter led a quiet life, stubbornly close-mouthed as to his past and employed as freight auditor for a Baltimore steam packet company.

John Celestina had been incarcerated throughout the period of the conspiracy trial. He was freed the day after the four hangings, upon condition that he leave the country within ten days. Through a New York attorney who called his case a "peculiar one," Celestina petitioned the government for compensation payable out of "secret service funds." Then, paid or not, Celestina disappeared, settling under an alias near New Orleans as a wealthy plantation owner.

Will Browning was denied the opportunity to reveal any of his secrets. He fell ill early in 1866, shortly after President Johnson nominated him for an American legation post in Mexico. For some days he was an ailing guest at Lola Alexander's home in New York, where she had two invalids on her hands, frail health having forced her husband to quit his federal post. Browning died upon returning to Washington. He was thirty-one.

The profiteers in whose scheming he had taken such an active role? Nothing in Hanson Risley's office that Friday, April 28, had identified Chief Detective Lafayette Baker as "Henry J. Eager." But the deal went ahead. Joseph N. Kein, a New York cotton broker with ties to the South, was briefly in the picture. His job, once the papers altered in Risley's office were back at Water Street, was to carry out a plan that James V. Barnes devised, ensuring safe shipment of Georgia's cotton for the Anglo-American merchant bankers, the "Henry Stewart" company, and other profiteers Barnes had so indefatigably served.

Thousands of bales were coming into Savannah from the Georgia hinterland by wagon teams, flatbottom boats, barges, and a war-damaged railroad undergoing hasty repair. "The war was over, we had to move fast," Barnes would recall. Throughout the recent days of fluctuating emotions for North and South alike, Barnes had kept strictly to business. "No sooner was the president dead than we got passes to go south."

The passes were secured for Barnes's employers by the dead president's old friend Orville H. Browning. Barnes had meanwhile arranged for the printing of 200,000 labels displaying the British flag. With a safe conduct pass and Barnes's labels stored in cartons, Kein had disembarked from the steamer *Fulton* at Savannah and at once began attaching labels to every bale of cotton within reach. "No one questioned our authority. We got [the cotton] out as fast as we could find transport. It was all consigned to the firm Brown and Shipley, Liverpool." Kein also recalled making the labels look still more authentic by countersigning them with fictitious names.

In later years Barnes told a National Detective Police investigator, "The bankers? They fared quite well. Some of the cotton was destroyed but most went out all right. About £250 million [sterling] worth before the bottom dropped out of the market."

CHAPTER 23

Web of Secrecy

On July 28, 1866, this exchange took place in the United States Senate:

> Senator Garrett Davis, KY: I have never seen myself any satisfactory evidence that Booth was killed.
>
> Senator Reverdy Johnson, MD: I submit to my friend from Kentucky that there are some things that we must take judicial notice of, just as well as that Julius Caesar is dead.
>
> Senator Davis: I would rather have better testimony of the fact. I want it proved that Booth was in that barn. I cannot conceive, if he was in the barn, why he was not taken alive. I have never seen anybody, or the evidence of anybody, that identified Booth after he is said to have been killed. Why so much secrecy about it? . . . There is a mystery and a most inexplicable mystery to my mind about the whole affair. . . . [Booth] could have been captured just as well alive as dead. It would have been much more satisfactory to have brought him up here alive and to have inquired of him to reveal the whole transaction . . . [or] bring his body up here . . . let all who had seen him playing, all who associated with him on the stage or in the green room or at the taverns and other public places, have had access to his body to have identified it.
>
> Senator Herbert B. Anthony, RI: I am happy to relieve my friend from Kentucky by informing him that a small part of the skeleton of Booth is in the anatomical museum of the Surgeon General.
>
> Senator Johnson: Who knows that?
>
> Senator Anthony: I do not know how it is identified, but it is certified to be that.

There was, in fact, widespread reluctance to accept what the government had put out about the fate of Lincoln's murderer, and it did nothing for officialdom's credibility that the contents of Booth's diary, by then known to be in War Department custody, were still withheld from the public. The first newspaper reports of Booth's possible escape placed him in Canada, then in Mexico by way of the Bahamas. In 1867 more persistent and persuasive accounts had him in Ceylon, the purport being that he arrived there from California, stopping on his transpacific passage at the Sandwich and Caroline Islands.

History provides no parallel for the enduring and ramifying pattern of concealment spun from the crime at Ford's Theatre. What had to be well and truly hidden were a planned political coup requiring Lincoln's physical abduction and the involvement or furtive endorsement of bankers, businessmen, military officers, newspaper chiefs, and even some of the victim's own friends and hangers-on; the names of those in political and war-profiteering circles wherein John Wilkes Booth significantly moved; the role played by the seductive Harriet "Lola" Alexander, whose words had tightened Booth's finger on the trigger; and the true identity of the man cornered, shot, and buried in the assassin's name. Captain James Boyd's children never saw their father again. They were told—unofficially, as far as can be discovered—that he was among the almost two thousand Union veterans who perished when the steamboat *Sultana* sank ten days after Lincoln's murder.

All that could be learned from a single interview given by Harriet Alexander, under assurance of confidentiality, was that she had posed as being one of King Leopold's illegitimate daughters and had written to Booth as "Lola." She also disclosed that friends in high places had protected her from exposure after Lincoln's death. Harriet died at her New York home on Fifth Avenue in May 1905. Three months later her body was transported to South Bend, Indiana, for interment in the Schuyler Colfax family plot.

Kate Scott, another of Booth's lovers, was awarded a lifetime pension by special act of Congress for her service as an army nurse. She had served for four months. She was carrying Booth's unborn child when, three months after his reported death at Garrett's farm, she received a letter "in handwriting unmistakably his," directing her to collect a certain package from an address in nearby Meadville and have it waiting for him by September. Kate followed his instructions. On the appointed date, her ghostly lover appeared, limping slightly and without a mustache. Kate Scott was to relate all of this in a sworn affidavit, while enjoying respectable prominence as a local historian and national secretary of the Association of Army Nurses of the Civil War. "[Booth] told me that he had made arrangements to go to India where he could live in peace, that he had ample funds in the Bank of England." He remained with her for a week and then was gone.

Less than a year after the trial of John Surratt, President Andrew Johnson was charged with "high crimes and misdemeanors." The impeachment hearing hinged primarily on constitutional issues, triggered by Johnson's attempt to remove Stanton from the War Department. Political ultras hunted for evidence of a criminal liaison between Johnson and John Wilkes Booth. To this end, they mounted the first and only congressional inquiry into Abraham Lincoln's assassination. The five-man panel, headed by Congressman Benjamin Butler of Massachusetts, leaked some of its anti-Johnson findings to the press. But there also appeared a reference to abduction plots known in advance to "a large class [of] . . . prominent persons," in effect "accomplices," and among them "was a John Celestina." Nothing else emerged from American history's first "assassination committee." It issued no report and before the end of 1867 went out of business.

Meanwhile, Booth's leatherbound little diary had become a matter of public knowledge. Some of its pages, everyone soon knew, had been knifed or scissored out. Stanton, in testimony before the House of Representatives' Judiciary Committee during its impeachment hearings, could not recall the date when he had first seen it. But he had since, on occasion, "examined it with great care, read over all the entries, and noticed that leaves had been cut or torn from it." Judge Holt swore that when Major Thomas Eckert, the diary's appointed custodian, gave it to him for possible use in the 1865 assassination conspiracy trial, the sheets were missing. The diary was not introduced at that trial. Holt's appearance before the Impeachment Committee was followed by that of Eckert, who was at that time a director of the Western Union Telegraph Company. In Eckert's prepared statement, he noted that when the diary first arrived, "The Secretary of War remarked on the absence of leaves and that care had been taken by Booth to destroy his records. I noticed also that a portion of the book was gone."

Then Lafayette Baker swept back on the scene. He had been out of sight since his expulsion from government employ after the affray with President Johnson over his practice of stationing spies on the White House grounds. His testimony before the Judiciary Committee made some of his listeners jump. When he had handed that diary over to Stanton, he said, the book was intact, with no pages gone. Colonel Conger, Baker's own handpicked detective at Garrett's farm, was brought in to contradict his old chief by swearing that when the diary was taken off "Booth," some pages were indeed missing. Luther Baker, the former chief detective's cousin, followed the same line. Lafayette Baker was later recalled and given a chance to recant. His responses this time were less assured, to the point of vagueness, but they did not amount to any clear departure from his earlier assertion that since he had last seen Booth's diary at the War Department in 1865, someone had sliced out dozens of its pages.

Two nights before Christmas 1867, someone stabbed Lafayette Baker as he stood outside his home at 1739 Coates Street, Philadelphia. The attacker fled. That same festive week, bullets flew at Baker's carriage as he took a ride. Early in 1868 he fought off an attempt to kidnap him. After being shot at again, he told a servant that they would get him yet, and when asked who "they" were, he replied, "My old friends."

"Old friends" included, Lafayette Baker's enemies were legion. The main army consisted of potential vengeance-seekers, hundreds jailed for disloyalty on Baker's command during the war. He had invited more trouble by his suicidal stand on the matter of the missing pages from Booth's diary. Also, he had lost heavily through disastrous investments of his own money, which included the $3,750 reward money for Booth's capture (Everton Conger got the lion's share of $15,000) and of Jennie Baker's inherited wealth. His endeavors to recoup were perceived by his partners in the now-dormant Henry J. Eager Company as tactics of fraud.

Early in the year, Baker was visited by Walter G. Pollock, a former NDP agent. There were other connections. Raised in childhood at R. D. Watson's home, Pollock had married Baker's sister-in-law. Pollock brought oysters and imported beer, and one January evening he and the Bakers dined at a rathskeller in Germantown. Baker was sick the next morning, and his doctor diagnosed ptomaine poisoning.

Walter Pollock called again. And again. And a comparison of medical reports with entries in Jennie Baker's private journal reveals that her husband's gastric upsets occurred whenever Pollock arrived with beer and oysters. By the onset of summer, Baker's physician suspected arsenic poisoning and prescribed an elixir. Thus precariously sustained, Baker had begun the task of framing in code and cipher his sensational intelligence. He feared that "professionals" were out to get him and at times suspected everybody, including his wife—whose proximity to Pollock, whether known to Baker, kindled Jennie's lust. But her diary, frank in its disclosure of Pollock's amorous attraction, would give no cause to assume that cuckoldry had blossomed into a murder pact. She seemed resigned to the death of her "Lafe," at least from the evening on which, reading the cards, as was her habit, she drew the ace of spades.

Baker would not, however, die a pauper. Briefly in early spring Pollock stayed clear of him, Baker apparently thriving on his absence. He went to New York and called on Richard Demill. Details of the deal he cut would remain obscure, but the result for Baker was a windfall of about $400,000—money from cotton sales that was supposed to have been split five ways within the "Henry J. Eager Company." Thus enriched, Baker returned to Coates Street. Shortly thereafter, so did Walter G. Pollock, with more oysters and imported beer, and when Jennie Baker, within forty-eight hours of Pollock's latest visit, wrote in her diary, "My love is dying—poor dear," she was not referring to her sinister seducer.

Yet Baker was not so easily disposed of. He hung on into June, when his wife wrote, "Lafe is changing his will so that someone else will get his papers and personal possessions." A neighborhood friend and former NDP cipher clerk, who paid a visit at the end of the month, found him with a stack of books at his bedside. He was "making marks in one, a cipher but a different cipher than I had ever seen." Baker gave him one of the books to take home. "It was an English military title." This, too, had cipher penned in it.

The next day, Baker suffered a relapse. His physician, William M. L. Rickards, rushed to Coates Street and found Baker suffering violent headaches, with an increasing paralysis, symptoms the doctor diagnosed as of meningitis. He relieved Baker's distress briefly by cupping and leeching along his patient's spine. But the leeches quickly died, and shortly after midnight, July 3, so did Baker, in fits of tremendous shuddering.

Many of the events during Lafayette Baker's final hours were recorded in court proceedings held October 14, 1872, to determine the legality of an unprobated codicil to his will. Conflict had flared between rival claimants to the sudden fortune he had left. Andrew Potter attended the hearing. Potter was one of Baker's early and most dogged proteges, and even in post–Civil War years the contemporary definition of a detective as "one whose occupation is to discover matters artfully concealed" fit Potter like a glove. As an official government bureau, the National Detective Police no longer existed, but "we had merely changed hats and badges. Almost without exception we went to work for the United States Detective Service, a private agency controlled by God knows who." Potter's latest task was at least a quasifederal assignment, inasmuch as it was authorized, albeit discreetly, by none other than President Ulysses S. Grant.

What led to it was the discovery in a War Department basement of a trunk full of papers left there for safekeeping by Colonel Levi C. Turner. He had been Judge Holt's second in command, army judge advocate, with wartime duties that often overlapped Baker's. After Turner's death in March 1867, those papers had escaped a formal inventory of his files and records, some of which centered on frauds and subversion. They included a fourteen-page memorandum that summarized Turner's conclusions about business affairs that he deemed scandalously improper. The memorandum, which soon vanished, was also supposed to have said that the parties involved would stop at nothing to keep their secrets safe, and that this ruthlessness might explain the premature death of William A. Browning.

Levi Turner died the year after Browning, from "apoplexy supervening typho-malarial fever." Since then, Lafayette Baker had died. For that matter, so had Edwin Stanton, on Christmas Eve 1869, within a week of his nomination by President Grant to a seat on the United States Supreme Court. An investigation was launched to ascertain whether any of these deaths were from other than natural causes, and to his old comrade-in-arms Lew Wallace, Grant gave nominal command of the probe. All of this was done behind the scenes. Surviving evidence that some such investigation was under way during the 1870s is too persuasive to dismiss.

Wallace was its "special judge advocate." He sat on the military court that tried the assassination "conspirators," whiling away the hours of testimony in sketching them. Wallace had also begun writing novels and was working on *The Fair God*. As well, he was now engaged in the practice of law in his native Indiana. A staunch Republican, he was, in 1872, actively seeking political office.

So, most of the field work was directed by the brothers Luther and Andrew Potter. Their team of "government detectives," five agents wearing imposing badges and eight phonographers busy with shorthand notebooks, logged more than two hundred interviews over a four-year period. Potter and his colleagues may have felt at times as if engaged in a chilling race against time, for even as they rode the trains to and from places as far apart as Rome, Georgia, and Escanaba, Michigan, death removed one potentially valuable witness after another.

Following an interview with John Surratt, unproductive because of a "holy vow" of silence he claimed to have made in exchange for his life, next on the detectives' calling schedule might have been Henri B. de Sainte-Marie, who had betrayed Surratt to superiors while both served in the Papal Guard. Sainte-Marie was living in Philadelphia, awaiting a claims court decision on his demand for more than double the $10,000 that the United States government had reluctantly agreed to pay for his informing on Surratt. He died suddenly in the street, aged forty-one.

Benjamin Ficklin was already difficult to reach, having resettled in the Far West to manage the San Antonio and El Paso mail line. Then it was too late, for on one of his infrequent visits East, he died in Washington—as a result, it was said, of a fish bone lodged in his throat.

From commercial agents, the detectives were briefed on the great cotton-for-pork deal, the artful combines of "Henry Stewart" and "Henry J. Eager." They got information about what had gone on at 178½ Water Street. An account of how the Savannah cotton was carried off under British insignia "flabbergasted" Andrew Potter, but he recovered to go after R. D. Watson in Kentucky. He returned East for a New York meeting at the Astor House with James V. Barnes, who needed little prompting to disclose how radical politicians of the North had collaborated with the business combine that Barnes had represented, to have Abraham Lincoln bundled out of office. Inevitably, the detectives' trail led to the Doylestown, Pennsylvania, home of Walter Grant Pollock, whose mother was the president's second cousin. On March 21, 1876, Pollock admitted to his visitors that not only had he been present when Lafayette Baker died, but that he was on the premises at the deaths of both William A. Browning and Levi Turner. Yet the circumstances in each case, he pleaded, were so painful a memory that he could not discuss them. Yes, he had studied pharmacy and had worked as a druggist before joining the National Detective Police. No, he was not a member of any conspiracy to poison anybody, and if they had any evidence that said otherwise, they had better turn it over to a grand jury. The detectives snapped back that they would, and when they accused him of feigning grief to avoid questions, Pollock drove them out.

The investigation records were assembled and studied in Lew Wallace's carriagehouse at his Crawfordsville, Indiana, home. The probers decided that only in the case of Baker's death were there sufficient grounds for murder indictments, and they recommended five, naming Pollock, James V. Barnes, John McGinnis, R. D. Watson, and his brother-in-law Doctor Henry Megill, of Owensboro, Kentucky. Baker, the Potters deduced, was murdered for having swindled those businessmen whose enterprise he had blackmailed himself into in the hours immediately following Lincoln's murder.

Of the five, Barnes might be treated lightly—he had volunteered much information about the profiteering schemes and their connection with plots against Lincoln and had pledged further cooperation in exchange for immunity and reward money.

Matters went no further. In a covering letter to the report and its recommendation for indictments, Lew Wallace advised Grant that since Barnes, then drinking heavily, might prove "a weak or recalcitrant witness," convictions were uncertain. Moreover, the accused were sufficiently wealthy and influential to hire first-rate lawyers. And if failure to convict would have "staggering political implications," conviction might be just as undesirable, for who could tell "what direction the testimony might take and just what previously undisclosed secrets might be dislodged by an astute defense?" It was best that the matter be dropped, "the report be sequestered." Grant agreed. He was a weary chief executive, ending two scandal-haunted administrations. On February 12, 1877, forty-eight hours after Andrew Potter arrived in Washington with his report and Wallace's covering letter, the White House announced that the president was packing and could see no visitors until further notice. Fully a week passed before Andrew Potter managed to lay the papers on the president's desk. They were received without enthusiasm, the detective would recall. He had come to conclude that for all the justice likely to result from his efforts to get at the truth, he might as well never have set up a single interview.

Barnes attempted a comeback in the business world. It failed, and he led a nomadic existence until his death in 1918. John McGinnis used a warm relationship that his wife, Lydia, had developed with Andrew Johnson during the latter's presidency to try and secure an overseas diplomatic post. He was unsuccessful but eventually ran a brokerage firm in New York City, with clients that included Robert T. Lincoln, the late president's son. Roswell Goodell—like McGinnis, once a partner of Lafayette Baker in his Henry J. Eager Company—settled in Colorado and achieved eminence in Denver banking society and Democratic politics. Hanson Risley also relocated to Colorado, as did Ward H. Lamon.

The Watson Provision Company dissolved in Watson's lifetime, but, as maps still show, local features of that tongue of terrain formed by the Mississippi River as it loops northwest into Missouri carry the Watson name.

As for Walter Pollock, little is known of his last years. Where and when he died are not known. He seems to have fit the character of a hit man. The detective Andrew Potter did not think that Baker's death had anything to do with Pollock's designs on Jennie Baker. "Pollock never mixed business with pleasure. Had it been called for by his employers, Pollock would probably have given Jennie arsenic, too."

CHAPTER 24

The Searchers

Amid the prevalence of stories alleging that the man shot at Garrett's farm was not Lincoln's killer, what brought relief to many, by appearing to settle things, was the well-publicized transfer of the body in 1869 from the old penitentiary grounds in Washington to the custody of the Booth family.

While Edwin McMasters Stanton ruled at the War Department, pleas to the government from Edwin Booth "on behalf of my broken-hearted mother" had gone unanswered. Not until Andrew Johnson's turn came for leaving office was consent finally given, as Edwin worded it, "to lessen the crushing weight of grief that is hurrying mother to her grave." When the remains arrived in Baltimore for interment in the family plot, they were removed from their plain deal box to a more elegant casket. According to the *Baltimore American,* all that could be seen was "a mass of blackened bones." Not surprisingly, as almost four years had elapsed since the time of death, no one admitted to the ill-lit undertaker's parlor could precisely recall that any of Booth's physical features were recognizable among the skeletal fragments finally coffined for Christian burial.

At about the same time as that somber event, but without equal publicity, the settlement of a court case, *Simonds v. Allegheny Valley Railroad Company,* in western Pennsylvania indicated that John Wilkes Booth might still be alive. It had to do with the company's construction of tracks across land that the actor, with Joseph Simonds and John A. Ellsler, had purchased five years earlier in hopes of realizing a fortune from oil. Simonds filed the suit as trustee for himself, Ellsler, and J. W. Booth. The case was decided in favor of the plaintiffs and duly recorded, without the slightest notation that Booth was deceased or Simonds acting for an estate.

In a letter to Richard Demill, dated October 12, 1870, "John B. Wilkes of Poona (Birdi), India," desired that monies held in trust for him be deposited in certain Canadian or American banks in the name of Elizabeth Burnley Wilkes, a British widow with whom "Wilkes" lived. The rest of the missive read:

> Justification for these actions is provided by this letter and other identification. . . . When these transactions are completed please let me know. . . . Banks which are solid and friendly should be used as we will want to transfer these funds out of the country. . . . Once the money is in Canada or England we can draw from it. . . . One bank which should receive a healthy sum is the Bank of Montreal as they have been quite helpful. The interest which has occurred should cover your cost but if you have added costs we will reimburse you. However, you have already received half the accrued interest and I do not anticipate further charges.

Demill knew what Wilkes was writing about. And undoubtedly, he spotted his "other identification" mentioned in the letter's first sentence, by using the same acrostic method that R. D. Watson's condemned brother had employed when he conveyed John Surratt's name. The initials to seven consecutive sentences in the letter from Poona spell the name of the man who murdered Abraham Lincoln.

Booth's Pennsylvania paramour, Kate Scott, had a brother-in-law, Frank A. Weaver. He was a politician and the editor of the *Brookville Republican,* and in 1870 he, too, had received a letter from John B. Wilkes of India. Wilkes wanted him to recover a wax-sealed, oilskin-wrapped package left behind in the Shenandoah Valley of Virginia, in a cave known locally as the Bear Hole. "Prior to going there, contact a Mr. Lewis Pence of Rockingham County. He knows the cave." The contents of the package had to do with claims of property in the United States. "I plan to be in Philadelphia in a year or so and it is essential that these documents be in my possession."

Pence was a farmer who had aided Confederate partisans in the Shenandoah Valley after Union soldiers slew his twelve-year-old son. And Pence always believed that one of three men he had guided along the trail from Rockingham County to Harper's Ferry in May 1865 was John Wilkes Booth. Weaver wrote to Pence, who replied that he would gladly find the cave when spring came. "I remember the man what was here in 1865 and can keep my own counsel." Pence did as he was asked and was well paid. But letters of gratitude he received from India became a source of anxiety in his old age, and he showed them to a lawyer friend named Henry Showalter, who at once advised him to destroy them. "If it was known that anyone in your family helped the assassinator of President Lincoln, it would not go good with you even at this late date. His full name was John Byron Wilkes Booth. He used the stage name of John B. Wilkes."

As promised in his letter to Weaver, John B. Wilkes was not long afterward in the United States, trying to effect the release of impounded funds. One day in 1873 he stepped into Groom's Carte de Visite and Photograph Gallery on Second Street, Philadelphia (a business that began after the date when "Booth" was shot at Garrett's farm), and had his picture taken: Negative No. 1292. In 1971, Doctor Lawrence Angell, the Smithsonian Institution's curator of physical anthropology and renowned in his field, compared this picture with known photographs of John Wilkes Booth. His verdict: The likenesses are "sufficiently similar . . . to allow the possibility that they are all pictures of one man, taken at different times of his life. . . . details of ear formation (strong antihelix), of the right eyebrow, and of the chin, appear very similar."

During the nineteenth century's last decades, efforts were made to ascertain whether the mysterious John Byron Wilkes of India was in fact John Byron Wilkes Booth, actor and assassin. One who wished to find out was William McKee Dunn, lawyer, educator, and U.S. congressman from Indiana, who succeeded Joseph Holt as judge advocate general of the army and served in two Republican administrations before retiring in early 1881. Dunn's curiosity was stimulated by the assortment of Lincoln-Booth relics and documents gathered within his office when, under Judge Holt's control, it was designated "Bureau of Military Justice." As judge advocate general, Dunn gave custody of this material to a fellow Indianian, John Simonton, who discharged this duty for forty years. Simonton appears to have talked of it too openly and placed his job at risk.

Upon retirement, Dunn moved to Virginia and began his memoirs. When ill health overtook him, he yielded the task to someone half his age, William Wood Parsons, who was—as Dunn had been before entering government service—a noted Indiana educator. At the time when Dunn engaged him, Parsons headed the Department of History and Economics at Indiana State Normal School (later Indiana State University). Within a year, he had some forty boxes of the judge's papers shipped to Terre Haute for study and organization. He was also soon in touch with Andrew Potter, not a native of Indiana but living in that state. The professor and the ex-detective pooled some, but by no means all, of their sensitive knowledge concerning Lincoln's murder and the true fate of his assassin. "I soon learned," Parsons was to write, "that it was an accepted fact among a group of people [McKee Dunn included] that Booth had escaped, to wind up in India as John B. Wilkes." Parsons learned a lot more that he could never publicly reveal. He was himself a strand in the quilt of secrecy.

There lived in Terre Haute one John Wilkes, who had emigrated from England in 1850 and worked throughout his adult life at the Eagle Iron Foundry in that city. John Wilkes Booth had stayed with the Wilkeses of Terre Haute at least once while on tour, and in those same pre-assassination years, the Wilkeses were also friendly with Harriet "Lola" Alexander, then living in South Bend. Her photo, found in Booth's room after the assassination, had been taken in a Terre Haute studio where John Wilkes was also photographed. Professor Parsons was uniquely placed to learn much of what it all meant, for he had married Wilkes's daughter Sarah. And it is beyond question that William Wood Parsons, historian and eventually college president, prominent banker, and founder of the Terre Haute Trust Company, knew long before his death in 1925 the astonishing truth about his wife's family.

Parsons guardedly collaborated with Andrew Potter in piecing together the itinerary of John Wilkes Booth during the first months when the world believed the assassin dead. After his final meeting with Kate Scott in Pennsylvania and some business in Canada, giving power of attorney to Joseph Simonds, his agent in the oil holding, Booth had left for the Bahamas and thence to Central America.

Parsons and Potter figured that there was a connection here with Harriet Alexander.

In December 1865 Harriet embarked on a voyage to the Caribbean. Ships' passenger lists affirm as much. The ever-probing Andrew Potter discovered that shortly before her departure, Harriet had drawn funds from a Baltimore bank. He was convinced that "she took money to Booth, who by then had assumed a new identity and was headed for California."

What was Booth's "new identity"? In the fall of 1886 Potter was summoned to Crawfordsville, where Lew Wallace asked him to find out if a John B. Wilkes, reported to have died in India three years earlier, might have been Lincoln's assassin. Wallace showed him letters from "Elizabeth Burnley Wilkes" of India to Grant, pleading with the former president to obtain the release of assets allegedly frozen under federal government orders at the close of the Civil War. Grant had met the lady in India during his celebrated journey around the world in 1877.

Other material Wallace displayed included a summary from the brokerage firm of Grant and Ward, listing assets of no less than $800,000 as belonging to John B. Wilkes in banks in the United States and Canada. The former president scribbled on one of the letters, "See what can be done for the lady." His own involvement was short-lived. Grant and Ward was a business house he had set up through his son, in a foredoomed effort to restore family fortunes. It succumbed to scandal in 1884, with the junior partner, Jeremiah Ward, sentenced to jail. And the following year, throat cancer took Grant's life.

Andrew Potter successfully bargained with Wallace for higher pay and began his quest. He was initially helped by John Foster, future secretary of state and grandfather of John Foster and Allen Dulles. It took him across the country to the West Coast, where, in San Francisco at the office of the British Consulate, he learned that a John Wilkes had applied for and received permission to enter Ceylon in 1866. But, as the consular ledger showed, this Wilkes claimed to be a British subject, born in Sheffield, England, December 15, 1822, to Samuel and Olivia Wilkes. And there was nothing faked about that data; it checked with records in London. Before long,

Potter and Parsons were poring over the will of India's John B. Wilkes because a man named George Forrester had come to Indiana seeking one of the heirs mentioned in it.

What finally emerged, unassailably documented, was proof that there had indeed been a transference of identity—in effect, a sale, for money had changed hands, probably from a high-level source, and was personally delivered by Harriet Alexander. The information presented in 1866 by "John Wilkes" to gain entry into Ceylon, then India, is identical with that still on record for Professor Parsons's father-in-law, the English-born John Wilkes who spent his entire adult life in Terre Haute, Indiana, and died there in August 1916, aged ninety.

As for the man who had assumed John Wilkes's identity, it was found that he was not a freeholder, and his will could not be executed in India. The case had been declared "nulla bono—in bonis cedere"; in a word, Wilkes was bankrupt. Lew Wallace, demonstrably active in all this commotion over the death of a presumed Englishman in a far-off land, had the will probated through a state court in the United States. Did Wallace, the novelist, savor a notion of an assassin exiled abroad, every man's hand turned against him? For at this very time, with *Ben-Hur* already behind him, Wallace had begun reworking the Wandering Jew legend into his next literary success, *The Prince of India.* At any rate, he was instrumental in securing sworn statements that established the authenticity of the will. Forrester was a witness when John B. Wilkes signed it in Bombay and he was now its executor.

And the will itself? We found a legally certified copy among other faded documents in a Midwest county courthouse. It is dated September 12, 1883, and bids disbursement of a total exceeding $160,000. Other than Elizabeth Burnley Wilkes, his "beloved wife and mistress," all named as principal legatees provably figure in the life of the actor John Wilkes Booth. They include Izola, Booth's first and perhaps only legal wife, and their daughter, Ogarita; Kate Scott of Brookville, Pennsylvania, and her daughter, Sarah Katherine. Nor was Ella Turner forgotten, Booth's lover who had tried suicide the morning after he murdered the president. And that she, too, had carried Booth's child on that long ago Easter weekend is indicated by the stipulation favoring Mary Louise Turner, identified, as were Ogarita and Sarah Katherine, as "the natural heir of my body." Fidelity is rewarded, $1,000 annually bequeathed to Henry Johnson, Booth's onetime valet, who had helped him escape and "to whom I owe my life." What went to Booth's other loyal companion in flight is not stated, but he is there, too, "Edwin Henson," one of the two witnesses, the cognominal alteration hardly less slight than the omission of the last name in the star signature of "John Byron Wilkes."

Fifty years separated the cease-fire at Appomattox and the sinking of the *Lusitania,* which pitchforked America into global war. It was a time span largely occupied by the Gilded Age, a period hardly conducive to the exposure of domestic secrets that might inflame or corrode. It was characterized by fiercely competitive business growth and a feverish chauvinism, with bipartisan politics riding both trends and nothing to be gained in gold or votes by raking over ashes of the recent past. If not ignored, the past was to be recalled in ways that hurt nobody's feelings. So the Civil War's military campaigns were refought, by and large, in neutral prose. Chivalry tinctured each published memoir and regimental reunion. Lindsay Lunsford Lomax attended his share of comradely gatherings, and the North saluted the South's diehard cavalry warrior by appointing him a commissioner of the battlefield park at Gettysburg and a member of the editorial board charged with the selection of records for a history of the Civil War. In these posts Lomax was unlikely to have been smitten with any urge to disclose what his sister and her husband had been up to in the old Van Ness mansion in Washington or what he knew about the escape of Booth, as confirmed in a telegram from John Mosby, who was then U.S. consul in Hong Kong.

Thomas T. Eckert was another of the close-mouthed school with wartime secrets, so much so that David H. Bates, his loyal associate at the War Department and afterward in the bomb-proof New York headquarters of the Western Union Telegraph Company, sometimes referred to him as "Silent Eckert." This reticence, by extension, muzzled Bates, too: The articles he put together in 1907 under the title *Lincoln in the Telegraph Office* were drafted virtually under Eckert's supervision. Eckert's memory or imagination supplied anecdotes that appear at times to have given Bates pause but, once published, were accepted without question. Following Eckert's death three years later, his sanity was argued by rival claimants to his millions, and it was said that the old man had ordered his bedroom windows darkened and mirrors covered because of the faces he saw in their glass.

And with a vibrant new century well under way, no one seemed to get excited over odd fragments of truth that began to slip out—for instance, that Stanton's War Department had known in advance of plots against the president, yet apparently took no preventive action. Bates, in plain English, referred to Eckert's "previous knowledge of the plot to kill or kidnap the President," whose life might have been saved had the broad-shouldered telegraph chief been in the box with him. (As we have seen, even after the fatal shot Eckert stayed clear of the theater.) In a series of articles published in 1887, "Colonel" William P. Wood wrote that on the secretary's authority, he had given Mary Surratt's brother guarantees that she would not be executed. After she was hanged, and presumably enraged over the betrayal, Wood appeared to be on the point of telling all. During the closing stages of the trial of Mary's son, Wood was reported as ready to at least show proof of that alleged previous knowledge. Wood's boast that he alone knew the full truth of the matter could not be swallowed without appropriate salt. But even apart from John S. Mosby's confidential assertion that Wood himself, accompanied by Booth, had approached him with kidnap proposals, the former Old Capitol Prison superintendent's claim that he rented a room at the Herndon House "to keep watch" on the conspirators raises the question of why, instead of being kept under surveillance, they were not promptly seized. Hundreds were thrown into Wood's prison on far flimsier grounds.

During the first decades of the last century, getting information on mysterious aspects of Lincoln's murder and the fate of his assassin was not always easy. In 1912 the judge advocate general was flatly denying that his office had any "official information concerning the pursuit and capture of John Wilkes Booth." Three years later Mary Stevens Beall of the Columbia Historical Society sought word to settle the "strong doubt" that Doctor John F. May, in a posthumous publication by the Society, said had existed over whether the body he was summoned to identify on the *Montauk* was actually Booth's. Although, officially, the judge advocate general "has charge of these records," his reply to Mrs. Beall was that "this office has no official reports or information concerning the capture and killing of Booth, nor as to what means, if any, were taken to identify the body of the man brought to the Navy Yard at Washington as that of the assassin."

In 1928, Martha Mills, widowed and close to ninety, was interviewed in Indianapolis by John C. Shaffer, editor-publisher of the *Chicago Post, Indianapolis Star,* and *Rocky Mountain News.* William W. Parsons of Terre Haute had briefed him on aspects of the untold Booth story, and with belief in the late educator's veracity tempered by professional skepticism, Shaffer questioned Mills searchingly. What she told him conformed with what he had learned from other sources, but she added more, about her last encounter with Booth. It had occurred six months after his supposed death. At his direction, they had met near the new Shakespeare monument in Central Park, which the proceeds from the attendance at his final New York stage appearance had helped fund, and they left for Canada, where "he had a power of attorney prepared for his business agent for the oil property." Martha and John Wilkes Booth spent two weeks in Montreal while he waited for mail addressed to "John Wilkes" at a post ofice. "Those were idyllic days and I never forgot them." Shaffer found no reason to disbelieve any of this, but, advised against publication, he, too, joined the tight-lipped band privy to secrets deemed most safe to divulge in the distant future, if at all.

Andrew Giles Potter lived into an often-troubled old age with philosophic courage and died in 1932 as the result of an automobile accident in Colorado. Potter was then ninety-two. His body was returned to Virginia for burial on the farm where he and his eighteen brothers and sisters had spent much of their childhood. His grave was relocated during the expansion of the Marine Corps base at Quantico, Virginia, in 1943. The bulk of Potter's papers went to Gaylord McCluer, a longtime friend and fiscal agent and Crawfordsville banker, who thereupon settled Potter's debts, which were considerable, for the old detective had lost heavily in the Great Depression. Potter's papers—those that had survived a fire when lightning struck Lew Wallace's carriagehouse, where they were stored—would rest in an attic for further decades, undisturbed and forgotten, and finally be scattered in three different directions, one portion purchased by Dr. Ray Neff and one portion going to McCluer's niece, Helen Lilienthal, wife of the first chairman of the United States Atomic Energy Commission. The third portion went to an unnamed woman in Connersville, Indiana.

Did Ulysses S. Grant know or suspect the true identity of India's "Wilkes"? It is impossible to tell. But that Wallace had a role in all this is not so astonishing. His penchant for intrigue is amply illustrated by his own detailed account of an attempt to undermine the Lincoln-Seward policy of neutrality with respect to the struggle in Mexico.

And the Wallace connection, as well as that of Grant and Ward, is firmly established in the correspondence of Robert Burns Stewart, a respected Midwest circuit court judge who died in 1970. Booth's assumption of another's identity, with the secrecy and furtiveness that inevitably ensued, had led to embarrassment and confusion among descendants on both sides. In 1930 Stewart, then a youthful attorney, tried to sort things out for a daughter of the Terre Haute Wilkes. A man had indeed fled the United States in 1866 and entered Ceylon. "He was using your father's vital information to circumvent entry requirements." He died in India and left an estate that was "originally handled by the banking firm of Grant and Ward of New York, who enlisted General Lew Wallace to handle matters in Indiana."

For the latter part of his life, Andrew Potter had enjoyed the skills and devotion of Susan Wade, a highly intelligent woman experienced in various types of shorthand, ciphers, and languages. Her son, Mark, served overseas with army intelligence in the Second

World War, and while on a mission in India, he and a friend paid a visit to Guwahati in the province of Assam. Since Victorian times this had been a British garrison town, then spelt *Gauhati,* which, roughly translated, means “the light of the east.” It is an ancient place surrounded on three sides by hills and bordered on the north by the great river Brahmaputra. On April 29, 1945, Wade wrote to his mother,

> We looked for the mausoleum everyone has been anxious to find. We did not find it. It is no more. The Brits built a road and the mausoleum was in the way so they took it apart and moved the bodies. The engineer who built the road sent us to the right people who took us to the cemetery where the bodies have been buried. The mausoleum was too tore up to put back together so they put them underground. I'm afraid the news is disappointing. I found the gravestone and it reads: John B. Wilkes 1822–1883, and that's it. As I recall, this could not be the man everyone thought because he was born in 1836 or 38, right? I took some pictures. We found the record and it gave the same date of birth, 1822, and his birthplace in Sheffield, England. I guess this ends it, right?

How readily Mark Wade might have thought otherwise had he seen the incontestable proof that “John B. Wilkes” of India was certainly not the John B. Wilkes of Indiana. That particular missing piece of the jigsaw fell into place when we acquired a copy of the death cerificate of John Wilkes of Terre Haute, with the data typed on the back, matching the credentials claimed by the man buried in the soil of Guwahati.

The old graveyard that stood near the Guwahati railway station is no more. On its site stands a building put up since the end of the Second World War and housing the Institute of Indian Engineers. Before its construction, little or no effort was made to remove any coffins, but many of the tombstones were transferred to other cemeteries, most to the “new” cemetery opened in 1882, where a number of them were cemented into the boundary walls. Still others were cast aside or carried off by laborers, and some were buried under earth filling. Recent attempts to find the John B. Wilkes stone, part of the mausoleum in which “Wilkes” shared occupancy with Elizabeth (Burnley) Wilkes's first husband, have not been successful.

Was the man whose last resting place that stone marked truly Abraham Lincoln's assassin? One thing is certain: After Lincoln's assassination, it contributed to peace of mind for many in the United States that the assassin be dead or be thought to be. So after that farcical business on the *Montauk,* he was officially pronounced dead, which safely ruled out further search or pursuit by authority. And this might have been expected to ensure that if he still lived, his lips would remain sealed. So there was great relief, with no one foreseeing the awkwardness ahead when Booth in distant exile would determine that women he had loved, children he had fathered, and friends to whom he owed his life would benefit from a fortune rightfully his but upon which he was unable to get his hands.

Much remains to be told. Riddles persist. What really happened in the Sewards' gloomy residence the night Booth shot Lincoln? Who exactly was the man hanged as Lewis Payne or Powell? Was there some high-level arrangement to shield Harriet "Lola" Alexander from the media of her day? Where are Thomas Eckert's papers? In January 1975 *Fortune* magazine named Alexander T. Stewart as a laureate in its business hall of fame, without reference to the complete disappearance of his business and personal papers, not to mention that of his body from its tomb. Had any minutes of those politically radical Strong Band meetings in New York been noted down, what would they have told us? As evidence implicates Edwin Stanton's agent, William P. Wood, in a conspiracy to kidnap Lincoln, how much should we assume that the secretary of war himself knew? What happened to the records of the brokerage firm of Grant and Ward? Questions abound. But the more questions the better. Today, as always, there are too many people who have a vested interest in preserving a standardized version of history. Instead of welcoming new discoveries, as genuine historians should, they ignore or even try to suppress fresh evidence that tends to contradict conventional accounts. This is particularly true, and a tragedy in itself, of questions at the heart of the Abraham Lincoln drama. Questions imply doubts, as well they should. This fact should not silence the questioner. As the sixteenth-century philosopher Francis Bacon said, "If a man will begin with certainties he shall end in doubts. But if he will begin with doubts he shall end in certainties."

COLBURN'S

UNITED SERVICE

MAGAZINE,

AND

NAVAL AND MILITARY JOURNAL.

1864, PART II.

LONDON:
HURST AND BLACKETT, PUBLISHERS,
SUCCESSORS TO HENRY COLBURN,
13, GREAT MARLBOROUGH STREET,

SOLD BY ALL BOOKSELLERS.

The *Colburn*'s volume in which Lafayette Baker secreted his startling intelligence about the plots against Lincoln.

574 NARRATIVE OF THE CAMPAIGN [Aug.

done so at a heavy cost of life and treasure. The Allies were well aware of this or they would not have commenced a campaign at the time they did. The assumption that the Danes would have been defeated is justified by the inferiority of their numbers to that of the Allies; and to military men this is the more certain, that the Germans are better disciplined, and in the case of a portion, if not the whole, of the Austrian force engaged, had had recent experience of actual warfare, whereas the Danish army was composed of soldiers young, middle-aged, and almost old, who had never seen a shot fired in anger. That the Danes would have fought bravely nobody doubts, but in war mere bravery is not sufficient to secure success. As it was, the troops suffered severely before the retreat was decided upon. The cold was intense; heavy falls of snow and severe frosts, followed by a partial thaw, which filled the air with a dense cold vapour that soaked in their clothes and chilled them to the bone, depressed their spirits to an extent which experience alone can enable a man to realise. Add to this that they were very inadequately sheltered at night from the inclemency of the weather, and it will be evident to the most unexperienced person, that even a few more hours would have rendered a considerable portion of the army unable to fight from mere sickness. That General Meza acted wisely in abandoning the Dannewerk will eventually be admitted even in Copenhagen, where the excitement was very great indeed on its first becoming known. His determination was approved by nearly every officer under his command competent to form an opinion, though there were some whose bravery was greater than their judgment, who gave way to expressions of indignation when they heard of what had been decided upon. It was asserted by Bishop Monrad that neither the Government nor the King had previously sanctioned the retreat; but it is impossible to reconcile this statement with the reports current in Schleswig that the King, when he visited the Dannewerk on the previous Sunday, agreed with Meza that the works were untenable by an army so small against an enemy so numerous. That the King did not order the retreat is possible: but that General Meza failed to give his Majesty his opinion on the subject is altogether improbable; we may fairly infer, therefore, that in what he did the Danish commander had the tacit approval of the King, if nothing more. However, it was necessary to sacrifice Meza to appease the excitement at Copenhagen, and he was sacrificed accordingly.

The Prussian attack on Missunde on the 1st of February doubtless had a motive, but it is not easy to discern what this motive was; but probably it was connected with an intention to cross at this point. However this may be, the result did not compensate for the loss of life it occasioned. The fight was chiefly carried on by means of artillery, and considering the fog that prevailed throughout the day, the Danes made good practice against the moving bodies of the enemy, who could only be seen at intervals. The

Baker's signature, written in invisible ink and chemically restored. Figures along the inner margin are part of his cipher message.

Chief Detective Lafayette Charles Baker.

The National Detective Police badge. Usually, NDP operatives wore it only when the need arose to impress or intimidate.

National Detective Police Agent Earl Potter.

St. Lawrence Hall, Montreal. Setting for the October 1864 secret conference between business and political agents of the North and the South. John Wilkes Booth was present, his bold signature unmistakable on the hotel register.

Henry Megill, M.D., was a brother-in-law of R. D. Watson and was a part of John Wilkes Booth's drug-smuggling system. He lived in Owensboro, Kentucky, and funneled desperately needed drugs to the Confederacy.

William A. Browning. An active operator in the clandestine meat-for-cotton deal.

Robert Daniel Watson, largest livestock-raising merchant in the midwest. He had heavily invested in the scheme, but grew nervous as to its outcome.

Beverley Tucker, the Confederacy's trade commissioner in Canada. Note glove on his right hand from which the thumb had been amputated.

You had better get [illegible] to copy this distinctly, and in large writing. I have written it thus for obvious reasons. Oct 31/64.

I have seen with my own eyes old Abe's written permission to pass the Blockade Squadron at Mobile, with vessels to take in supplies (meat) & bring out cotton.

Beverley Tucker's exultant report to Richmond of having seen Lincoln's written permission to raise his naval blockade of the South, allowing the exchange of meat for cotton.

Izola Mills Booth, aspiring actress until she married John Wilkes Booth and helped him smuggle medicine into the South.

Mount Olympus, the home Booth secured for Izola. Near Harper's Ferry, it became a way station for Confederate agents. Privately owned, the house still stands.

A band of secessionist smugglers at St. Michaels, Chesapeake Bay, Maryland, photographed by NDP operatives disguised as itinerant cameramen. Group includes David Herold, John Celestina, and Edwin Hynson, later involved in Booth's plot to kidnap Lincoln.

James V. Barnes (left), pivotal figure in the meat-for-cotton plan. With him Mary Cook, his future wife, and an NDP agent named Walter Buckman.

Alexander T. Stewart, prince of New York retail merchants and shadowy string-puller behind the great exchange scheme.

One of R. D. Watson's mercantile steamboats tied up at Watson's Landing, Kentucky.

The old Van Ness place, whose subterranean quarters were renovated for the captive Lincoln. It stood scarcely 300 yards from the White House.

Martha Mills was related to Booth's wife and among his lovers. She overheard Barnes call him useless as kidnap ringleader. She would accompany Booth to Montreal when the world believed him dead.

Captain James Boyd shortly after his official release on Secretary of War Stanton's orders. After supplanting Booth in the plot to kidnap Lincoln, he served as the assassin's surrogate on an autopsy table.

Boyd's wife, Caroline, left to care for her seven children until her death five months before Boyd's.

Watson's anxious note to John Surratt at a critical moment for the profiteers. Surratt was their special courier while serving Rebel and Union interests—the ultimate triple agent.

New York
March 19th 186[illegible]

Mr J. H. Surratt

Dear Sir

I would like to see You on important business, if you can spare the time to come on to New York. Please Telegraph me immediately on the reception of this whether you can come on or not & much oblige

Yours &c—

R. D. Watson

P.S.

Address Care Demill & Co.

178 1/2 Water St.

Benjamin Ficklin, Pony Express cofounder, Confederacy procurement wizard, blockade-running shipowner, and Lincoln assassin suspect. Described by a witness as having "the appearance of a refined pirate."

Harriet "Lola" Alexander of New York—intimate of Andrew Johnson and also of Booth, to whom she wrote a fatally taunting letter. The same Terre Haute photographer took the picture of John Wilkes on page 236.

Ford's Theatre, looking south from F Street.

The Seward home, setting for a bizarre domestic tragedy that itself became woven into the Lincoln murder cover-up.

R. D. Watson's home on Watson's Bar, Kentucky.

Edwin McMasters Stanton, an inscrutable warlord. He was outwardly loyal to Lincoln, for whom he had once voiced sneering contempt.

Chief Detective Baker and subordinates Everton Conger and Luther Baker plan the manhunt. From a photograph by Alexander Gardner.

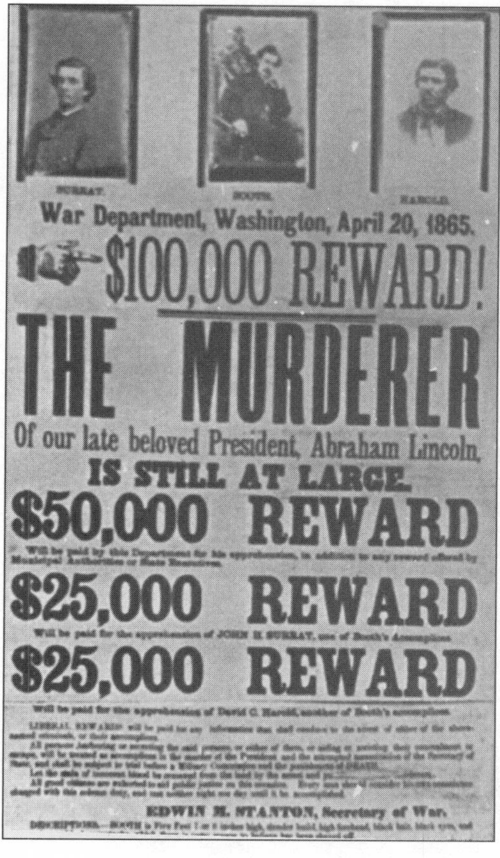

David E. Herold. To keep secret the fact that he had been seized within forty-eight hours of the assassination, manacles were cropped from his photo to accommodate the reward poster five days later.

Steam tug *John S. Ide* leaving Washington for Belle Plain with the New York Cavalry in pursuit of Booth. NDP tug *Jennie Baker* in foreground.

Edwin Hynson, a diminutive, prayerful secessionist. He was loyal to Booth and his true companion while on the run.

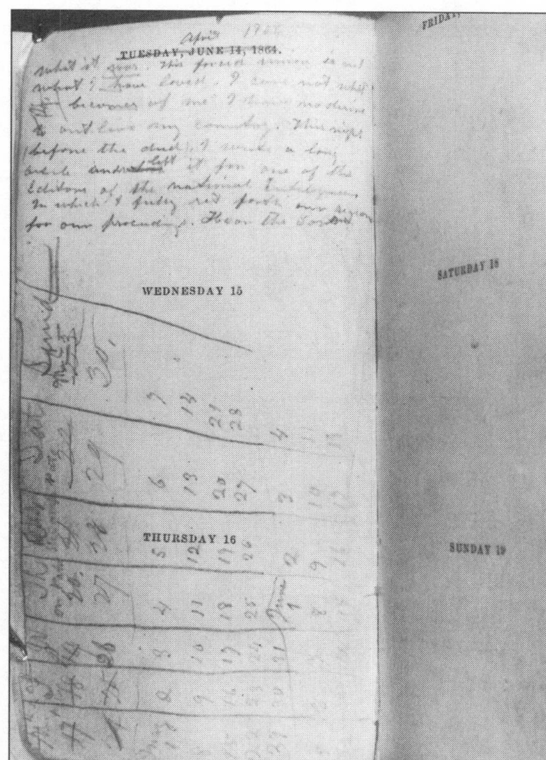

Booth's makeshift calendar. Locations while a fugitive are marked over dates along the top line.

Cleydael, King George County, Virginia. Summer home of Doctor Stuart, empty and abandoned when we took this shot in 1980. Today, renovated and in private hands.

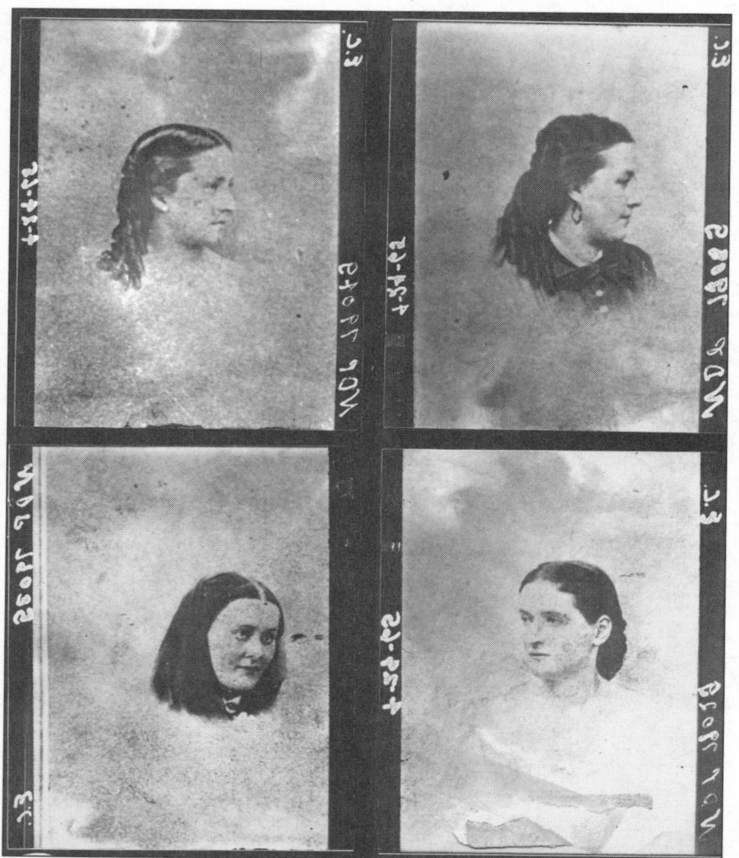

Photos from Booth's diary. Initials and dates in the margins establish time of diary's discovery as three days before it was supposedly taken from Booth's pocket. The woman bottom left is Kate Scott, who met Booth while an army nurse stationed for three months near Washington.

Whippet Nalgai was of Pamunky Indian and Portuguese stock. A valuable scout for the NDP, he found Booth's diary and took it to the detectives halted at King George Court House.

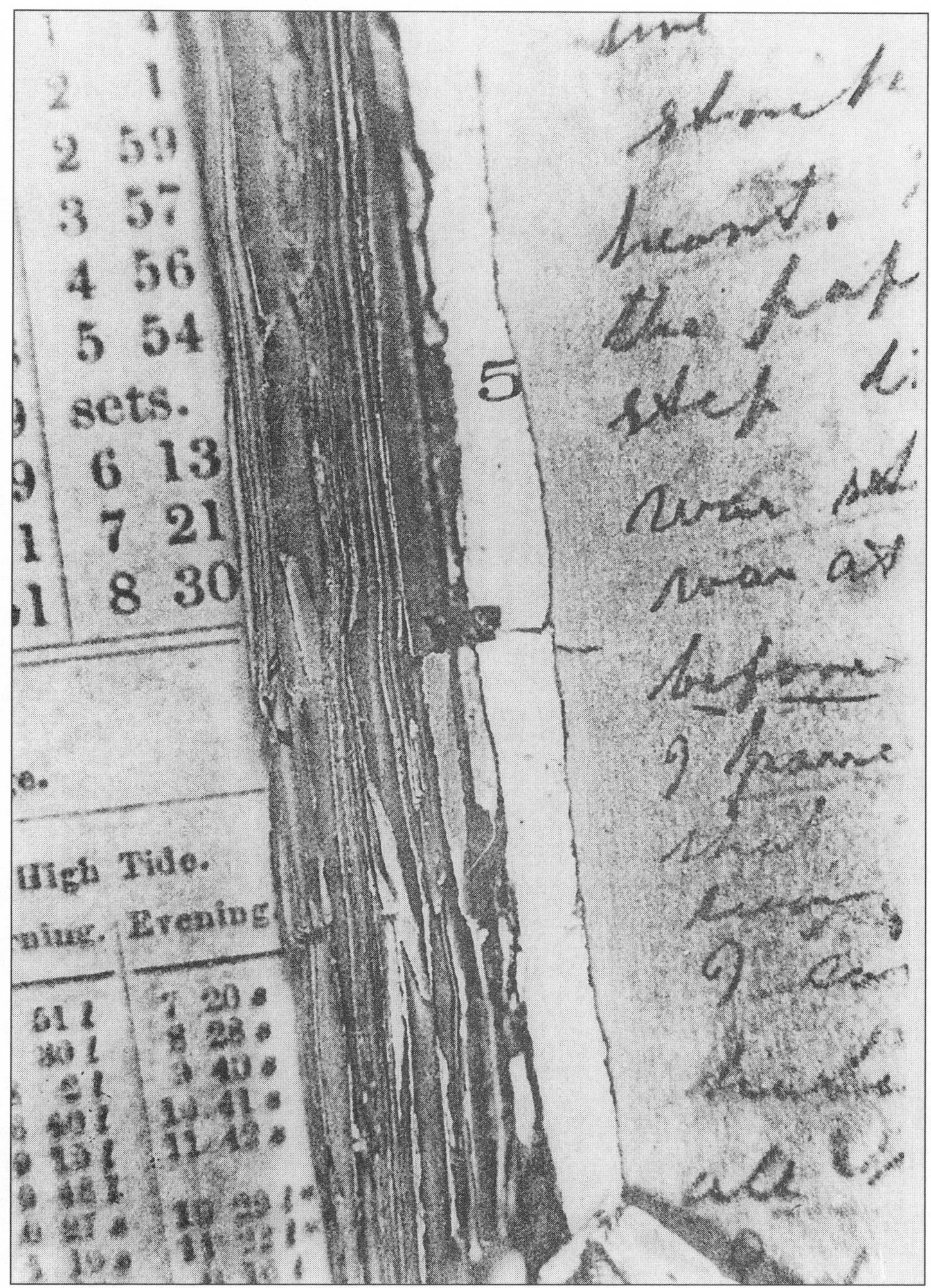

Close-up of stubs left in Booth's diary. The item is on display beneath today's Ford's Theatre, but permanently sealed for preservation.

The last days of Garrett's farm. No trace of it now remains.

a.

b.

c.

d.

a. One of three cotton permits, each for 10,000 bales of cotton, signed by Lincoln and altered after his death. **b.** Chemical application revealed R. D. Watson's name under Henry J. Eager's on the permit one hundred years after its "erasure" with a scraper. **c, d.** The permit facilitated these cotton orders between Eager and H. A. Risley. In the lower left corner of the latter are the names of other parties to the deal.

Roswell E. Goodell. A partner in the "Henry J. Eager" company who traveled abroad after the Civil War, settled finally in Colorado as a millionaire banker and a pillar of Denver society.

Thomas J. Caldwell. Shipping agent at 178½ Water Street, New York. Deployed vessels for Lincoln's kidnapping and took the Lincoln cotton passes to Washington for surreptitious alteration.

NDP agent Robert "Rob Rover" Bernard and (right) John Celestina. Mistaken for Celestina, the detective was arrested.

Death of J. Wilkes Booth according to an illustration in Baker's postwar memoirs. The unknown artist was apparently unaware that Booth had shaved off his mustache.

The monitor *Montauk* (left) on which the body brought back from Garrett's farm was identified as Booth's.

An illustration from Baker's memoirs purporting to show the autopsy on the *Montauk* in process.

Dr. John Frederick May who, upon seeing the body, refused to believe it was Booth. He then said it was, by virtue of a scar on the back of its neck.

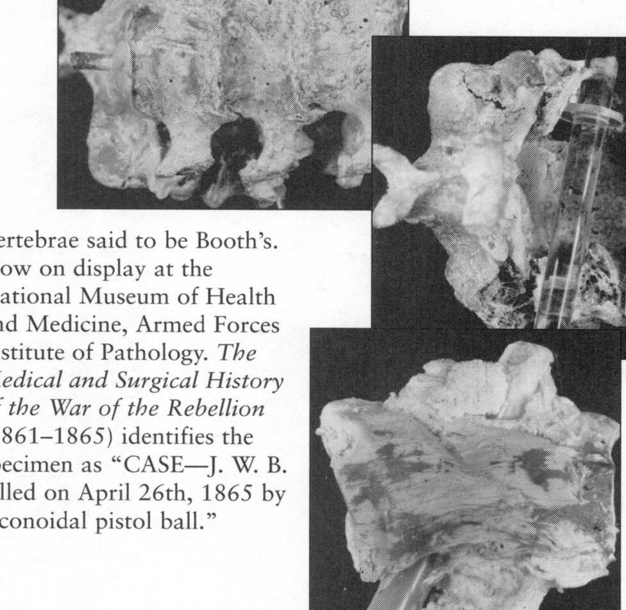

Vertebrae said to be Booth's. Now on display at the National Museum of Health and Medicine, Armed Forces Institute of Pathology. *The Medical and Surgical History of the War of the Rebellion* (1861–1865) identifies the specimen as "CASE—J. W. B. killed on April 26th, 1865 by a conoidal pistol ball."

Walter G. Pollock, NDP agent whose own words and other testimony identify him as something of a "hit" man.

Lafayette Baker's wife Jane (Jennie) left a highly revealing diary in NDP hands.

John Wilkes (1822–1916), whose identity Booth assumed to gain entry into India.

Beside the seated man, Richard Cage, stands Henry Johnson, once Booth's valet. He was freed to set up a popular hairdressing salon in Washington and helped Booth escape.

"The Bear Hole," a cave near Swift Run Gap in the Blue Ridge Mountains, where Booth, Hynson, and Johnson sheltered several days. Andrew Potter, detective, shouldered camera equipment uphill to take this picture, indicating that he and fellow sleuths were on no mere spelunking expedition.

Rebel partisans led Booth to the Rockingham County, Virginia, farm of Lewis Pence (shown with wife). Pence guided Booth's party north to Mount Olympus.

Booth's bed at the Pence place.

John Wilkes Booth, probably in 1862.

John Byron Wilkes of India. This picture was taken in 1873 in Groom's Studio, Philadelphia, eight years after Booth reportedly was killed.

ROBERT BURNS STEWART
Times Building
Brazil, Indiana

January 7, 1930

Mrs. Elizabeth Bossom
1633 South Third Street
Terre Haute, Indiana

Dear Madam:

Allow me for a moment to review the situation. Mrs. Wilson claims that your father, Mr. John Wilkes (sometimes also spelled WILKS) who died in Terre Haute in August of 1916 was the same man who was reported to have died in Assam, India in October of 1883. The claim is made that the alleged death in 1883 was some sort of Machiavallean conspiracy to allow Mr. Wilkes and his family to utilize funds held by the government of the United States. These funds, it is further alleged, had accrued during the Civil War as a result of the contraband trade. It is further alleged that the death in India was faked and that Mr. Wilkes came to Terre Haute and took up residence so that a will which had been executed in India could be probated and monies previously frozen could be released. To support this claim Mrs. Wilson has presented a document which, it turns out, is genuine in its source but certainly erroneous in its content, which shows that Mr. John Wilkes fled the United States in 1866 or thereabout, and entered the Colony of Ceylon, claiming British citizenship and giving his place of birth as Sheffield England, the date of his birth as December 15, 1822, and the names of his parents as Samuel Wilkes and Olivia Barber Wilkes.

I am now settling an estate having to do with the Mr. Wilkes of India. That case was originally handled by the Banking firm of Grant and Ward of New York, who enlisted General Lew Wallace to handle matters in Indiana. The case was later handed over to me and the file contains a number of documents which are both informative and interesting in regard to Mr. John Wilkes who allegedly died in India in 1883. I could show certain of these to your attorney but some could not properly be disclosed. I'm sure you understand. A man who held a life estate in a trust stemming from that legacy died last October here in Clay County. The trust will now be dissolved in accordance with the stipulations set forth in the trust. If you wish to get further information on that trust, have your attorney contact me or Mr. Gaylord McCluer of Crawfordsville. Mr. McCluer is a banker and custodian of the trust and can probably supply information of value.

A mr. Andrew Potter assisted General Wallace in the investigation of the circumstances of the death of Mr. Wilkes of India and now resides in Virginia. His address is:
Mr. Andrew Potter
c/o Paul Potter
Potters Store
Noakesville, Virginia

Portion of a letter that links Grant, Lew Wallace, and Detective Andrew Potter with the estate of India's John Wilkes.

Judge Robert B. Stewart wrote the letter while a young Indiana attorney in 1930.

Six women whom "John B. Wilkes" in far-off India named as legatees in his will: **a.** Izola Booth; **b.** Ogarita, daughter of Izola by Booth; **c.** Kate Scott; **d.** Booth and Kate Scott's daughter, Sarah Katherine; **e.** Ella Turner; **f.** Booth and Ella Turner's daughter, Mary Louise.

William Wood Parsons, president of Indiana State Normal School, now Indiana State University. Following his retirement in 1921 resumed his own investigation of the Booth mystery. He had married John Wilkes's daughter.

Andrew Giles Potter in retirement. The NDP's most enduring and tenacious agent, he died in a car accident in 1932.

Two gravestones, one in Guwahati, India (above), the other in Terre Haute, Indiana.

Notes on Sources

From whatever perspective, any serious study of Abraham Lincoln's assassination and important circumstances that surround it must be undertaken with ready access to the Investigation and Trial Papers Relating to the Assassination of President Lincoln, commonly called the Lincoln Assassination Suspects (LAS) Files. Microfilmed as Microcopy 599, they are at the National Archives and Records Administration (NARA) in Washington, D.C. This also applies to the Case Files of Investigations by Army Judge Advocate Levi C. Turner and Lafayette C. Baker, 1862–1866, Records of the Adjutant General's Office, NARA. The title of this collection is abbreviated to the Turner-Baker Papers. In addition to these federal materials is the rich treasure trove of records and memorabilia housed in the Neff-Guttridge Collection, recently acquired by the Indiana State University (ISU) Cunningham Memorial Library, Special Collections Division, Terre Haute, Indiana. A principle component of this collection is research gathered by Andrew Potter, a former United States government detective (Potter Papers).

Introduction

Lincoln's reading preferences are detailed in William D. Howells, *Life of Abraham Lincoln* (1860). The erroneous insertion of Herold's name in a passage from Booth's diary appears in Philip Van Doren Stern's introduction to the 1954 facsimile edition of Benn Pitman's (hereinafter *Trial*) *The Assassination of President Lincoln and the Trial of the Conspirators* (New York: Funk & Wagnalls, 1954). Prominent among writers who, it seems, have accepted without question accounts of the assassin's alleged last words is William Hanchett, professor emeritus, San Diego State University. His "The Eisenschiml Thesis," in *Civil War History* (September 1979), and *The Lincoln Murder Conspiracies* (Urbana, Ill.: University of Illinois Press, 1983) portray an unconscious Booth revived sufficiently by water splashed on his face to make "remarks" about his mother, betrayal, love of country, and so on. In conclusion, Hanchett states, "There is no disagreement among the three officers present, Doherty, Baker and Conger," as to Booth's last words. Not so. Lieutenant Doherty, in his official report of the capture, says nothing of last words and in a later interview denies that there were any, except "useless, useless." Also see his account to Secretary Stanton, April 27, 1865, Records of the Office of the Adjutant General, NARA. Officialdom's denial of access to government files is made clear in Inventory 179 of Record Group (RG) 94, prepared 1949, NARA.

Chapter 1

For the first published account of Lafayette Baker's encoded assertions, the discovery of the codicil to his will, and the court transcript, see Robert H. Fowler, "Did Stanton Plan Lincoln's Murder?" *Civil War Times* (August 1961). Fowler, a veteran journalist and founder of Historical Times, Inc., was the periodical's publisher and first editor. Reactions to that issue's content appeared in the October and December issues. (The history professor who apparently considered Lincoln's murder a hypothetical case was William S. Baring, University of Florida.) The discovery of the Baker codicil hearing triggered a curious train of events. In 1972 Fowler was succeeded as editor of *Civil War Times Illustrated* (the title had been lengthened) by twenty-six-year-old William C. Davis. Davis, for no apparent reason other than the private expression by an unnamed Philadelphia City Hall employee of his opinion "that the documents were not genuine and might have been planted there for Fowler to see," generated his own suspicions. These grew to a point where more than twenty years after the 1961 *Civil War Times* article, he wrote that "many researchers" (himself included?) had sought the hearing record in Philadelphia but could not find it. Even as Davis was publicly declaring that his editorial predecessor had been duped, the transcript was indeed available for study, having been typed by Gina Giordana from the original at Philadelphia City Hall in 1936 under the WPA program, and was filed with the Works Progress Administration Papers as WPA (1936)-400 (1868)–(C. C. 1872). Yet Davis, by that time a prolific writer on Civil War battles, the executive director of Historical Times, Inc., and a Pulitzer Prize nominee, was so convinced that the certifiably authentic Baker codicil hearing transcript was false, he took the unusual step of refuting the material that had so sensationally dominated the August 1961 issue of *Civil War Times*. For Edwin Stanton as enigmatic but indefatigable war bureaucrat, see Albert E. Johnson, the *Evening Star*, January 11, 1896; W. T. Sherman to U. S. Grant, May 10, 1865, Sherman Mss., Library of Congress; and "Two Letters from General Sherman," *Journal of Southern History* 20. Also, see *Personal Memoirs of Ulysses S. Grant* (New York: C. L. Webster, 1885); George H. Curtis, *Life of James Buchanan*, vol. 2 (New York: Books for Libraries Press, 1970); "Recollections of Lincoln Usher," *New York Daily Tribune*, September 13, 1885; and Benjamin P. Thomas and Harold M. Hyman, *Stanton: The Life and Times of Lincoln's Secretary of War* (New York: Alfred A. Knopf, 1962).

Chapter 2

The St. Lawrence Hall meeting. Our account of this historic, yet historically overlooked, secret business conference is drawn from a number of separate sources, as well as the confidential NDP interviews in the Potter Papers. Those include interviews with R. D. Watson, October 15, 1875, and Dr. Luke Blackburn, October 18, 1875, whose signature also graces the torn portion of the hotel register. Blackburn was later a governor of Kentucky. "D. A. MacDonald," William A. Browning's alias, is signed directly above "J. W. Booth." Dialogue around the conference table is described in Beverley Tucker's triumphant report to the Richmond government, intercepted at Washington and now on official record in the LAS Files, NARA. Also see Jane Ellis Tucker, *Beverley Tucker: A Memoir* (Richmond, Va.: Frank Baptist Printing Company, 1893), and "Beverley Tucker's Canadian Mission," *Journal of Southern History* 29 (1963). In J. B. Jones, *A Rebel War Clerk's Diary at the Confederate States Capital* (Philadelphia, Pa.: J. B. Lippincott & Co., 1866), the entry for January 23, 1864, referring to Jeff Davis's reluctant decision to approve exchanges of cotton for northern meat, reads, "Men in high positions in Washington wink at this traffic and share its profits. I hope we may get bacon without strychnine." That for October 29, 1864, a week after the St. Lawrence Hall meeting, reads, "Bev. Tucker has made contract for Confederate States govt. with ——— & Co. of New York to deliver bacon for cotton, pound for pound." For Luke Blackburn's concern over the plight of prisoners of war, see his letter to Judah Benjamin, August 29, 1864, copy in the Filson Club, Louisville, Kentucky. A slim biography is Nancy D. Baird, *Luke Pryor Blackburn* (Lexington: University Press of Kentucky, 1979). An imagined visit to the St. Lawrence Hall is provided by E. C. Guillet, *Pioneer Inns and Taverns,* vol. 2 (Toronto, Canada: Ontario Publishing Company, 1956).

Chapter 3

Great trading triangle: See Harold Woodman, *King Cotton and His Retainers* (Lexington: University Press of Kentucky, 1968); "The Federal Government and Confederate Cotton" by A. S. Roberts, *American Historical Review* XXXII (1927); G. R. Woodfolk, *The Cotton Regency 1865–1880* (New York: Bookman, 1958). Lincoln's "the temptation is so great" is from R. P. Basler, *Collected Works of Abraham Lincoln,* vol. VI (Newark, N.J.: Rutgers University Press, 1953–1955). Also see David Cohn, *The Life and Times of King Cotton* (New York: Oxford University Press, 1958). The vital importance of cotton to both warring sides is further emphasized in "Lincoln and the Cotton Trade," *Civil War History* (March 1961); F. L. Owsley, *King Cotton Diplomacy* (Chicago: University Press of Chicago, 1959); *Inside the Confederate Government: The Diary of Robert G. H. Kean, Head of the Confederate Bureau of War* (Westport, Conn.: Greenwood, 1957). Wrote Kean, March 15, 1863, "The President [Jeff Davis] has yielded at last on the subject of getting meat from the enemy for cotton." Also see E. A. Pollard, *The Lost Cause* (New York: Books for Libraries Press, 1866); and Clement Eaton, *A History of the Southern Confederacy* (New York: Macmillan, 1954). "The alternative is presented of withholding cotton from the enemy or risking the starvation of our armies," wrote G. W. Randolph to Jefferson Davis in October 1862, in *War of the Rebellion: A Compilation of the Official Records of the Union and Confederate Armies* (hereinafter OR), Ser. 4, vol. 2. Also see *Papers Relating to the Commissary Department, C.S.A.,* Virginia Historical Society, Richmond, Virginia. Captured rebel papers giving the first full disclosure of the Confederacy's fatal wartime famine appeared in the *New York Herald,* July 21, 1865. Lincoln's letter citing "pecuniary greed" as a possible aid in confronting the Union's financial crisis is an essential key to the understanding of his risk-fraught cotton policy. See Abraham Lincoln to Major General Edward Canby, December 12, 1864, in *The Works of Abraham Lincoln,*

Letters and Telegrams, vol. IV, eds. John H. Clifford and Marion Miller (New York: Newton and Cartwright, 1908). "Rob Rover," one of Lafayette Baker's agents in Canada, was William Robert Bernard, born in Brookville, Pennsylvania, in 1838. His wartime experiences are recounted in a personal memoir provided to us by his granddaughter Margaret Summerson, of El Paso, Texas, also the source for Bernard's telegrams to Lafayette Baker. The hotel register page bearing Booth's signature and others of significance passed into the hands of Charles Brombach, Philadelphia, whose typewritten monograph "The Canadian Phase of Lincoln's Murder" (1953) is in the Special Collections Department, Columbia University Library, New York. The torn page fits the stub left in the St. Lawrence Hall register for the period, in the Archives of Canada, Ottawa. Additional material on this instance of wartime espionage, with its "Booth should be watched" telegram to Lafayette Baker, is in the Potter Papers. For valuable insights into John Wilkes Booth's character and professional career, see Stanley P. Kimmel, *The Mad Booths of Maryland* (New York: Dover, 1969); Francis Wilson, *John Wilkes Booth* (Boston and New York: Houghton Mifflin, 1929); Ella V. Mahoney, *Sketches of Tudor Hall and the Booth Family* (Belair, Md.: Tudor Hall, 1925); and Asia Booth Clarke, *Passages, Incidents and Anecdotes in the Life of Junius Brutus Booth.* Edwin Booth's condescending introduction of his brother onstage appears in Eleanor Ruggles, *Prince of Players: Edwin Booth* (New York: W. W. Norton, 1953). Booth's demonic performance in Albany in February 1861 is in Kimmel, *The Mad Booths of Maryland.* Toppling Richmond into the pit is described in a clipping from the *Boston Commercial Bulletin,* citing the *New York Herald,* undated, probably May 1865. For further examples of the onstage John Wilkes Booth, see the *New York Herald,* March 18, 1862; the *New York Times and Messenger,* March 23, 1862—"his combat with Richmond is frightfully real"—and *Wilkes' Spirit of the Times,* March 20, 1862. That Booth "looked beautiful on the platform" is in Ellsler, *Stage Memories.* For Booth in militia ranks, see Petersburgh (Virginia) *Daily Express,* November 28, 1859, quoted in *Lincoln Herald* (Spring 1976). That Booth was married is indicated in correspondence between Mrs. Elijah B. Rogers, friend and neighbor of the Booths, with Stump Forward, 1886, Booth Family Papers, Library of Congress (hereinafter LC). Also see Izola Forrester, *This One Mad Act: The Unknown Story of John Wilkes Booth and His Family* (Boston, Mass.: Hale, Cushman and Flint, 1937). Booth's cliff-top refuge, Mount Olympus, still stands at Bolivar, near Harper's Ferry. The Potter Papers contain documentary and photographic evidence of Booth's pro-Confederacy smuggling. A significant portion of them consists of original ledger pages and correspondence of the Passamaquoddy Bay–based nineteenth-century Canadian ship-owners James and John Chaffey. The material was supplied to us by a direct descendant of the family. In an editorial entitled "Caveat Emptor," *Civil War Times Illustrated*'s William C. Davis, in its August 1977 issue, pronounced the Chaffey papers "a hoax." He gave no indication that he had ever set eyes on them but expanded his pronouncement with "clumsy fakes . . . the Chaffey company never existed. . . . a spectral firm." William Hanchett, in *Lincoln Murder Conspiracies* (Urbana: University of Illinois Press, 1983), echoed Davis's words, a sad example of inept "research" slavishly perpetuated. For competent data on Chaffey and

Chaffey, see E. C. Wright, *Planters and Pioneers, Nova Scotia 1749–1775* (Wolfville, Nova Scotia: E. C. Wright, 1978); J. C. Lorimer, *History of Islands and Islets in the Bay of Fundy* (St. Stephens, New Brunswick: *St. Croix Courier,* 1876); and Martha F. Barto, *Passamaquoddy: Genealogies of West Isles Families* (St. John, New Brunswick, Canada: Lingley Printing, 1975), all of which mention the Chaffey mercantile interests. For good measure, there are informative Canadian news clippings, early New Brunswick probate records, and Chaffey company account books in the New Brunswick Museum. For Booth's oil investments, see John A. Ellsler, *Stage Memories,* ed. Effie Ellsler Wesson (1950); Hildegarde Dolson, *The Great Oildorado* (New York: Random House, 1959); "Booth in the Oilfields," by E. J. Miller, *Pennsylvania Historical Magazine* 21 (July 1954); Joseph H. Simonds to D. V. Derickson, April 25, 1865, LAS Files, NARA. For Booth's western tour, see J. W. Booth to J. Ellsler, January 23, 1864, Western Reserve Historical Society, Cleveland, Ohio; Edwin Adams to "My Dear Rearkirt" [Eckert?], April 17, 1865, LAS Files, NARA. Browning's pro-rebel background: He is charged with Confederate sympathies in A. M. Swan to Benjamin Butler, September 14, 1867, Benjamin Butler Papers, LC. Peregrine Browning family papers, also LC, contain samples of rebel poetry. For Ringgold Browning's military service and contraband activities, see Compiled Service Records of Confederate Soldiers and also Unfiled Papers and Slips, etc., War Department Collection of Confederate Records, NARA. William A. Browning's letter asking Secretary Stanton to release his brother, October 20, 1863, and delivered in person by Gov. Andrew Johnson, is in the Turner-Baker papers. For more on Ringgold Browning's rebel service, see the Union Provost Marshal's File of Papers Relating to Individual Civilians, NARA.

Chapter 4

That Stanton had habitually opposed any large-scale exchange of prisoners is in Thomas and Hyman, *Stanton: The Life and Times of Lincoln's Secretary of War* (New York: Alfred A. Knopf, 1962), and OR Ser. 2, v. 11. The *New York Times,* August 23, 24, and September 5, 1864, and the *National Intelligencer,* September 12 and 14, 1864, give ample impression of how the prisoner problem weighed on Lincoln's mind. For a useful chronology on this issue, see Clement Eaton, *A History of the Southern Confederacy* (New York: Macmillan, 1964). For details on the raid, see Virgil C. Jones, *Eight Hours before Richmond* (New York: Holt, 1957), and the *New York Times,* March 7 and 10, 1864. Opposing aspects of the controversy over documents allegedly taken from Dahlgren's body appear in Virgil C. Jones, *Eight Hours before Richmond* (New York: Holt, 1957); Dowdery and Mannering, eds., *The Wartime Papers of Robert E. Lee* (New York: Da Capo Press, 1981); and Van Diver, ed., and Josiah Gorgas, *Civil War Diary* (1947). D. S. Sparks, ed., *Inside Lincoln's Army: The Diary of Marsena R. Patrick* (New York: T. Yoseloff, 1964), cites an officer who accompanied the expedition as expressing his belief that the documents were genuine. Another Union officer, General Meade, thought so, too, because of "Kilpatrick's reputation and collateral evidence in my possession," *Life and Letters of General George Meade* (Baltimore: Butternut and the Blues, 1996). On this point, see also John S. Mosby to Major Stiles, *Letters of*

John S. Mosby, edited by Adele H. Mitchell (Stuart-Mosby Historical Society, 1986). The undercover activities of Andrew Johnson's confidential aide are outlined in several memoranda among the Potter Collection, especially the detective's interview, April 26, 1876, with John C. Van Duzer, whose wartime military commission had been arranged with the help of R. D. Watson and Orville H. Browning. For Van Duzer's misuse of the military telegraph, see *The Photographic History of the Civil War,* vol. 8, ed. Francis C. Miller (New York: Castle Books, 1957), and OR Ser. 1, vol. 17, pt. 2. The financier Jay Gould, a postwar partner of Eckert in the creation of the Western Union Telegraph Company, had "rigged up a telegraph system by which he learned in advance of Union victories and defeats"; see Richard O'Connor, *Gould's Millions* (Garden City, N.Y.: Doubleday, 1962). Exploiting "unbridled Yankee avarice" is a proposal of Francis Ruffin to Secretary of War James Seddon, February 8, 1864, OR Ser. 4, vol. 3; and Col. Lucien Northrop correspondence, *New York Herald,* July 21, 1865. For Booth's throat trouble, see the *New Orleans Times,* March 20, 21, and 27, 1864. "Seeking an end to this madness," Booth said in a letter to Browning. Undated, but almost certainly April 14, 1865, this remarkable missive, revealed here for the first time, was discovered in Browning's room after his death. It fell into the hands of his brother Ringgold, and in 1872 Andrew Potter had a true copy made, from which a further copy was notarized for Potter's friend Gaylord McCluer, a Crawfordsville, Indiana, banker. It is in our possession as part of the Potter Papers.

Chapter 5

Celestina and the *Indian:* The schooner's seizure and disposal are traced through OR, *Navies,* Ser. 1, vols. 9 and 10; also Records of the District Courts of the United States, Admiralty Case no. 114, NARA. Details on Celestina (Joas Celeste), including his smuggling background and the *Indian*'s mission, are assembled from NDP reports and memoranda in the Potter Papers. See also the Union Provost Marshal's File, Confederate Records, NARA; and "The Unknown Conspirator," by Philip V. D. Stern, *American Heritage* (February 1957). Barnes's early life is briefly detailed in the only published obituary to follow his all but unnoticed death, an undated clipping from the *Crawford County Gazette* (Illinois), 1916. Autobiographical material that Barnes volunteered to Detective Andrew Potter, July 12, 1876, was supplemented almost exactly one hundred years later via tape-recorded interview with his centenarian son George Henry Barnes, March 13 and 15, 1975. Alexander T. Stewart: The founding father of American retail commerce has been favored with no serious biography. For sidelights and insights, it is necessary to navigate the literature on nineteenth-century business development and practice. The following are useful: *Frank Leslie's Popular Monthly* (June 1876); M. H. Smith, *Twenty Years among the Bulls and Bears of Wall Street* (New York: American Book Company, 1873); and a profile from *Belfast News* (Ireland), July 15, 1876. A clipping from an unidentified Philadelphia newspaper article, dated August 31, 1877, deems Stewart "one of the meanest men and merchants that ever lived. He squelched hundreds of smaller dealers without compunction and ground his employees into the very dust of humiliation and impecuniosity." As for his hold over the president's wife, see

Justin and Linda Turner, eds., *Mary Todd Lincoln: Her Life and Letters* (New York: Alfred A. Knopf, 1972). His peculiar business moves are debated in Brown Shipley, Liverpool, to Brown Brothers, New York, April 28, August 12, and October 1, 1864; and Brown Brothers to Brown Shipley, October 14 and December 5, 1864, *Brown Brothers Harriman Historical File,* New-York Historical Society, New York. Brown's banking family: Edwin J. Perkins, *Financing Anglo-American Trade: The House of Brown 1800–1880* (Cambridge, Mass.: Harvard University Press, 1975); Aytoun Ellis, *Heir of Adventure: The Story of Brown, Shipley and Company* (London: Issued privately, 1960); J. A. Kouwenhoven, *Partners in Banking* (Garden City, N.Y.: Doubleday, 1909). For the orgy of gold gambling, see William A. Fowler, *Ten Years in Wall Street* (Hartford, Conn.: Worthington Dustin, 1870), and R. Sobell, *Curbstone Brokers: The Origin of the American Stock Exchange* (New York: Macmillan, 1970). For Lincoln's ardent view of an appropriate retribution, see D. L. Thomas, *The Plungers and the Peacocks: 150 Years of Wall Street* (New York: G. P. Putnam & Sons, 1967). The most persistent and well-informed of lobbyists pestering the president on cotton matters was the New England textile merchant and economist Edward Atkinson. See Harold F. Williamson, *Edward Atkinson: The Biography of an American Liberal, 1827–1905* (New York: Arno, 1972). Letters unavailable to Williamson, showing the logic and thrust of Atkinson's arguments to Lincoln, are July 8, 19, and August 13, 1864, LC. Also see Gideon Welles, *Diary* (1911), entry for July 5, 1864; and Ludwell H. Johnson, "Contraband Trade during the Civil War," *Mississippi Valley Historical Review* 49 (March 1962).

Chapter 6

For details on the Wade-Davis Bill, consult Nicolay and Hay, *Abraham Lincoln: A History,* 10 vols. (New York: Century, 1890), vol. 9; and William F. Zornow, *Lincoln and the Party Divided* (Norman: University of Oklahoma Press, 1954). An intimidating force: The nature and influence of the radicals in Lincoln's political party have been examined from different perspectives: see T. Harry Williams, *Lincoln and the Radicals* (Madison: University of Wisconsin Press, 1941); Michael L. Benedict, *A Compromise of Principle* (New York: Norton, 1974); G. McWhiney, *Grant, Lee, Lincoln and the Radicals* (Baton Rouge, La., 1964); and "Who Were the Senate Radicals?" by E. D. Gambrill, *Civil War History* XI (September 1965). For Wade's outburst, see the *Congressional Globe,* 38th Congress, 2d Session; and for Sumner's fears, see Edward L. Pierce, *Memoirs and Letters of Charles Sumner* (New York: Arno Press, 1969); and David Donald, *Charles Sumner and the Rights of Man* (New York: Knopf, 1970). The radicals "persistently urged a vigorous policy suited to remorseless revolution and violence," according to one of the breed: George W. Julian, *Speeches on Political Questions 1850–1868* (New York: Hurd and Houghton, 1872). Lincoln was "fully aware that they would strike him down if they durst," wrote the attorney general in Lincoln's first administration, Howard K. Beale, *Diary of Edward Bates, 1859–1866* (Washington: Government Printing Office, 1933). "A little bloodletting" is from Mary K. George, *Zachariah Chandler, a Political Biography* (Lansing: Michigan State University Press, 1966). Wade's "deluge the whole land in blood" was reported in the *Cincinnati Daily Gazette,*

September 26, 1863. Also see Hans Troufesse, *The Radical Republicans: Lincoln's Vanguard for Racial Justice* (New York: Knopf, 1968). Brushed aside unsigned: Nicolay and Hay, *Abraham Lincoln;* John Hay, *Letters of John Hay and Extracts from Diary* (Washington: Printed but not published, 1908); James G. Randall, *Lincoln the President,* vol. IV (New York: Dodd Mead, 1945–1955). Reference to Henry Winter Davis's voice is in Noah Brooks, *Washington in Lincoln's Time* (New York: Century, 1895). For the Wade-Davis Manifesto, see the *New York Tribune,* August 5, 1864; *Appleton's Cyclopedia of Biography* (New York, 1864); Williams, *Lincoln and the Radicals;* and Benedict, *A Compromise.* "Boded no good" is from an unidentified clipping enclosed with Thurlow Weed to William H. Seward, August 10, 1864, Seward Papers, University of Rochester Library. Alexander Stephens's affirmation of cotton as "the tremendous lever" is in the *New York Times,* October 19, 1864. Concerning a letter from 178 1/2 Water Street, New York City directories from 1865 through 1867 show the Demills as lawyers and merchants at that address. The New York Demills during the Civil War were of the family that six years later produced Cecil B. DeMille of motion picture fame. Background material is at the Brooklyn Public Library and at the Brown Public Library, Washington, North Carolina. This and other Demill letters were offered to us for high-price purchase at Sikeston, Missouri, in July 1988. Their nature was sufficient to establish their authenticity, but doubt clouded their provenance, and while copies were obtained, no sale resulted. Inquiry pointed to Emsy H. Swaim (1896–1982), an Eden, Texas, attorney and collector of Lincoln assassination memorabilia, as their earlier owner. A sampling of the agitated correspondence among Republicans who feared defeat in the 1864 national election was published in the *New York Sun,* June 30, 1889, as a collection of letters illustrating the "secret movement to supersede Abraham Lincoln in 1864." Lincoln's "I am a beaten man" is cited in Francis Lieber to Charles Sumner, August 31, 1864, Frank B. Freidel, *Francis Lieber, Nineteenth Century Liberal* (Baton Rouge: Louisiana State University Press, 1943?). Published documentation on the militant Strong Band is slight. See "A Strong Band Circular," by George W. Smith, *Mississippi Valley Historical Review* XXIX (March 1943); also Zornow, *The Party Divided.* "What are you going to do in this chaos?" was asked by Lieber of Sumner, August 31, 1864, cited in Freidel, *Francis Lieber.* Prediction of political unrest was made in England by Edward Pierrepont, future U.S. attorney general, and relayed back home. See Brown Shipley to Brown Brothers, July 29, 1864, in Brown Brothers-Harriman Historical File, New-York Historical Society. For "atrocious conspirators," see Ward Lamon pamphlet, Rare Books Division, LC. The meeting at Judge Field's is referred to in Lieber to Sumner, August 31, 1864. Also note George Wilkes to Elihu Washburne, August 31, 1864, Washburne Papers, LC; John A. Stevens to Benjamin Butler, August 27, 1864, Butler Papers, LC, i; and the *New York Sun,* June 30, 1889. "Really a planned coup," said James V. Barnes, in an interview with Andrew Potter, 1876, Potter Papers. The discovery made by congressional investigators that prominent northerners were "accomplices" in a plot against Lincoln was reported in the *New York Times,* November 1, 1867. "On his way lower down," wrote Henry W. Davis to S. F. Du Pont, August 31, 1864, Letters of Admiral Du Pont,

Hagley Museum and Library, Wilmington, Delaware. William P. Wood's undercover work while nominally in charge of the Old Capitol Prison is affirmed in Levi Turner to E. M. Stanton, November 7, 1865, Turner Letterbook, NARA. Also, Wood's obituary in the *Evening Star,* March 21, 1903, and "In Pursuit of Booth Once More," by Curtis C. Davis, *Maryland Historical Magazine* 79 (Fall 1984). A meeting with Mosby: The Booth-Wood-Mosby rendezvous is described by Mosby in a personal interview with Caroline Long Harper, August 1913, transcript provided by her great-granddaughter. Mosby repeats this account of the Lincoln kidnap conspiracy in a suppressed chapter of his memoirs. Caroline Harper's research concerning Abraham Lincoln was incidental to her main purpose, an investigation into the wartime murder of a German Brethren Church elder named John Kline. For Samuel B. Arnold, see his *Defense and Prison Experience of a Lincoln Conspirator,* ed. Charles F. Heartman (Hattiesburg, Miss.: The Book Farm, 1943). An unpublished memoir by "John Henry Stevenson," almost certainly Michael O'Laughlen, describes Booth as telling Arnold and O'Laughlen that he had been approached by a high government official who offered to pay him for kidnapping the president. "A provisional government would be designated by Congress." The memoir was transcribed by Lottie Eaton, foster child of Elmira Brandt of Davenport, Iowa, the sister of a Lafayette Baker detective. Copy furnished to us by the Brandt family. For Davis's "wring from that old fool," see J. D. Hayes, ed., *Samuel Francis Du Pont, Selected Civil War Letters* (Ithaca, N.Y.: Cornell University Press, 1969). Insight into the radicals' mood at this stage and what, in their perspective, were to be Lincoln's obligations once reelected is provided by George Julian, *Speeches on Political Questions* (1872). That there was "a conspiracy . . . formidable and vicious" is in Nicolay and Hay, *Abraham Lincoln,* vol. 4. Governor Andrew's involvement is described in Henry G. Pearson, *The Life of John Andrew.*

Chapter 7

Cotton sought after and brought out: Tyler Dennett, *Lincoln and the Civil War, in the Diaries and Letters of John Hay* (New York: Dodd, Meade & Company, 1939); "O'Connor, Lincoln, and the Cotton Trade," *Civil War History* (March 1961); L. H. Johnson, "Contraband Trade during the Last Year of the Civil War," *Mississippi Valley Historical Review* 49 (March 1962); and the same writer's "Northern Profits and Profiteers: Cotton Rings of 1864–65," *Civil War History* 13 (June 1966). Also see E. M. Coulter, "Commercial Intercourse with the Confederacy," *Mississippi Valley Historical Review* 388; and for the busy ringmaster, Hanson Risley to Thurlow Weed, summer 1864, Weed Mss., University of Rochester Library. Hay letter, September 26, 1864, is in *Letters of John Hay and Extracts from His Diary,* 3 vols. (1908). The men have Lincoln's ear: Richard Demill to Henry Megill, September 12, 1864. Megill was R. D. Watson's brother-in-law, a physician, a contrabandist, and an investor in the meat-for-cotton deal (Demill Papers). White House fiat: The cotton regulations are House Exec. Docs., 38th Congress, 2d Session, which also show the executive order permitting one-third payment for rebel cotton in the form of supplies. It also appears in Basler, *Collected Works,* vol. 8. Additional material in Johnson, "Northern Profits and Profiteers." Details on the negotiation and scheming toward a mammoth deal of pork for cotton are found in detective interviews with Govin, Kein, Barnes, Watson, and Megill in the Potter Papers. Henry Stewart Company: Its only mention in any published work is in Oscar A. Kinchen, *Confederate Operations in Canada and the North* (North Quincy, Mass.: Christopher Publications House, 1970). James Watson's last letter, with its hidden name and the location of John Surratt, is in the Neff-Guttridge Collection, thanks to the generosity of Watson descendants. For intriguing data on Surratt, see Detective Andrew Potter's 1875 interview with James V. Barnes, who identified the Montreal businessmen's treacherous courier as "Charley Armstrong." Surratt's use of this alias is confirmed in the diary of Edwin Gray Lee, microfilm copy in the *Southern Historical Collection,* University of North Carolina, and excerpted in "Sidelights—Who Hid John H. Surratt?" *Maryland Historical Society Magazine* LX (June 1965). Also see Surratt's own words from his Rockville, Maryland, lecture, the *Evening Star,* December 7, 1870, and the interview with Hanson Hiss, *Washington Post,* April 3, 1898, in which he speaks of his "pockets . . . full of Uncle Sam's gold furnished me by my government." This instance of intercepted enemy dispatches may be the one Charles Dana recalled for Ida Tarbell in 1896. See Charles A. Dana, *Recollections of the Civil War* (New York: Appleton, 1898). For the agent's "capture" and "escape," see Gen. C. C. Augur to Secy. Stanton, November 12, 1864, enclosing a report of Col. H. H. Wells with the papers found on "Peterson," War Department Records, NARA. Also see the *Washington Evening Star,* November 15 and 17, 1864. Lincoln's telegram: Dated November 6, 1864, addressed to Admiral Farragut, and transmitted through Gen. Edward R. Canby at New Orleans. The president's follow-up letter to Canby, with his stated belief that rebels had forged his signature, is dated December 12, 1864, in Basler, *Collected Works,* vol. VIII. Cotton at Mobile: Coded telegram, General R. Taylor to secretary of war, Richmond, November 18, 1864, *Telegrams to the Confederate Secretary of War,* NARA. The secretary's reply, November 29, 1864, is in *Telegrams Sent by the Confederate Secretary of War,* NARA. In the same assemblage of Confederate records filed under the general heading of Records of the Office of the Secretary of War, NARA, can be found additional telegrams on the subject, sent by General Dabney H. Maury and including his report of suspended action off Mobile.

Chapter 8

Death threats abounded. A plot against Lincoln's predecessor, James Buchanan, is mentioned in Ward H. Lamon, *Recollections of Abraham Lincoln 1847–1865* (Lincoln: University of Nebraska Press, 1994). The letter pronouncing Lincoln "a dead man in six months," dated January 4, 1864, is no. 29176 in the Lincoln Collection, LC. The advertisement of an assassin for hire appeared in the *Selma (Alabama) Morning Dispatch,* December 1, 1864. The western editor calling for a dagger thrust was Brick Pomeroy, whose inflammatory words are cited in the *Buffalo Commercial Advertiser,* November 5, 1864. For the president's protection, see *Indiana Historical Publications,* vol. 5, lecture by R. W. McBride, late Union Light Guard before Century Club, Indianapolis; "Experiences as a Member of Lincoln's Bodyguard," by Smith Stimmel, *North Dakota Historical Quarterly* XXXVII (January

1927): pt. 11. For Lincoln's indication on a military order that he wishes no escort, see Basler, *Collected Works,* vol. 11. The old Van Ness place is described in Frank Carpenter, *Carp's Washington* (New York: McGraw-Hill, 1960); Felix Stidger Report, Turner-Baker Papers; Elizabeth L. Lomax, *Leaves from a Washington Diary;* T. B. Peterson, *The Trial of the Alleged Assassins and Conspirators* (Philadelphia: T. B. Peterson and Brothers, 1865); "Recollections of Mansion Square," by Mary F. (Green) Stone, unpublished memoir in the Virginia Historical Society, Richmond; Memoranda in the Potter Papers.

Chapter 9

Reviewing contracts: Hanson Risley's methods, including erasures and alterations, and the nature of abuses arising therefrom, are outlined in U.S. Congress, House Reports of Committees, 38th Congress, 2d Session, no. 24, "Trade with Rebellious States." Also see 7th Special Agency, Records of the Department of the Treasury, NARA. War Department a stumbling block: Records of the Adjutant General, General Order 285, October 6, 1864, signed by E. D. Townsend. That the president pressured his secretary of war into line is shown by D. Randolph Martin to W. P. Dole, November 14, 1864, in 7th Special Agency Records, RG: 366, NARA. Incredible results: For more on Joseph H. Maddox, see R. Lamon to W. Lamon, January 20, 1865, Lamon Mss., Huntington Library, San Marino, CA. Copious evidence of Maddox's business and espionage activities appears in 51st Congress, 1st Session, Ex. Doc. 101, April 8, 1890; Turner-Baker Papers; and Seventh Special Agency Records, Treasury Dept., NARA. The Poughkeepsie merchant Robert E. Coxe was represented in Washington by Lincoln's lobbyist friend Orville H. Browning. Coxe's contract is recorded in "Trade with Rebellious States" and Basler, *Collected Works,* vol. 8. Also see Coxe's statement, "made voluntarily at the direction of the Secretary of War," May 10, 1865, LAS Files. Coxe is mentioned in B. Tucker to his brother, June 17, 1864, LAS Files B. That Booth's wardrobe was lost is reported in the *New York Herald,* November 15, 1865, citing the *Quebec Morning Chronicle,* July 17 and 19, 1865. For Booth in New York, see Kimmel, *The Mad Booths of Maryland,* and Samuel Chester's testimony, in Peterson, *The Trial of the Alleged Assassins and Conspirators.* Booth's onstage "fire and elan" is in the *New York Times,* November 29, 1864, and Odell, *Annals of the New York Stage* (New York: Columbia Press, 1927). "God judge me": Booth's written outburst is in General Records, Department of Justice, NARA. A squad of experienced detectives: Robert A. West to Nicolay, November 30, 1864, Nicolay Mss., LC. "Your life is sought after," wrote Lamon, *Recollections.* Lamon as bodyguard is in Dennett, *Letters and Diaries of John Hay.* Lamon professed to have good reasons for uneasiness in a letter to Nicolay, December 15, 1864, Nicolay Mss., LC. Officers reacted angrily: Union protests in OR Ser. 21, vol. 39, pt. 2. Confederate protests, ibid., and vol. 41, pt. 4. Also see OR Ser. 4, vol. 3, "baseness of Judas Iscariot" is cited in "Trade with Rebellious States," and the impassioned appeal to get the law repealed in General C. C. Washburn to Congressman E. B. Washburne, December 25, 1864, Washburne Mss., LC. Greedy cotton rings: Welles's warning is in Beale, *Gideon Welles Diary,* and Sherman's alarm in a letter to W. P. Fessenden, January 19, 1865,

OR Ser. 1, vol. 47, pt. 2. That the president was "determined to have the cotton come," said by Congressman Oakes Ames, is reported in E. Atkinson to H. Risley, 7th Special Agency Records, NARA.

Chapter 10

Uncontrollable fate: Booth's letter to his mother is in the General Records of the Department of Justice, RG60, NARA. Although sealed within the same envelope containing Booth's November 1864 declaration, the different appearance of its ink and that of his signature indicates that it was added to the earlier effusion when the envelope was reopened. Tug of war on again: Benedict, "A Compromise of Principle," *Congressional Globe,* 38th Congress, 2d Session (January 1865). That "military men" infiltrated Booth's plans to abduct the president is reported by George A. Townsend in the *New York World,* May 10, 1865. For Ringgold Browning, brother of Andrew Johnson's private secretary, see Confederate Service Records and Turner-Baker files 3312, 3313, B648. They include Browning's statement, December 13, 1864, Johnson's application for Browning's release, and President Lincoln's endorsement of it. Also see Unfiled Confederate Papers, Microcopy 247, NARA, which shows Browning, as confined to prison, "lieutenant and adjutant to Col. Mosby." Prisoner of War Boyd: See the *Washington Evening Star,* October 31, 1864; and Register of the Old Capitol Prison, page 304, part 783, NARA. When Boyd surrendered himself to Colonel Edward Hatch, 2nd Iowa Cavalry, at Jackson, Tennessee, in July 1863, he applied for permission to take the oath of allegiance in hopes of gaining a parole to stay with his consumptive wife and seven children. For Boyd's transfer to Washington on a special order from Secretary Stanton, see Case 4013, Turner-Baker Papers. Across one of its documents is penciled "Wm. B. Earle, Park Hotel, New York." Earle was the NDP agent attached to the supposed turncoat Boyd as his "control." In Record of Passes Signed by the Secretary of War January 1st, 1864—March 23d, 1865 (NARA), Earle's name is close to Boyd's. While "confined in a separate cell" as a prisoner of war, Boyd worked for his Union captors, at least as a telegrapher for Major Eckert. He was one of a dozen telegraphers along Chesapeake Bay's eastern shore in early 1865. See William R. Plum, *The Military Telegraph during the Civil War in the United States* (New York: Arno Press, 1974). Booth in southern Maryland: See O. H. Oldroyd, *Assassination of Abraham Lincoln* (Washington, D.C.: Published privately, 1901); Arnold, *Defense and Prison Experiences.* Free and unmolested passage: Basler, *Collected Works,* vol. VIII, where the name of the recipient of the contracts and passes is given as Henry J. Eager. The name was actually that of R. D. Watson, later erased after Lincoln's murder. See also detective interviews with Barnes, Watson, and Kein.

Chapter 11

Moribund little port: Eyewitness accounts of the activity at Port Tobacco came from a cotton broker and commercial agent named Missionary E. Martin, who had been delayed there while en route to Richmond for completion of a cotton-for-meat contract with the rebel government. See J. L. McPhail to Secy. Stanton, LAS Files; *Trial of John Surratt in the Criminal Court for the District of Columbia,* 2 vols.

(Washington, D.C.: Government Printing Office, 1867); R. M. Smoot, *The Unwritten History of the Assassination of Abraham Lincoln* (Baltimore: John Murphy, 1904); and G. A. Townsend in the *Cincinnati Enquirer,* April 14 and 19, 1892. The web of communication posts is described in Capt. W. N. Barker's "report of the signal corps" for the quarter ending March 31, 1864, Turner-Baker Papers, NARA; Capt. J. L. Smith's report of the signal corps in Richmond and on the Potomac, December 21, 1864, Letters Received by the Confederate Secy. of War, War Department Collection of Confederate Records, NARA. OR, Ser. 1, vol. IV, and Ser. 1, vol. V; Thomas A. Jones, *John Wilkes Booth* (Chicago: Laird and Lee, 1897). For Mosby's guerrillas in the Northern Neck, see V. C. Jones, *Ranger Mosby* (Chapel Hill: University of North Carolina Press, 1944); and OR, *Navies,* Ser. 1, vol. V. Also, *Confederate Veteran* 40 (1952). Tidwell, Hall, and Gatty, *Come Retribution* (Jackson: University of Mississippi Press, 1988), provides valuable details on the Confederacy's "signal corps" network. For Forrest, the greatest actor, see *Washington Constitutional Union,* January 17, 1865. "Thinks I live upon him," John Wilkes Booth wrote to Junius B. Booth, January 17, 1865, Seymour Theatre Collection, Princeton University Library. "An armistice would be death," Francis Lieber told Halleck, February 4, 1865, Lieber Papers, Huntington Library, San Marino, California, quoted in F. Friedel, *Francis Lieber* (1948). *The Peacemakers of 1864;* Basler, *Collected Works,* vol. 8; James G. Randall, *Lincoln, the President,* 4 vols. (New York: Dodd Mead, 1944–1955), vol. 4; Nicolay and Hay, "Abraham Lincoln," *Century Magazine* (May 1884). For the radicals' resolution in Congress, see Basler, *Collected Works,* vol. 8. "Humble rail-splitter" was the term used before a Boston audience by William L. Garrison, February 4, 1865, reported in *The Liberator* (Boston), February 10, 1865. The storms are detailed in the *Congressional Globe,* 38th Congress, 2d Session. Newspapers of the period report the political turmoil, and for a foreigner's view of the worsening situation, see Charles A. P. Marquis de Chambrun, *Impressions of Lincoln and the Civil War* (New York: Random House, 1952). The intensification of the radicals' warfare against Lincoln is described in Benedict, *A Compromise of Principle.* "He must accept our views" comes from "A Russian Estimate of Lincoln," by Benjamin Thomas, *Bulletin of the American Lincoln Association* (June 1931). For Wade's belief in congressional primacy, see his letter to B. Storer, December 17, 1866, Storer Mss., Historical and Philosophical Society of Ohio, Cincinnati. The petition for divine removal of an unsatisfactory chief executive was made by Owen Lovejoy at a National Republication Party convention in Pittsburgh, February 22, 1856, and quoted by Julian, *Recollections.* The change in Booth is reflected in Simonds's letters to the actor, January 6, 24, and February 21, 1865, LAS Files, NARA. G. A. Townsend tells of "unwilling military men" in the *New York World,* May 10, 1865. Also see Lafayette C. Baker, *History of the United States Secret Service* (Bowie, Md.: Heritage Books, 1992). Ella Turner's note is in LAS Files, NARA. The War Department's grand inquisitor, from L. E. Chittendon, *Recollections of President Lincoln and His Administration* (1891). For the inventories Baker filed as the agent in charge of abandoned rebel property, see Baker, *Secret Service,* 567–571, in which same work he justifies the practice of domestic spying in wartime as follows: "When war, especially the most fearful form, a civil conflict, exists, the unnatural condition of things calls for the detective service, to watch and bring to justice the enemies of the state." Backwater to the cotton tide: For fuller detail on this significant, yet often ignored, congressional investigation, including correspondence and testimony of Lafayette Baker and Hanson Risley, see Hearings and Report, "Trade with Rebellious States," 38th Congress, 2d Session, House Report 24, LC.

Chapter 12

Information about Harriet "Lola" Alexander appears within NDP reports and the correspondence of the Potter Papers, with firm corroborative evidence in the research of Doctor William W. Parsons (1854–1925), a prominent Indiana educator during the last century's early decades. Correlative material is also found in an unpublished chapter of the memoirs of John S. Mosby, lawyer, diplomat, and former Confederate partisan leader. Copies of letters from "Lola" to Booth are in the Potter Papers. Early background on this genuine "mystery woman" is found among census records and genealogical records of the Stover family, Botetart County, Virginia. Her letter to William A. Browning, enclosing a valentine, is among the Potter Papers. James W. Boyd's bid for freedom is attested to in the Andrew Potter monographs, Potter Papers; in Boyd family letters; and in correspondence with his Union captors, Turner-Baker Papers, File 4013; also J. Holt to E. Stanton, March 24, 1865, citing Boyd to William P. Wood, December 4, 1864, in *Record Book of the Bureau of Military Justice,* vol. 15 (January 1865), NARA. Boyd's release on oath, February 15, 1865, "by order of the Secretary of War," is recorded in the Old Capitol Prison records, NARA. Boyd in New York: Almost immediately after his release, Boyd called at 178 ½ Water Street, as revealed in Richard Demill to Henry Megill, Watson Provision Company, one of the letters offered to us for sale in Sikeston, Missouri. It also connects Boyd with his control, William B. Earle. For the Belleville showdown, see Barnes to Watson, March 1, 1865; Watson family papers; and the John Shaffer interview with Martha Mills, 1926. Shaffer was a prominent Midwest newspaper proprietor and editor. A copy of his interview is among the research materials left by Professor William Wood Parsons and secured by us via Parson's widow and their protege Richard Gemmecke (1898–1972), an Indiana historian and the first dean of arts and science at Indiana State University. Shortly before his death, Gemmecke was preparing to publish, including the letter from "Lola" to Booth, revelations that could "change recorded history. . . . I am on the verge of a historical coup the magnitude of which frightens me." Much of the material was destroyed by Gemmecke's widow, but several key documents escaped the flames (authors' interview with Mrs. Conrad Gemmecke, February 13, 1987). Evidence that six NDP operatives, including Earl and Andrew Potter, were given military commissions is in R. B. Moore, Indiana State Library, Indianapolis, to Gaylord McCluer, Crawfordsville, Indiana, October 23, 1940, Potter Papers. For the plight of the rebel troops on limited rations, see Kean, *Diary.* Richmond's approval of barter for bacon from whatever quarter is in Seddon to Gen. Lee, February 19, 1865, OR Ser. 4, vol. 111. Tucker's fears that his plan will be "botched" is in Tucker to R. M. T. Hunter, February 2, 1865, in Salmon Chase Mss., LC. The original letter from Cape Girardeau is in the Neff-Guttridge Collection. Edgar P. Stringer, to whom Barnes refers to as an aid in the fulfillment of contracts, from his office at No. 8, Austin Friars, London, founded the Mercantile Trading Company specifically to do business with the Richmond government. See Records of the Inspector General, Confederate Papers Relating to Intercepted Correspondence; Individuals or Business Firms; Correspondence and Reports of the Confederate Treasury in NARA. Stringer is also mentioned in OR, *Navies,* Ser. 2, vol. 2.

Chapter 13

Fifty determined men: T. Ewing to E. M. Stanton, February 22, 1865, Ewing Mss., LC. For Weichmann, see F. R. Riswold, ed., *A True History of the Assassination of Abraham Lincoln and of the Conspiracy of 1865,* by Lewis J. Weichmann (New York: Knopf, 1975). Compare Weichmann's version of his role with D. H. Gleason's "The Conspiracy against Lincoln," *Magazine of History* (February 1911); and the Gleason statement, LAS Files, NARA. That it took a pointed summons from Lincoln to make sure of Andrew Johnson's presence at his own inauguration, see Basler, *Collected Works,* vol. 8. Evidence of a previous connection between Andrew Johnson and Booth appears in a sworn affidavit published in the *Chicago Tribune,* July 27, 1868 (editorial comment two days later), with the affiant's name omitted. The additional publication, to support the affidavit's soundness, of a dated letter (name again omitted) to President Lincoln, requesting promotion, made it easy to establish the affiant's identity as that of Lieutenant James H. Woodard, sometime military aide to Andrew Johnson. Booth and Johnson had become "boon companions," according to veteran newsman Don Piatt, writing to Joseph Holt, January 13, 1889, Holt Papers, LC. For cotton contracts, see House Reports, 38th Congress, 2d Session, March 1865; and Williamson, *Edward Atkinson.* Stanton intervened: See Lamon, *Recollections;* Philip Van Doren Stern, *An End to Valor* (Boston: Houghton Mifflin, 1958); Basler, *Collected Works,* vol. 8; Stanton to Gen. Dix, April 22, 1865, Stanton Papers, LC. The considerable evidence that Andrew Johnson was intoxicated includes Senator Zachariah Chandler's letter to his wife—the new vice president was "too drunk to perform his duty"—March 6, 1865, Chandler Mss., LC. Also see de Chambrun, *Impressions.* Enraged by Lincoln's veto: Lamon, *Recollections.* That the real purpose of Washburne's trip to City Point was to counteract Lincoln's veto is shown in "George Julian's Journal—Assassination of Lincoln," *Indiana Magazine of History* XIII (December 1915). For Grant's special order, see OR Ser. 1, vol. 46, pt. 2; and Lincoln to Grant, "what form you choose," Basler, *Collected Works,* vol. 8. That Lincoln had broken the law was asserted by Congressman George Julian, whose daughter provided extracts of his diary for publication in *Indiana Historical Magazine of History* XI (December 1915). Claude Bowers, preparing his book *The Tragic Era,* borrowed the 1865 diary and photographed its pages without Grace Clark's knowledge. Citations here are from both versions. It "frightens me," wrote R. D. Watson to his wife, may be found in the correspondence and diary of Caroline Dickerson, Watson's sister-in-law, Watson family papers. For shipping orders to take on special cargo, see Thomas Caldwell to Captain Scott, Neff-Guttridge Collection; Chaffey business ledgers show Caldwell's connection with the Indian Island shipping firm. Also see Leeds interview, Potter Papers. The United States Coast Guard located Okahanikan Cove for us. The meeting at Gautier's is described in Pitman, *Trial;* statements, LAS File; and Arnold, *Prison Experiences and Defense.* Also, see John Surratt lecture, Rockville, Maryland, the *Evening Star,* December 8, 1870. An unpublished version of Surratt's lecture, identifying the interlopers as rebel prisoners of war specially released for employment in the Lincoln kidnap plot, is among the Potter Papers. The undertaking more complicated, fears Arnold, in a letter found in Booth's room after the assassination, LAS Files, NARA. Surratt's movements are traced in detective reports, Potter Papers, and Surratt lecture reported in the *Washington Evening Star.* "Make the terms lenient" is in Beale, *Gideon Welles Diary.* The reference to Grant and bacon is in the *Baltimore American,* March 23, 1865. Also see "Julian's Diary" in *Indiana Historical Society, Magazine of History* XI (December 1915), for the radicals' belief that Lincoln's purpose at City Point was to have Grant annul his special order. For Hanson Risley's involvement in the president's trip, see Risley to Abraham Lincoln, March 23, 1865, Lincoln Collection, LC. The defiant Confederate Congress Resolution, March 14, 1865, is reported in the Richmond press. Also see Frank E. Vandiver, *Their Tattered Flags* (1870), and E. A. Pollard, *The Lost Cause* (1870). That the rebels were preparing to "astonish the world" is in the *Washington Morning Chronicle,* February 17, 1865. For Secy. Trenholm's stop-gap legislation, the Act to Raise Coin, see his letters of March 17 and 22, 1865, to the Treasury Agent at Marshall, Texas, and on March 22, 1865, "to the Banks and private capitalists in the Confederate States," Letters sent by the Confederate Secretary of the Treasury, NARA. Ficklin's responses under questioning, May 16 and June 12, 1865, are in LAS Files, NARA. Also see Richard Lester, *Confederate Finance and Purchasing in Great Britain* (Charlottesville: University of Virginia Press, 1975). Ficklin's western frontier enterprises are mentioned in Ray Bliss, *Pony Express—The Great Gamble* (Berkeley, Calif.: Howell-North, 1959). Ficklin's disclosure of having signed a contract with the rebel government is in his application for a passport: Letters Received by the Confederate Secretary of War, NARA. Also see W. B. Webb's *Handbook of Texas* 6, Austin (1952); *The Texas Almanac for 1870,* Galveston; and detective reports, Potter Papers.

Chapter 14

That Lincoln went to City Point "with the most liberal views towards the rebels. He wanted peace on any terms" is found in William T. Sherman, *Memoirs,* 2 vols. (1957). Also see Beale, *Gideon Welles Diary;* Ficklin hid in New York, reported NDP agents, Potter Papers. The meeting at the Astor between Ficklin and Watson is described in the Watson family papers. For "J. W. Booth and lady," see Alfred Smith to E. M. Stanton, April 18, 1865, LAS Files, NARA, and "William" to E. M. Stanton, Telegrams Received by the Secretary of War (bound), NARA. Booth's signature in the register of the Aquidneck Hotel wound up in the Oliver R. Barrett Collection, auctioned 1952. See also the *Lincoln Herald* 51, no. 4 (December 1949); Martha Mills interview with John Shaffer; and "Lola letters," copies in the Potter Papers. Watson is registered at the St. Lawrence Hall under his own name.

Surratt is "John Harrison." Booth signed in as "John White." See the St. Lawrence Hall register for April 1865, Canadian Archives, Ottawa; and undated "memorandum of facts" by Barney Devlin, LAS Files, NARA. For Booth at the National Hotel, see a run-down on his arrivals and departures, November 1864–April 1865, LAS Files, NARA. The impact of a cease-fire on the cotton market is stated in Edward Atkinson to John McCulloch, April 4, 1865, Letters Received by Secretary of the Treasury, NARA. For word from Liverpool on business failures, see correspondence April–May 1865 in Brown Brothers Harriman File, New-York Historical Society. Diplomatic records in NARA contain a report from the American consul in Liverpool, indicating a scare in business circles resulting from any moves toward peace. Dated February 1865, it reads: "No event since the war commenced produced so much excitement in Liverpool as news of peace negotiations going on in Hampton Roads. It amounts to a panic on the cotton market."

Chapter 15

For Seward's accident, see "The Stabbing of Lincoln's Secretary of State," by John K. Latimer, M.D., *Journal of the American Medical Association* (April 12, 1965); also, excerpts from Fanny Seward's diary, *American Heritage* (October 1959). For Weitzel's failure to order prayers in Richmond and Stanton's consequent anger, see Dana, *Recollections;* and David H. Bates, *Lincoln in the Telegraph Office* (New York: Century, 1907). Basler, *Collected Works,* vol. 8; and Dana to Stanton, April 7, 1865, Stanton Papers, LC, deal with Lincoln's move to recall the Virginia legislature. His improved grooming was noted by William Doster, *Lincoln and Episodes of the Civil War* (New York: Putnam's Sons, 1911). For his speech, see Basler, *Collected Works,* vol. 8, and the *Evening Star,* April 11, 1865. "Opposition is forming hourly," reports the *New York Tribune,* April 11, 1865. Stanton "most disconcerted" is in Sumner to Chase, April 12, 1865, Chase Papers, LC. For cabinet distress over Lincoln's action in Richmond, see Beale, *Gideon Welles Diary;* Stern, *An End to Valor;* and Thomas and Hyman, *Stanton.* Benjamin French, "Facts Worthy of Record" memoir in the New-York Historical Society, reported on Wade's "The sooner he is assassinated": Lincoln's anxious messages to Weitzel are in Basler, *Collected Works,* vol. 8. Stanton's own version of how he dictated to Lincoln is in his testimony before the Andrew Johnson Impeachment Committee, House Report No. 7, 40th Congress, 1st session. Lincoln's telegram to Weitzel countermanding his earlier instructions was the president's last, according to Bates, *Lincoln in the Telegraph Office.* Beale, *Welles Diary,* notes McCulloch's apparent dilemma over the Savannah cotton. Grant revoking his earlier order was reported in the *Philadelphia Daily Evening Bulletin,* April 13, 1865. The scrap of paper with "We must get the permits" is in LAS Files, NARA. For Browning at the White House and his involvement with Ficklin and the cotton deals, see the *Diary of Orville H. Browning,* 2 vols., ed. T. C. Pease and J. G. Randall (Springfield: Illinois State Historical Society Library, 1925–1933). Lamon's explanation for being in Richmond the night of the assassination is in Lamon, *Recollections.* The *Port Tobacco Times,* March 30, 1865, reported the Watkins killing. Boyd told of the incident in letters home, Boyd Family Papers, Neff-Guttridge Collection. That Confederate General Richard Ewell, in

Washington following his capture, was overheard saying that "within ten days we would see something we did not dream of," is in LAS Files, as is a prophecy voiced by other captured rebel officers that "agencies in the North that people knew nothing about would strike at the proper time." Booth was at the commissary of prisoners when he talked of a "big undertaking," according to the Memorandum of Evidence against John Wilkes Booth Furnished by Col. John A. Foster, April 25, 1865, LAS Files, NARA. The end of factitous fortunes is reported in the *Alexandria Gazette,* March 22, 1865. That Colfax was with Harriet Alexander in New York is disclosed in "Mrs. Col. Alexander" to John McCulloch, April 12, 1865, Letters Received by the Secretary of the Treasury, NARA.

Chapter 16

Colfax was at the White House, according to Willard H. Smith, "Schuyler Colfax," Indiana Historical Collections, Indiana Historical Society, 1952. Also see John Starr, *Lincoln's Last Day* (New York: Stokes, 1922). The cabinet meeting is noted in Beale, *Welles Diary,* vol. 11 (1960); David Donald, ed., *Salmon P. Chase.* For Grant turning down the theater invitation, see Horace Porter, *Campaigning with Grant* (1897). Booth was last at breakfast, Zachariah Chandler told his wife, Chandler Papers, LC. For Booth's subsequent moods and movements that morning, see the Pumphrey testimony; Pitman, *Trial;* and LAS Files, NARA. "Mortified bravo" is from G. A. Townsend, *New York World,* cited in Baker, *Secret Service.* "Shortened fuse" was the effect of Junius Brutus Booth's letter, to which he testified, LAS Files, NARA and in Pitman, *Trial.* That Booth left a card is in LAS Files, Reel 15, NARA. Also see A. Swan to B. Butler, September 14, 1867, Butler Papers, LC, and Booth to Browning, certified copy, Neff-Guttridge Collection. For Ella Turner, see the *New York Daily Tribune,* April 17, 1865. The president's afternoon is noted in John Starr, *Last Day* (New York: Stokes, 1922), and William Crook, *Through Five Administrations* (New York: Harper and Brothers, 1907). The frequently aired story of a Lincoln visit to the War Department, with doubtful inferences drawn, rests on shaky ground. Dana, *Recollections,* says nothing of such a visit. Maunsell B. Field, *Memories of Many Men and Some Women* (1874), has Lincoln in the Telegraph Office of the War Department exchanging pleasantries with Charles Tinker, the telegrapher, but this was the morning of April 13, as Tinker himself testified, lecturing in Brooklyn on February 12, 1907; David H. Bates, *Lincoln in the Telegraph Office,* locates the president there before the White House cabinet meeting. Secretary Stanton testified before a congressional committee in 1867 that Lincoln's last appearance at the War Department was April 12. Grant sets the time of his announced decision not to join Lincoln at Ford's Theatre as just after the forenoon April 14 cabinet meeting. A. E. H. Johnson statements, the *Evening Star,* February 15, 1896. Superintendent Richards charged "special policeman" Parker with negligence, but years elapsed before he was dismissed from the force. He was not questioned at the conspiracy trial; neither was the coachman, Burke. Photostats of Parker's record are in the New York Public Library, Manuscripts Room. For Parker and Charles Forbes, White House footman, addressing the coachman, see the statement of Francis P. Burke, LAS Files, NARA, and *Trial of John Surratt.* The footman, Forbes, was at the theater with the Lincolns, but no testimony was taken from him either. Booth's "worked to capture" is from his diary, original at the Lincoln Museum beneath Ford's Theatre but cited in numerous published works. For the fretting outside Ford's, see statements of Sergeant R. H. Cooper and Private L. M. Dye, April 22, 1865, LAS Files, NARA; and Dye's letter to his father. *New York Tribune,* April 21, 1865; also the *Washington Daily Union,* which identifies Dye as of the Pennsylvania Independent Artillery. The soldiers were not on guard duty. Writing to his brother Edwin, October 20, 1862, Junius Brutus Booth Jr. alluded to the younger brother Joseph's "insane manner . . . I do not say positive insanity but a crack that way, which father had [and] I fear runs through the male portion of the family, myself included," Walter Hampden Library, Players Club, New York. For Ford's stagehands under backstage pressures, see Edward Spangler statement, LAS Files, NARA, and Pitman, *Trial.*

Chapter 17

The Sewards' domestic secrets can be glimpsed in an NDP interview with Emerick Hansell; G. Van Deusen, *William H. Seward* (New York: Oxford University Press, 1967), and Seward Family correspondence, University of Rochester Library (microcopy in LC), especially [Mrs.] Frances Seward to her husband when Augustus was at West Point, December 17, 1842: "I shall never become reconciled to the path you have chosen for him. My continuous anxiety is wearing away my health." The description of Seward's attacker from those officially circulated first appeared in the *Washington Daily Morning Chronicle,* April 18, 1865. Fanny Seward's cry was first revealed by Fred Seward's wife two years after the event in *Trial of John Surratt.* Details on Secretary Seward's wounds are found in "The Stabbing of Lincoln's Secretary of State" by John K. Lattimer, M.D., *Journal of the American Medical Association* (April 12, 1965). A newspaper article by G. A. Townsend said, "a wire instrument to relieve the pain Seward suffered prevented the knife . . . from striking too deep." This led (or contributed) to an impression that Seward wore a neck brace. Townsend erred. There is no indication in doctors' testimony or in Fanny Seward's diary that Seward wore any device other than wire ligatures to hold the jaw in place. In a handwritten memoir, Huntington Library, Gideon Welles refers only to "a steel wire frame attached to the jaw." See also "The Treatment of Fracture of the Lower Jaw by Interdental Splints," by T. B. Gunning, *New York Medical Journal* IV (1867); "Full Particulars of the Attempted Assassination of Secretary Seward, His Family and Attendants," by T. S. Verdi, in the *Western Homeopathic Observer,* St. Louis, May 15, 1865. Gunning describes the zig-zag wound to Seward's face as appearing "to have been made by one sweep of the knife. . . . it split the cheek." Fanny Seward's "Diary," which she self-edited weeks after events, appeared in *American Heritage* (October 1959), but also see her account, "to the best of my recollection and belief," Martin Luther King Library, Washingtoniana Division, Washington, D.C. This latter writing, though done three weeks after the attack, predates the "diary" 's coverage of it. Hansell's version of the occurrence was obtained by detectives in a confidential interview, Potter Papers. Details on Ford's Theatre come from *Restoration of Ford's Theatre,* Dept. of the Interior,

Washington, D.C. The following provide essential information on the physical effects of Booth's bullet: "The Wound That Killed Lincoln," *Journal of the American Medical Association* (February 15, 1964); "Assassination and Death of Abraham Lincoln," by Charles Leale, M.D., Adgt. General Records, Special File, NARA; Lincoln Memorabilia, *Bulletin of the History of Medicine* XXXII (1958); and "Medical Aspects of the Assassination of Abraham Lincoln," Proceedings, *Royal Society of Medicine* 47, London (1954). Hoofbeats passing eastward are recalled by W. S. Burch, April 21, 1865, LAS Files, NARA; also in the *Washington Daily Morning Chronicle,* April 21, 1865. A rider seen leaving the side of the theater simultaneously with Booth's departure from its rear is reported in *Leslie's Weekly.* Also see statement of Benjamin Gilbert, another F Street resident, and Colonel Foster's April 21, 1865, "summary of evidence." F Street's eastward slope and condition are described by Henry E. Davis, "Ninth and F Street and Thereabouts," *Records of the Columbia Historical Society,* vol. 5, 239–240. Edwin Hynson is repeatedly identified as Booth's companion in NDP reports, Potter Papers, especially that of an interview with Ringgold Browning, October 7, 1870. That Browning "hired the horse" is shown by Police Superintendent Richards to Col. Ingraham, Provost Marshal, April 16, 1865, LAS Files, NARA. The whistle-blowing is well attested to, in Burch statements, LAS Files, NARA, and the testimony of J. B. Stewart, *Trial of John Surratt.* For gas lamps going out, see the B. B. French Diary, LC; also affidavit of the lamplighter, Kauffman, May 11, 1876, Ford's Theatre Collection, Washington, D.C. They could have been extinguished by the closing of a valve in the city gasworks, then located just west of the Capitol. G. A. Townsend told of the telegraph blackout in *New York World,* May 2, 1865. Eckert was to brush this off in testimony taken before the Judiciary Committee, House of Representatives, in the Investigation of Charges Against Andrew Johnson (Impeachment Hearings). The superintendent of the commercial line at Washington, William H. Heiss, would recall closing down the telegraph by short-circuiting the wires, but he did not ever make clear whether he was so ordered or acted upon his own. See letters to the authors from the Heiss family, Neff-Guttridge Collection. For how Stanton and Eckert reacted to the shooting at Ford's, see recollections of the War Department clerks Sterling and Johnson, the *Evening Star,* April 14, 1918, and Eckert's own account in the David H. Bates Papers, LC, Rare Books Division. Stanton's arrival at the Sewards' and apparent reluctance to head for Ford's are in Gideon Welles's memoir, Huntington Library. Chase's decision to wait until morning is in *Diary and Correspondence of Salmon P. Chase,* Washington Govt. Printing Office, 1903. What occurred at the Navy Yard Bridge has never been positively established. One has to consider: F. A. Demond to F. L. Bates, June 16, 1916, Swaim Collection, Georgetown University Library, Special Collections; Sgt. Silas Cobb statement, LAS Files, NARA; Lieut. David Dana, *Boston Sunday Globe,* December 12, 1897. The statement in the LAS Files is undated and unsigned. Stanley Kimmel, *The Mad Booths of Maryland,* thought, "the failure to question Cobb immediately after the crime is as perplexing as the failure to question [special policeman] Parker." If the statement is indeed genuinely Cobb's, it casts further doubt on officialdom's story, for, at least as reported in the *Evening Star,* May 17, 1865, Cobb said after seeing a picture of David Herold that "I did not think he was the man" who crossed the bridge a few minutes after Booth. Evidence from separate sources places Booth on the road to Upper Marlborough. Commander Foxhall Parker to Stanton, Navy Dept. Records, NARA; the Montgomery Meigs diary, LC; and the Polk Gardner statement in LAS Files, NARA, affirm this route. That Booth left the Marlborough Turnpike but still headed generally southeast rather than south—in other words, bound for the Patuxent River—is evident from the reported midnight exchange with a local farmer whose wagon had broken down. See William P. Wood to Levi Turner, April 23, 1865, LAS Files, NARA; also, federal agents Allend Kirby to Wood, Adjudication of Claims, Adgt. General's Office, NARA. Information on the kidnap vessels was taken from NDP detectives, Potter Papers. With Celestina, the other Chaffey captain on the abduction assignment was John Scott, a cousin of Kate Scott, Booth's Pennsylvania paramour. Reference to a seaman named Scott at Mary Surratt's house on April 14 is found in *The Trial of John Surratt.*

Chapter 18

Corp. James Tanner, a shorthand clerk on the scene at Stanton's Petersen House command post, later said that enough evidence was quickly assembled to hang Booth. "It was well and certainly known that Booth was the assassin before twelve midnight," wrote police chief Richards to Louis Weichmann, December 24, 1900, in Riswold, ed., Louis Weichmann, *A True History of the Assassination* (New York: Alfred A. Knopf, 1975). A penciled note for telegraphic dispatch from Richards to Baltimore, New York, and Philadelphia police chiefs is in Benjamin Butler Papers, LC. For the War Department clerks at Stanton's door, "They say it is a man named Booth," the *Evening Star,* April 14, 1918. A newspaperman's inventory of what was found in Booth's room appears in George S. Bryan, *The Great American Myth* (New York, 1940). The envelope with a sketch map and James V. Barnes's name and address is in LAS Files, NARA, preceded by the notation: "Of no importance to this investigation." For the stableman John Fletcher's statements, see LAS Files, NARA, and his testimony in *Trial of John Surratt.* That Fletcher first talked to the police is shown by his name on the police blotter as a caller between 11 P.M. and midnight on April 14, 1865. What he told them is not known, since the earliest Fletcher statement in official records is dated eleven days later. For Booth at Doctor Mudd's, see his statement to Col. Henry H. Wells, April 22, 1865, War Department Records, NARA, and Capt. George Dutton's affidavit, April 23, 1865, testimony, Pitman, *Trial.* Stanton wrote to Charles Adams, London, April 15, 1865, that the murder was plotted in Richmond, Stanton Papers, LC. Stanton's story of lurking prowlers is in O. H. Browning's diary. The War Department's denial that the doorbell was out of order is in the *Evening Star,* April 14, 1918. Stanton's son never thought anybody lurked outside the house, according to a biographical sketch of Stanton in Woolcott Mss., Rice University, Houston, Tex., cited in Thomas and Hyman, *Stanton.* For Welles ridiculing Stanton's precautions, see his unpublished memoir, Huntington University. "A more glorious death," wrote Lieber to Sumner, April 23, 1865, referring to Lincoln's murder. See Friedel, *Francis Lieber.* For the radicals' conviction that their cause benefited from Lincoln's death, see Sumner to John Bright, May 1, 1865, cited in Donald, *Charles Sumner and the Rights of Man* (1970). See also Claude Bowers, *The Tragic Era* (New York, 1929); also George Julian, *Political Recollections*. The *New York Daily Tribune,* April 17, 1865, was one of several newspapers that made reference to Ella Turner's suicide attempt. That he heard "a man named Boyd was said to be the assassin" was stated by Dr. Mudd to a congressional investigator, December 1867. The involvement of a "Boyd" is also suggested in OR Ser. 1, vol. 46, pt. 3. The murderers have gone southeast, wrote J. L. McPhail to Gen. B. B. Hough, April 15, 1865, and see Montgomery Meigs to Col. Newport, April 16, 1865, Unbound Telegrams Received by the Secy. of War, NARA. Booth's attempts to reach the Patuxent are apparent from Lieut. Dana to J. Holt, October 3 and 23, 1865, Adjudication of Claims, Adj. Gen. Records, NARA. Also, Dana's reminiscences in the *Boston Sunday Globe,* December 12, 1897. A penciled note found among the Ewing Papers, LC, says that Dana told a local, Leonard Robey of Bryantown, that Booth had not intended to go by Mudd's, "as he had gotten the boat and had intended to cross [the Patuxent] twelve miles above Mudd's house." Details on David Herold come from a detective interview with one of his sisters, August 22, 1873. For his schooling, see Georgetown University student records. City directories prove that Booths were the Herolds' neighbors. Also, see Turner-Baker Papers, File 635T. As for Herold at Nailor's Stables the day of the assassination, he would have been there in the morning, about 10:30, certainly not while Atzerodt was there—in a statement, April 23, 1865, LAS Files, NARA. And at the trial of John Surratt, the stableman testified, "I never saw the two of them together that day at all." For the alleged discoveries in Room 126 at the Kirkwood, see testimony of John Lee, Pitman, *Trial,* and especially his unpublished statement, Turner-Baker Papers, and LAS Files, NARA, to the effect that on his first visit to the room, "the first thing that attracted my attention was a large navy revolver and a dark coat hanging on the wall." The clerk with him testified to seeing only the revolver. When asked by the military court to describe the appearance and the location of Room 126, Lee gave such a mangled response that no one present could make sense of it.

Chapter 19

Stanton's summons to Baker, April 15, 1865, is in War Department Telegrams, NARA. For Baker's prewar career, which included vigilante activity in San Francisco and fur trapping in Michigan, see an autobiographical memoir given to Andrew Potter by the NDP agent W. R. "Rob Rover" Bernard, Potter Papers. For Ficklin's arrest and a description of the papers found on him, also O. H. Browning's prompt appearance in his defense, see Ficklin to De LaRue, April 15, 1865, LAS Files, NARA, which also includes the letter introducing Ficklin to Brown Brothers. Details on Watson's midnight visitor are in the Potter Papers. In the coded material of Lafayette Baker, he refers to "my partners Goodell and McGinnis," whose names appear in full with "Henry J. Eager" on No. 17468, Cotton and Captured Property Records, NARA. For Herold in handcuffs before his picture appeared on a reward poster, see Potter Papers; Herold's statement, LAS Files, NARA. Reference to Herold's capture, with details on the photography process, is in E. M. Schaeffer,

M.D., to O. H. Oldroyd, March 22, 1910, Oldroyd Papers, Neff-Guttridge Collection. To account for the fact that a pair of fugitives showed up here, the myth took hold that currents must have swept Booth and his companion upriver from their hiding place near Pope's Creek and landed them on the same Maryland shore. An analysis of tidal and wind conditions then prevailing shows that this was not possible. See "Booth Crosses the Potomac: An Exercise in Historical Research," by William A. Tidwell, *Civil War History* XXXVI, no. 4 (1990). Booth was not seen at Nanjemoy Creek; Herold was. The boarding of the *Indian Prince* is described in L. M. Angelicus to O'Bierne, April 30, 1875, Adjudication of Claims, Adj. General's Office Records, NARA. Also see the John Leeds interview, Potter Papers. Booth's diary is in Lincoln Museum, beneath Ford's Theatre. The word *ship* under the date "18," penciled as are Booth's other words, has faded over the decades but is still visible.

Chapter 20

Concern for the security of certain documents is seen in David C. Mearns, *The Lincoln Papers: The Story of the Collection,* 2 vols. (Garden City, N.Y.: Doubleday, 1948). For Richards on the carpet, see Stanton Papers, LC, and LAS Files, NARA. The superintendent's request for a horse for going after Ringgold Browning is to Ingraham, April 16, 1865. Richards's telegram about Bishop is to Carmichael, Baltimore Police Marshal, April 15, 1865, Butler Papers, LC. Police discovery of Booth's saddle blanket is reported on the Washington Detective Police Blotter for April 15, 1865, NARA. The name of Etta is unknown, complained John Kennedy, New York police chief, to Col. J. A. Foster, LAS Files, NARA. Also see Andrew Potter to William McKee Dunn, April 29, 1883, Potter Papers. Arrest of the Greens after the detective's discovery of "excavations for a storm sewer" is described in an Andrew Potter memoir, Potter Papers, and also in LAS Files, NA. Also see Peterson, *Alleged Assassins.* Arnold talked too freely, wrote Secretary Stanton to McPhail, April 18, 1865, Stanton Papers, LC. Stanton to Gen. L. Walker, Telegrams Collected by the Office of the Secretary of War, NARA, called "the proceeding outrageous. Take Arnold into your custody, double iron him. Prohibit the publication of his examination or any facts relating to him." See Arnold's "confession," *Baltimore American,* January 19, 1865. For Gen. Seward's statement that no affidavits were taken from his family, see LAS Files, NARA. Britton Hill told Stanton that he had gone to the Sewards' at 9:30 the morning after the crime and interrogated the house boy and the army nurse. "You had just left," Stanton Papers, LC. Concerning the reliability of the surviving Sewards as witnesses, it should be noted that Fred Seward, in his memoirs, mentioned a letter he said his mother had written. It is oddly detailed, unlikely to have been composed by a woman mentally and physically prostrate and herself on the brink of death. Fred Seward's biographer indicates that he was not altogether trustworthy in his recollections and letters. See *Frederick W. Seward, Reminiscences of a Wartime Statesman and Diplomat, 1830–1915* (New York: Putnam, 1916). "Yet I am not sure," ventured Pvt. Robinson, May 19, 1865, Peterson, *Alleged Assassins.* Fanny Seward's failure to identify Payne as her father's attacker is from Dr. Verdi's article in the *Republic* 1 (July 1973), and

Major Seward's "I'm mad!" from his testimony, Pitman, *Trial.* For details on the Hansell coincidence, see the Emerick Hansell death certificate, Vital Records Division, District of Columbia Health Department; also see the *New York Post,* April 15, 1865. Several newspapers carried the story of Hansell's "death" within hours of the attack at Seward's. We obtained copies of family letters in 1975 through the assistance of Dr. Donald Hansell and Amelia Gale King, of Rensselaer, Ohio. Also see Andrew Potter's interview with Emerick Hansell, Potter Papers. Ordeal of the hooded prisoners is described in Arnold, *Defense and Prison Experiences.* For detail on the mystifying Lew Payne, see "Lewis Payne, Pawn of John Wilkes Booth," by Leon O. Prior, *Florida Historical Quarterly* (July 1964); "An Epistle of the Civil War," unpublished memoir by Elizabeth Payne Lomax, Neff-Guttridge Collection; and William E. Doster, *Lincoln and Episodes of the Civil War* (1915). Stories told of Payne/Powell traceable to Major Eckert, who had exclusive charge of the prisoner, show conflicts that cast doubts on his veracity. For example, among items in the David H. Bates Papers, LC, is Eckert's claim to have found Payne's revolver, buried under a tree in southeast Washington. Bates did not use this in *Lincoln in the Telegraph Office,* probably because it was said in 1865 that Payne had left the weapon at Seward's home. Allegedly found there, it served as evidence to hang him. Neither can one easily accept another of Eckert's assertions, made years after the executions. Payne told him that he and Booth had listened to Lincoln speak and that Booth had sworn, "That will be his last speech." Eckert had said nothing of this when the situation might have required it, during the conspiracy trial.

Chapter 21

Commander Foxhall Parker reported the collision at the mouth of the Patuxent River to Gideon Welles, OR, *Navies,* Ser. 3, vol. 5. A detailed account of the routes taken by the four fugitives was sent by Andrew Potter to Osborn Oldroyd, Potter Papers. See also Oldroyd, *Assassination;* George A. Townsend's article "How Booth Crossed the Potomac" in *Century* (April 1884); and Townsend's account in the *Cincinnati Enquirer,* August 3, 1884. That Stuart set Booth's leg is claimed by T. C. De Leon, *Belles, Beaux and Brains in the Sixties* (New York: G. W. Dillingham, 1907), and in a telephone interview, 1978, with Stuart's granddaughter, Rosalie Stuart. Also see Miriam Haynie, *The Stronghold: The Story of the Historic Northern Neck of Virginia* (Richmond, Va.: Dietz Press, 1959), and articles in *Northern Neck Historical Society Magazine* by T. Benton Gayle. David Herold's companion "told the doctor his name was Boyd," in Herold's statement, LAS Files, NARA. Most or all of the King George County people were rounded up during a second foray by Luther Baker and a small cavalry detachment. William N. Walton, a *New York Herald* reporter, accompanied them. On May 4, 1865, his account contained the first reference to a bitterly sarcastic "thank you" note signed "Stranger" and addressed to "Dr. Stewart." It was said to have enfolded five dollars. The War Department produced a second note, with Stuart's name again misspelled but this one with two and a half dollars. Confusion resulted, uncomfortably displayed by Eckert while testifying before the Andrew Johnson impeachment committee. Both notes have long vanished. Prentiss Ingraham, responsible for "Pursuit and Death of John Wilkes Booth," *Century* (January 1890), wrote more than one hundred wildly exaggerated novels supposedly based on the life of Buffalo Bill Cody. His Ruggles tale in the *Century* article has Booth saying, immediately after crossing the Rappahannock, "I am safe in glorious old Virginia, thank God," where he had in fact been since crossing the Potomac. While Booth "had shaved off his moustache," according to Ruggles, Bainbridge gives the assassin a "long dark mustache . . . straggling . . . he was constantly pulling it into shape." All of which, if not totally dismissable, is additional evidence of two pairs of fugitives. Herold's "he said his name was Boyd" is in Jett's statement, LAS Files, NARA, and in Pitman, *Trial.* "This good man labored" is from Gen. W. S. Hancock to "The Colored People of the District of Columbia, Virginia, Maryland and Alexandria" in the *Washington Morning Chronicle,* among other local newspapers, April 21, 1865. The account of the discovery of Booth's diary, with photograph of the scout Nalgai, is in the Potter Papers. The *New York Daily Tribune,* April 24, 1865, reported: "Assassin's Coat Found . . . A detective of the War Department returned from Virginia Sunday night with an ulsterette belonging to the assassin. . . . in the pockets were his personal papers." The alarm in Stanton's office is described in an unpublished portion of George Julian's journal, April 24, 1865, Neff-Guttridge Collection. Though Stanton ordered Booth's diary sealed away at once, the *Baltimore Advertiser,* April 29, 1865, noted that "a diary [of the assassin] is in the possession of the War Department." Glass plates of the women's photos, prepared at the Army Medical Museum photo laboratory and each with Dr. Edward Curtis's initials and the telltale date plainly visible, are in the Neff-Guttridge Collection. The women in the photos have been repeatedly misidentified, thanks largely to Francis Wilson, *John Wilkes Booth* (Boston and New York: Houghton Mifflin Co., 1929). Wilson's guesswork is obvious from his 1927–1929 correspondence with actor William Seymour and War Department clerk John D. Randolph, Princeton University Library. No doubt should exist that one of the photographed ladies is Kate Scott, of whom an identical picture is among the Kate Scott Papers.

Chapter 22

"Testimony is so conflicting," wrote Col. Wells to Col. J. H. Taylor, April 28, 1865, War Department Records, NARA. "My father introduced him to me as Mr. Boyd, an old soldier," says Wm. H. Garrett in "True Story of the Capture of John Wilkes Booth," *Confederate Veteran* 29 (1921). Also see Rev. R. B. Garrett in the *Indianapolis Bulletin,* November 12, 1896; Garrett to McKee Dunn, January 13, 1880, LAS Files, NARA; R. Garrett to J. B. Bentley, February 7, 1882, Virginian Historical Society, Richmond; and Frank A. Burr in the *Boston Sunday Herald,* December 11, 1881. Kate Garrett told Burr that the stranger was mustached and was introduced by Pvt. Jett as a wounded Confederate soldier named James W. Boyd. For Lieut. Doherty's orders, see his report to brigade headquarters, War Department Records, NARA; OR Ser. 1, vol. 46; and Doherty to Andrew Johnson, Adjudication of Claims, NARA, Microcopy 503. Versions differ as to what took place at Garrett's farm, including the dialogue through the barn door. The significant point on which all agree is that no names were uttered until Herold's emergence and the shooting. For Herald's assertion that he had known the other man in the barn as Boyd, see Peterson, *Alleged Assassins,* and Pitman, *Trial.* Information on Doctor Charles Urquhart's life and career comes from the Archives of the University of Pennsylvania, Philadelphia; information on Gay Mont, Rappahannock Academy, was provided by James S. Patton and Carrol M. Garnett, an Urquhart descendant, at a gathering to honor the doctor's memory, Germanna, Virginia, April 12, 1983. Also see L. B. Anderson, M.D., *Brief Biographies of Virginia Physicians of Olden Times,* vol. 1 (Richmond: Southern Clinic Printing, 1889). Urquhart died on July 7, 1866. Lieut. Doherty wrote of Baker making off with Booth's body in a letter to President Andrew Johnson, December 23, 1865, Adjudication of Claims, NARA, which also contains Doherty to Stanton, March 24, 1866, on the same subject. Proceedings on the *Montauk,* detailed in "Identification and Autopsy of John Wilkes Booth: Re-Examining the Evidence," by Leonard F. Guttridge, *Navy Medicine* 84, no. 1 (January–February 1993). For background on May, see E. F. Cordell, *Medical Annals of Maryland* (1903). Also note letters to the *Washington Post*'s "Close at Home" section, June 25, July 16, August 13, and September 3, 1995. After taking a picture of the body, the photographer Gardner returned to his studio with a government detective assigned to accompany him, even into the darkroom. Complying with orders, the detective took the plate and a print to Lafayette Baker's headquarters on Pennsylvania Avenue. Along the way, he peeked inside his package and recognized Booth's likeness, "except that the moustache was untidy." See D. M. Katz, *Witness to an Era: The Life and Photographs of Alexander Gardner* (New York: Viking, 1991). Alexander Gardner's thoughts on that Thursday would be interesting to know. But in 1867 he closed his gallery and headed west as a field photographer for the Union Pacific Railroad. He died in 1882, and, as far as is known, neither he nor Timothy O'Sullivan, who became a photographer of natural splendors, left written word regarding the picture they took on the *Montauk.* What happened to it after reaching the War Department is unknown. The *Montauk* captain's sense of outrage colors his letter to the Navy Yard commandant, April 29, 1865, quoted in H. B. Hibben, *History of the Washington Navy Yard* (Washington, D.C.: Government Printing Office, 1890). Also see Charles Paullin's "The Navy and the Booth Conspirators," in *Illinois State Historical Society Journal,* September, 1940. Montgomery's complaint at being kept uninformed is quoted in Izola Forrester, *This One Mad Act* (Boston, Mass.: Hale, Cushman and Flink, 1937). "Booth"'s burial is described in the Eckert-Bates memoranda, LC: also by Stanton, Eckert, and Lafayette Baker, Impeachment Hearings. The media reported a burial in the Potomac River; for example, *Frank Leslie's Illustrated Newspaper,* May 28, 1865; and the *New York Commercial,* April 28, 1865, which says that the body was sunk "by authority of the War Department with only two persons present, Detective Baker and another man, and they are sworn to secrecy." That Dr. Woodward autopsied more than one body as Booth's is revealed in E. Schaeffer to O. H. Oldroyd, Oldroyd Papers. Schaeffer was a hospital steward assisting Woodward at the Army Medical Museum. The cotton permits and passes are in Cotton and Captured Property Records, RG 56, NARA. The permits are numbered 17656, 17468, and 17500.

The contracts are numbered 16911 and 18568. In these papers appear the names of Goodell, McGinnis, Caldwell, and Ward Lamon. The letter from "Henry J. Eager Co. to Hanson Risley, April 27, 1865," is in Records of the Civil War, Special Agencies of the Treasury Department, 7th Special Agency. The erasures and substituted names were discovered in 1970 and 1971 with the help of NARA staff. See Ray A. Neff to Mark Eckhoff, Director, Legislative, Judicial and Diplomatic Records Division, NARA, November 27, 1970; Eckhoff to Neff, December 1, 1970; Walter R. McNutt, Chief, Document Reproduction and Preservation Branch, NARA, January 26, 1971. Ultraviolet, infrared, and high-contrast photographic techniques were used and the entire process conducted in a NARA laboratory with federal technicians present. Of hundreds of exposures, fifteen clearly showed the original name: R. D. Watson. Lola's invitation to Will Browning is signed "Mrs. Col. Alexander" and is in the papers of Andrew Johnson, LC. The informer James Owen's death is stated in Old Capitol Prison Records; Owens left a wife and six children. The official published version of the trial as edited by Benn Pitman under Col. Henry L. Burnett's supervision contains differences, some significant, when compared with the handwritten transcript and with Peterson, *Alleged Assassins.* For example, while the army nurse Robinson's testimony in the handwritten transcript and in Peterson clearly indicate that Seward was not the third man in the secretary's bedroom rushing to aid Robinson, the major's name is parenthetically, and repeatedly, planted in the Pitman version as if identified by the witness. Pitman described how the trial was recorded in "Behind the Scenes of the Conspiracy Trial," where he asserts that "the whole trial was conducted on the theory that the assassination of the President and attempted assassination of Wm. Seward was the culmination of an organized conspiracy . . . and that Jefferson Davis and other chiefs of the Southern Confederacy at Richmond and in Canada were the instigators." *Tyler's Quarterly,* XXII, No. 1, July, 1940. That a daguerreotype was sent to Washington by Payne's family is supported by Gen. Vogdes to E. A. Hitchcock, August 29, 1865, and Hitchcock to Stanton, October 30, 1865, Hitchcock Papers, LC. The photo of Private Lewis Powell, an able Mosby scout, is in the Neff-Guttridge Collection. The *Cincinnati Gazette,* May 28, 1867, reported that the condemned four expected reprieve "up to the moment they were swung off" and also intimated that a hundred armed men were in Washington the night of the assassination to assist in the crime and that one of the prosecutors at the trial knew that "government personages beyond suspicion had knowledge of the attempt." For Anna Surratt's desperate efforts to save her mother, see Guy W. Moore, *The Case of Mrs. Surratt* (Norman: University of Oklahoma Press, 1954), and David DeWitt, *The Judicial Murder of Mary Surratt* (Baltimore: J. Murphy, 1895). John Surratt's movements in Canada are noted in *Diary of Edwin Lee,* microcopy in the University of North Carolina Library, Chapel Hill. See also "Sidelights—Who Hid John Surratt?" *Maryland Historical Magazine* (June 1965), and the *Evening Star,* December 7, 1870. The *New York Times,* December 10, 1870, quotes Surratt as saying that while secreted in Canada, he was assured until the last minute that his mother would be saved. NDP interview with Surratt, May 11, 1876, reveals his expectation of immunity in exchange for a "holy vow" not to tell his secrets. His assertion that the government appeared "willing and anxious" for him to stay abroad, culminating after a curious delay in his seizure and shipment home, can be tracked in American Catholic Historical Association Documents, vol. 1, U.S. Minister to Papal States. Also see 39th Congress, 2d Session, House Exec. Docs. 1, 9, and 25. For press comments on the government's apparent reluctance to proceed with Surratt's trial, see the *New York Herald,* May 19; the *Baltimore Sun,* May 29; and the *Washington Daily Morning Chronicle,* May 30, all 1867. The Potter Papers supply glimpses of Celestina's postwar maneuverings.

Chapter 23

For Senator Davis's puzzlement over "secrecy," see the *Congressional Globe* (July 28, 1866): 4292. His question is echoed by the *Louisville Journal,* January 18, 1867, and other current newspapers in stories of Booth seen in Ceylon. Kate Scott's sworn statement, October 27, 1910, describes her relationship with Booth, Kate Scott Papers. Additional documents with photos are in the Neff-Guttridge Collection. The Jefferson County Historical Society holds pertinent material. Also, see Kate Scott, *A History of Jefferson County* (Syracuse, N.Y.: D. Mason and Co., 1888). For her nurse's pension, see Senate Report No. 1853, 50th Congress, 2d Session. Besides Butler, the Assassination Committee members were Samuel Shellabarger, Ohio; George Julian, Indiana; Hamilton Ward, New York; and Samuel T. Randolph, Pennsylvania. For portions of testimony leaked, see the *New York Times,* November 1, 1867. For testimony on Booth's diary by Holt, Stanton, Eckert, and Lafayette Baker, see Impeachment Hearings. In 1977 we received permission from the U.S. National Park Service to photograph the diary, page by page. Copies of the negatives were turned over to the Department of the Interior, with enlarged copies sent to the Library of Congress and the Lincoln Memorial Library in Harrogate, Tennessee. Following this, the FBI did its own photographic study of the diary, briefly enlisting our help, and finally reported that a total of 43 full sheets (86 pages) were "missing from the diary." See File No. 95-216208, October 3, 1977. Much of what we learn of Lafayette Baker's last years is drawn from a diary purportedly his wife's and very likely authentic. Jane ("Jennie") Baker was born to Cadwalladar Curry, like the Chaffeys a Passamaquoddy Bay shipowner. Sent to Philadelphia as a ward of related Currys, she married Baker on Christmas Eve, 1852, as reported three days later in the *Philadelphia Public Ledger.* After Baker's death, Jennie left for the West and married a Simon Dietz. There is some evidence that he, and possibly Jennie, died in the San Francisco earthquake. In 1975 Dietz's greatgranddaughter gave us Jennie Baker's diary, its pages heavily stained but not entirely illegible. The physical attacks on Baker are mentioned in it and Walter Pollock implicated as both seducer and poisoner. Diaries as sources are often suspect, as they should be, but we have no reason to believe this one is other than genuine. The transcript of the court hearing on the unprobated codicil to Baker's will was typed in 1936 by Gina Georgiana under the Works Progress Administration program. It is filed in WPA Papers, Philadelphia City Hall, catalogued as WPA (1936)-400 (1868-CCC-1872). Also see detective interviews with Benjamin Brewster and Walter C. Marshall, Philadelphia attorneys who represented Baker in the months before he died. Levi Turner's abhorrence of cotton speculators was expressed in a reply to a seeker after cotton permits who promised to put $200,000 in his pocket "and no one the wiser." See Turner-Baker Papers, File 2719. Turner is said to have written a fourteen-page memorandum exposing scandalous war profiteering. Notebooks used by the detectives in their investigation are among the Potter Papers, as are transcribed copies of interviews. For Ficklin's postwar activities, see the *Texas Almanac* for 1870, Austin, Texas. His death was reported in the *Washington Evening Star,* March 13, 1871, and Henri Sainte Marie's in the *New York Times,* September 12, 1874. Additional confirmation of this probe came from James V. Barnes's son during an audiotaped interview, May 15, 1975, and research conducted by Professor William W. Parsons. A copy of Lew Wallace's covering letter advising that the report be "sequestered" is among the Potter Papers. Lydia McGinnis's affectionate letters to Andrew Johnson are in his correspondence, LC.

Chapter 24

For Edwin Booth's effort to have the body turned over to his family, see his letter to Andrew Johnson, February 10, 1869, cited in George S. Bryan, *The Great American Myth* (New York: Carrick and Evans, 1940). Also see Kimmel, *The Mad Booths of Maryland,* and Izola Forrester, *This One Mad Act.* Eyewitness accounts in *Maryland Historical Magazine* 8 (1913), and the *Baltimore American,* February 17, 1869. For the Allegheny Valley Railroad Company case, see records in the Venango County Courthouse, Franklin, Pennsylvania. The Wilkes letter, with its scarcely concealed "J. W. Booth," and other letters from Wilkes of India dated in the 1870s were seen (and copied) by us when they were offered for sale. The letters were in their original envelopes bearing genuine Indian stamps of the period (Queen Victoria's head portrayed), franked, and watermarked. In addition to the acrostic "hidden" name of Booth, the subject of each letter has no relevance other than to John Wilkes Booth's known business activity. The Bear Hole, or "Bar Hole," as locally pronounced, is a limestone cave in the Blue Ridge Mountains near Elkton (formerly, Conrad's Store). Inaccessible in winter and in midsummer, it is close to Hawksbill Creek, another feature mentioned in material from independent sources that convincingly identifies three men as Booth, Hynson, and the faithful Henry Johnson, all of whom sheltered more than a week in the cave. That local partisans who modeled themselves after Mosby's band led the three down the forested western slopes to Louis Pence's home is confirmed by detective interviews with Pence, July 15, 1867, and July 26, 1873, Potter Papers, and Henry Showalter to Pence, Kate Scott Papers. John Simonton, custodian of Booth relics and records for more than forty years, was threatened with dismissal if he talked, according to a penciled note in the margin of a book among the Cazenove Lee collection at the Alexandria, Virginia, Library. After Simonton's death, his papers, like so much other telltale material to do with Booth and the assassination, went up in flames. Professor Parsons's second wife burned most of his papers after his death. Surviving documents reflect his own research, not to mention his kinship as son-in-law of John Wilkes (1825–1916) of Terre Haute, whose identity Booth had assumed upon leaving the United States. Parsons inherited valuable research papers from William McKee

Dunn, with which former judge advocate general Andrew Potter maintained a friendly and revealing correspondence. See Potter's letters to Dunn, August 19, 1884; June 19 and August 21, 1885; September 16 and September 28, 1886; and July 6, 1887, Potter Papers. In an undated letter, they discuss Professor Parsons's belief that Harriet Alexander took money to Booth in the fall of 1865. The specific dates of her departure and return, as agreed upon by Potter, Dunn, and Parsons, are found in the microfilmed Passenger Lists (New York), NARA. Details on Grant and Ward are found in a seminar paper, "Grant and Ward: Anatomy of a Fraud" by Karen Wendell, Smith College, 1977. New York newspapers covered the scandal throughout May 1884. See also W. S. McFeely, *Grant: A Biography* (New York: Norton, 1981). The involvement of Grant and Ward, also Lew Wallace, is soundly supported by evidence from independent sources. We located a copy of the will of John B. Wilkes, Bombay, in the business papers of the Indiana Circuit Court judge Robert Stewart (1898–1970), attorney for Elizabeth Bossom, the Terre Haute John Wilkes's daughter. Stewart's papers, like those of Willam W. Parsons, irrefutably link Booth, Wilkes, Lew Wallace, and Andrew Potter in the whole astonishing mix. See Stewart's letter to Mrs. Bossom, January 7, 1930, Neff-Guttridge Collection. Our copy was obtained from the executor of her estate and was authenticated by Robert Stewart's widow, who kindly granted us two personal interviews. Also see Andrew Potter's account of his search to establish the true identity of the man named Wilkes in India, whose will listed legatees provably connected with John Wilkes Booth, Neff-Guttridge Collection. The account acknowledges the assistance of yet another Indianian, John Watson Foster, diplomat, lobbyist for foreign governments, future secretary of state, and grandfather of Allen and John Foster Dulles. A copy of Mosby's telegram to Lunsford Lomax, March 5, 1884, conveying news of Booth's death the previous October, was supplied by Lomax's great-grandson Ken Hadow, Charlottesville, Virginia. "Guess this ends it," Mark Wade wrote to Susan Wade, April 29, 1945; copy furnished us by Myrtle Moore, Greencastle, Indiana, whose foster daughter Mark Wade married. Same source for the photo Wade took of "Wilkes"'s grave in India. Location of the grave was further assisted by correspondence in March 1988 with H. K. Gogoi, National Bank for Agriculture and Rural Development, Guwahati, Assam Province, India.

Index

NOTE: Page numbers in *italics* indicate illustrations.